Praise for *The Right Hand of the Lord Is Exalted*

"The anti-traditional mentality that breaks with the constant Tradition of the Church is at the very root of the unprecedented crisis that, for the past sixty years, has infected at all levels the life of the Catholic Church. Aurelio Porfiri's book *The Right Hand of the Lord Is Exalted* gives us comprehensive and informative insights into the arduous endeavors of several members of both the clergy and the laity to reestablish the Church's constant doctrinal and liturgical Tradition as the consistently proven way for overcoming the crisis. It is praiseworthy not to forget those persons who, despite their limitations and defects amid the heat of the fight, left us an example of their love for the Church."

— ✠ *Athanasius Schneider,* Auxiliary Bishop
of the Archdiocese of St. Mary in Astana

"Congratulations to Maestro Porfiri on an important, inspirational and precious book on matters of profound importance to many Christians, and others of good will. I recommend this book highly to traditional Catholics, but also to every reader who wishes to understand more deeply the modern struggle between tradition and modernity. Bravo, Maestro, and much thanks for this brilliant jewel of a work!"

Dr. Robert Moynihan, Ph.D., Founder and
Editor-in-Chief, Inside the Vatican

"Porfiri has performed a service for the Church by providing this high-level survey of the traditionalist phenomenon, from modernism to *Traditionis Custodes.* Although other books and biographies provide more extensive details about aspects of the story, Porfiri's text will serve as an excellent introduction that surveys all the pieces of this great puzzle."

— *Brian M. McCall,* Editor-in-Chief, Catholic Family News

"In his book on the post-conciliar Church and traditionalism, Aurelio Porfiri offers a historical outline that helps us to understand the crisis in the Church in the last decades. He traces the so-called traditionalist world, to which he does not belong, and focuses on the topics that demand a greater dedication by the Church: the correct interpretation of Vatican II without a rupture with the precedent Magisterium; the dignity and beauty of classic liturgy which cannot be compared; and a critical attitude toward the Godless ideologies that often dominate the modern world. "

— *Don Manfred Hauke*, *Professor of Dogmatics,*
Theological Faculty of the University of Lugano, Switzerland

"Anyone who wants to address the subject of the Church of Rome as it is and to try to understand in which direction Peter's boat is moving, will find great help in this book that Aurelio Porfiri has compiled. Porfiri has reconstructed the decades of turbulence following the Second Vatican Council and how the Council was interpreted and applied—with not a few betrayals of the intentions of the council fathers, the pontiffs who lived at that time, and the texts themselves.

The author focuses on what is called the 'traditional world,' one with often indistinct boundaries, as it includes those who think that the last legitimate pope was Pius XII and those who accept subsequent popes and the Council, but claim the right, never abolished, to celebrate according to the traditional Mass.

Here is a work that those interested in the life of the Church cannot miss,."

— *Marco Tosatti*, *author of* Viganò vs. the Vatican

"Aurelio Porfiri, musician, scholar, writer and chronicler, summarizes, succinctly but fully, many of the important developments, twists, and turns that have taken place in the Church since the Second Vatican Council, not only liturgically but on a wider canvas. He has striven, in this book, to take a balanced, unbiased look at the great chasm that has opened up in the Church since the Council and Pope Paul VI decided to open the door to changes which, in turn, have been radically and destructively perverted and abused ever since. The simple fact is that, before the Council, the Church was growing exponentially everywhere, and, after the Council, she has suffered the worst collapse in her entire history—not so much a decline in numbers as a complete 'free fall.' The problem, as Porfiri demonstrates, is that those now in authority in the Church seem to be completely blind to the disaster that has been unleashed by their radical misinterpretation of the Council. In exploring the movements, growing rapidly everywhere, that oppose this radical revolt within the Church, he discovered the so-called traditional movement. It is a movement, as he shows, that, in essence, is really no more than an attempt to renew the Church along the lines of historical Christianity and not along the lines of the empty experimentalism and facile novelty that has predominated since the Council. He recognizes the reality that a great divide—in effect, a schism—has been created within the Church between those who believe and accept historic Catholicism and those who reject it in favor of a superficial, neo-modernist experiment that has failed, again and again."

—*James Bogle*, *barrister, writer, historian, and former president of the International Una Voce Federation*

"We often speak of 'Catholic traditionalism' without knowing exactly what it is. Reference is made, generically, to the 'Latin Mass' (without taking into account the fact that even the reformed Mass can be celebrated in Latin), and it is imagined that traditionalists are all, more or less, followers of Msgr. Lefebvre. Aurelio Porfiri helps to clarify. He goes to the origins of the traditionalist phenomenon and draws a useful map for orienting oneself between the different sensitivities—because traditionalism is not a monolith but rather resembles an archipelago. The merit of the book is that it is not for specialists but is within everyone's reach—written not in a partisan spirit but in an authentic love for the Church."

—*Aldo Maria Valli*, *former Vaticanist for the Italian National Television and editor of the blog* Duc in Altum

"One need not be a Catholic 'traditionalist' to benefit from this book by Maestro Aurelio Porfiri. Serious students of Catholic history will be enriched by this compelling narration of the events and personalities of the Catholic traditionalist movement. Porfiri not only presents the story of Archbishop Lefebvre; he also covers other important Catholic traditionalists such as the Abbot de Nantes, Archbishop Thuc, and Romano Amerio. Porfiri does not identify himself as a traditionalist, but he, like every true Catholic, is devoted to Catholic tradition—whether in sacred music, art, liturgy, or theology. *The Right Hand of the Lord Is Exalted* should be read by all Catholics who wish to understand Catholic traditionalism, its leading proponents, and its historical development."

— ***Robert Fastiggi,*** *Ph.D., Professor of Dogmatic Theology, Sacred Heart Major Seminary, Detroit*

THE RIGHT HAND OF THE
LORD IS EXALTED

Aurelio Porfiri

THE RIGHT HAND OF THE LORD IS EXALTED

A History of Catholic Traditionalism from Vatican II to *Traditionis Custodes*

SOPHIA INSTITUTE PRESS

Manchester, New Hampshire

Sophia Institute Press
Box 5284, Manchester, NH 03108
1-800-888-9344
www.SophiaInstitute.com

Sophia Institute Press is a registered trademark of Sophia Institute.

paperback ISBN 978-1-64413-838-0

ebook ISBN 978-1-64413-839-7

Library of Congress Control Number: 2024936652

First printing

Contents

Preface

AURELIO PORFIRI WAS BORN in the ancient, working-class neighborhood of Rome, Trastevere, which makes him a true Roman. As a musician, he was a student of the maestro Cardinal Domenico Bartolucci, the last great director of the Sistine Chapel. He authored hundreds of compositions as well as a history of Catholic sacred music, published by the Catholic Center of the Chinese University of Hong Kong, in both English and Chinese, under the title *Forever I Will Sing*. I met him many years ago, and I still remember the beautiful concerts he directed in the Basilica of St. Chrysogonus of the Trinitarian Fathers, where the remains of Blessed Anna Maria Taigi lie, a saint quite dear to him, as is the Servant of God Rafael Merry del Val, Secretary of State to St. Pius X, who until his death in 1930 exercised his apostolate among the youth in Trastevere.

Although from Trastevere, life has launched him to the ends of the world, all the way to Macao and Hong Kong. Aurelio Porfiri has progressively enlarged his field of interest, though never renouncing his music, to include current religious and cultural themes. His reflections have appeared in books, magazines, and online publications, both in Italy and abroad. What has led him to intervene is above all the devastation of sacred music and liturgy in recent decades. The postconciliar years were a period in which we witnessed a revolution in the Church, carried out in the name of the "Spirit of the Council," which often contradicted the very documents it claimed to be promoting. The existence of this religious revolution and the search for a reference point to anchor oneself brought Porfiri to the discovery of the so-called "traditionalist" world, to which he never belonged, but within which he has lived and continues to live and participate, at times with great suffering, until finally deciding to reconstruct its history. Porfiri is not a historian in the strict sense of the term, but rather an attentive witness and chronicler of history, who in this book carries out his task magnificently — namely, that of narrating what he has seen with free and independent judgment.

The traditionalism that concerns Aurelio Porfiri is the movement born in reaction to the Second Vatican Council, especially after the liturgical reform of Paul VI in 1969. It must be said, however, that contemporary traditionalism is the offshoot of a broader cultural school that began in reaction to the French Revolution, and which is nourished by a profound theology of history often unknown to modern day neo-traditionalists. The founding fathers of traditionalism, in this perspective, are not only eminent authors like Joseph de Maistre and Juan Donoso Cortés, but also great Popes of the eighteenth and nineteenth centuries, above all Bl. Pius IX and St. Pius X, who in the Apostolic Letter *Notre Charge Apostolique*, of August 25, 1910, stated that "the true friends of the nations are neither revolutionaries, nor innovators, but rather traditionalists."

We cannot understand Msgr. Marcel Lefebvre without taking into consideration the *Cité Catholique* founded in 1946 by Jean Ousset. One must remember the activity of Professor Plinio Corrêa de Oliveira as well, dating back to the 1930s, who set himself in direct continuity with the counterrevolutionary thought of the preceding century. These Catholics who were labeled, or defined themselves as, "intransigent," "ultramontane," "integralist," "counterrevolutionary," "traditionalist," "anti-Modernist," were and are first and foremost Catholics. What ought to characterize them is not the polemical labels but their true faith in the Church. I, too, while not refuting the label "traditionalist" that has been attributed to me, would define myself using the words of St. Pacian of Barcelona: *Christianus mihi nomen est, catholicus cognomen* [Christian is my name, Catholic is my last name].

The religious and cultural crisis has penetrated even within contemporary traditionalism, dividing it into groups and currents. Porfiri was struck by these divisions and observes how there exists today not Catholic traditionalism, but rather many traditionalisms, often interacting with each other in "remarkable tension," which these pages register meticulously. Beside the more or less well-known institutes and groups that move within the institutions of the Church, there are also those on its margins or even outside it: sedevacantists, sedeprivationists, sedematerialists, sedeobstructionists. These groups often have subgroups that not infrequently are pitted against each other. Porfiri gives voice to each of them, but the risk of remembering all of them, avoiding judgments of merit, is that it can feed the dialectical confusion that he rightly laments, and which led him to undertake this research.

His attempt at the historical reconstruction of a movement this complex remains nonetheless the work of a pioneer, and for this it merits appreciation. Maestro Porfiri is not a traditionalist, but neither is he an anti-traditionalist. He loves the tradition but refutes what he defines as the "pathology of traditionalism." Professor Andrea Sandri identified three steps to this pathology, which exploded above all in the post-Covid era: the negation of the visible Church, the reduction of the ecclesiastical order to one's own reference group, and a political-apocalyptic worldview culminating in the elevation of political action to the "great sacrament" of liberation (*Vigiliae Alexandrinae*, June 29, 2021). A tendency derives from this which forgets that Christianity is an institutional and orderly reality, and which moves the frontier of tradition from supernatural life, which passes into the background, to the fight for the liberation of the world from a great political conspiracy. Grace ends up entirely in an exterior realm in this battle, in which salvation must be grasped by man through militancy against a power that is evil not due to its abuses, but in its essence.

It is no wonder that we find within the traditionalist movement figures of great intellectual and moral caliber, next to characters who have sought only to carve out a bit of notoriety, drawing to themselves fragile and disgruntled people. Aurelio Porfiri's book, written with the good sense of a true Roman, is also an invitation to meditate on the fragmentation of a world which, in its quest for purity, too often falls into the abyss of chaos. "The one who must be careful," writes Porfiri, "is precisely the one who considers himself purer, because at the top of the mountain of St. John of the Cross balance is more precarious and the air becomes rarefied" (*Stilum Curiae*, October 29, 2022). Maestro Porfiri is also fond of a phrase by Gustave Thibon: "Nothing is in greater need of purification than what we call purity." This means that to judge purity, one needs a heart free of evil and not to hate one's friends nearby more than one detests one's distant enemies. For this reason, it was commanded to leave to God the judgment of the intentions of our brothers in the faith.

Pope Francis's motu proprio *Traditionis Custodes* of December 16, 2021, confirmed by the rescript approved by the Holy Father on February 21, 2023, seemed to go in the direction of dismantling traditionalist groups. But it is legitimate to ask if certain criticism by traditionalists of their persecutors, allowing for legitimate resistance of unjust restrictive measures, differs from the persecutors' position only in their exterior attitude, while the interior disposition of the soul remains quite similar.

Aurelio Porfiri concludes his book by stating that the question of Catholic traditionalism appears as a thorn in the side of the postconciliar Church. After ten years of Pope Francis's pontificate, it is difficult to foresee the future developments of this path which, as he rightly observes, will nonetheless be tied to the figure of the new Pontiff. It is true. In the Church, the Pope as Vicar of Jesus Christ can at times be a problem, but he is also always the solution to every problem.

Roberto de Mattei

THE RIGHT HAND OF THE
LORD IS EXALTED

Introduction

CATHOLIC TRADITIONALISM IS MUCH more complex a topic than some would like to think. First of all, Catholic traditionalism does not exist. Rather, there exist Catholic traditional*isms*, which are often irreconcilable with each other and which fight each other with ferocity. In this book I have tried to account for this phenomenon with as much objectivity as I could, considering groups that are far from my sensibilities. Many topics were left out and some movements were given greater space than others. This was inevitable, but I believe that in the book there are many points of departure for those wishing to delve deeper.

I do not define myself as a traditionalist, even if some may think I am one. Obviously, many ideas held by a certain type of traditionalism are also my own, and in some respects, I am more of an "extremist" than mainstream traditionalism purports to be. But I do not like labels, nor do I like being part of a group or of various coteries. I enjoy friendship with many who are cited in this text or who hold them in high esteem, recognizing our communality of ideas and ideals. I believe this has not impeded me from being objective, insofar as a historian can be. Whether I have succeeded or not is for the reader to judge.

Before I begin, I think it is important to define which Catholic traditionalism we shall be discussing. This obviously is distinguished from, for example, that which found itself confronting the Modernist storm, Catholic integralists represented in the work of Msgr. Umberto Benigni (1862–1934), whose *Sodalizio Piano* and whose journalistic work (*Corrispondenza Romana*) attempted to create a bulwark against the violent winds of the Modernists.

What does the term *traditionalism* (or traditionalisms), of which we shall be concerned, connote? The date of departure for our enquiry, 1962, makes clear that a common and extremely important element for all these movements is criticism of the Second Vatican Council. The way in which the council was criticized obviously admitted notable differences among those who, for example, recognize its validity while judging it deleterious for the life of the Church, and those who consider it to be entirely invalid.

Then there is the other central question, with various nuances, regarding the liturgy: the desire to continue to participate in the preconciliar Mass (we shall call it the Tridentine Mass, traditional Mass, or Mass of St. Pius V, all imperfect names nonetheless).

Then there is the question of the Church's relationship with the world. The way in which this question is treated by traditionalism is that we should not simply accommodate to the world but ought to advocate an identity emboldened by the Christian message and try in every way to reestablish the Christian civilization exemplified by medieval Christendom.

Naturally, these are not the only important questions, but in my estimation they are certainly the main ones by which we can measure the complex phenomenon which is Catholic traditionalism.

Aurelio Porfiri
Easter Sunday, March 31, 2024

CHAPTER 1

The Beginning of the End ... Or Not?

THE PRIEST SHUFFLED AROUND the church mumbling some prayers in front of each of the sacred images he met every few steps. He almost seemed to levitate above the floor of the ancient church in which Mass had just been celebrated for the feast of Our Lady of Mount Carmel, as on every July 16. The song of the *introit* had been going through his mind, which used the verses of the poet Sedulius, *Gaudeámus omnes in Dómino, diem festum celebrántes sub honóre beátæ Maríæ Vírginis* ... and yet, for reasons that will soon be clear, he meditated much more on the words of the offertory song, *Recordare, Virgo Mater ... Remember, O Virgin Mother, to speak in our favor before God to remove his wrath toward us.* Yes, the wrath of God.

Precisely that is what our priest thought he had felt, he who had given himself to God at a young age because he wanted to find answers to his many questions. And not evasive answers; he wanted God to speak to him in a clear and radical way, by means of gestures and rites and the prayers of the Church. For this reason, he did not enter a diocesan seminary, as had other young men, but chose a traditional order that had permission to celebrate the traditional Mass and liturgy, that which some improperly call "Tridentine" or "Latin." A venerable rite which, thanks to the papacy of Benedict XVI and his motu proprio *Summorum Pontificum* of July 7, 2007, was liberated from the various former restrictions imposed by a hierarchy that was (almost) entirely in favor of implementing the liturgical reform inspired by the Second Vatican Council. A reform that had led to the abandonment of Latin, Gregorian chant, and the venerable rites that had withstood centuries. A rite that had saturated our culture.

Our priest needed more, as did the many faithful who at that moment watched him with dismay. Precisely on that day of the feast of Our Lady of Mount Carmel, 2021, the Holy Father, Pope Francis, had promulgated a new motu proprio which, ironically, was called *Traditionis Custodes*. In that document, one did not read of encouragement to those who were faithful to the traditional liturgy; quite the contrary, they were placed under accusation. Whereas Pope Benedict XVI had established that there exists only one Roman Rite with two forms, the ordinary form (the Mass of Paul VI) and the extraordinary form (the traditional Mass), now Pope Francis was making it clear: "The liturgical books promulgated by the Holy Pontiffs Paul VI and John Paul II, in conformity with the decrees of the Second Vatican Council, are the sole expression of the *lex orandi* of the Roman Rite." Moreover, in the motu proprio, the formation of new communities within traditional orders was prohibited, and those who might wish to celebrate the traditional Mass were placed under more stringent control.

If the message of this motu proprio just promulgated was not clear enough, the *Letter of the Holy Father Pope Francis to the Bishops of the Entire World in Presentation of the Motu Proprio "Traditionis Custodes" on the Use of the Roman Liturgy Prior to the Reform of 1970* must certainly have been. In this document we find unequivocal expressions:

> An opportunity offered by St. John Paul II and, with even greater magnanimity, by Benedict XVI, intended to recover the unity of an ecclesial body with diverse liturgical sensibilities, was exploited to widen the gaps. . . .
>
> I am . . . saddened that the instrumental use of *Missale Romanum* of 1962 is often characterized by a rejection not only of the liturgical reform, but of the Vatican Council II itself, claiming, with unfounded and unsustainable assertions, that it betrayed the Tradition and the "true Church."

The intention of the Pope is quite clear: those who find spiritual nourishment in the traditional Mass must quickly return to the ranks of the conciliar Church and stop creating divisions, thinking they are representatives of a supposed "true Church" in opposition to the conciliar Church. Unfortunately, the Holy Father, at least until now, has not deplored with the same force the much more serious and extensive exploitation of the new Mass, abuses which by now have become customary.

The faithful asked what the motives were that had now led to this closure with respect to the traditional Mass, in contrast to the opening offered by Francis's predecessor, Benedict XVI, who in his motu proprio *Summorum Pontificum* of 2007 brought about a truce in the Church and a more favorable treatment of those who could not accept the revolutionary state that seemed to have overtaken vast sectors of the Church. The intention of this document was to render freer and more straightforward the celebration of the Mass according to the Missal of 1962, the one which preceded the liturgical reforms following Vatican II. The reform was not without problematical aspects of great concern, though it had positive features as well. The reaction that took place after the council caused many divisions, the most famous being that of the French bishop Marcel Lefebvre. We will have to discuss his case in more depth later.

We were speaking about the deviance of the postconciliar period. Pope Francis stated the following during a conference on sacred music at the Augustinianum in March 2017 on the occasion of the fiftieth anniversary of *Musicam Sacram*, one of the first documents applied to the liturgical reform:

> The various protagonists of this area, musicians and composers, directors and chorists of *scholae cantorum*, liturgical animators, can give a precious contribution to the renewal, especially qualitative renewal, of sacred music and liturgical song. To encourage this path, an adequate musical formation must be promoted, also for those who are preparing to become priests, in dialogue

with the musical currents of our time, with the
contribution of the various cultural fields, and
with an ecumenical attitude.

Certainly, here too, as in other writings of the Pontiff, there
is liberty in interpretation that renders arduous the decoding
of the practical sense of what the Pope means to say. What
does he mean, for example, when he speaks of "musical currents of our time"? This is not easy to understand. However,
although the Pope is a son of the council in every sense of
the word, he is also therefore a son of that postconciliar op-
timism that continues to drive a certain narrative in favor of
this event (to the discredit of a more rigorous analysis of what
really happened, both positive and negative), and cannot but
recognize that mediocrity, superficiality, banality have set in.
These elements are not limited to sacred music, but given
that it is intimately united to the liturgy, they could not but
touch the celebration itself. And why ask musicians, cantors,
and organists to give their contribution when one well knows
it has not been requested, when experience shows that quite
often it is the clergy (de)formed in the postconciliar period
that is the number-one enemy of the dignity of the liturgy?
It echoes that other document of the same Pontiff, in which
he speaks of China and the Chinese people in these terms:
"On the civil and political level, Chinese Catholics are good
citizens, they love their country and serve their countrymen
with commitment and honesty.... This can require of them
the effort to say a critical word." A critical word? It would
probably be their last.

The crisis in the Church is not an invention of traditionalists longing to continue to say their Mass in Latin, but has been certified by the facts, by the collapse in participation in the sacraments, by the increasing irrelevance of the Church in society, by the fact that more and more church buildings are being converted for various and sundry uses because they lack faithful who would pray in them. Eliminating traditionalists will not resolve the problem, because they did not create it; like many others, they are *victims* of it.

Our priest continued to pray unperturbed and to finger his rosary beads. All the while outside, Rome offered one of those evenings in which the sky seemed to turn an all-consuming red. That sky then seemed to invade the church and paint it in hues that recalled the Passion of the Savior and of all those who, despite the world's opposition, desired to stay united to Him.

If the faithful seemed dismayed, he, the priest, was not. He had awaited that document for months. There had been inklings, leaks from the Vatican. Important prelates had been taking an especially harsh tone toward traditionalists lately. Even so, it seems that within the Curia too, not all were in agreement on the opportune nature of restrictions of this type. Not everyone in Rome shares the current Pontiff's harsh attitude toward traditionalists. Yet all can find common ground in the clear idea that at the origin of it all there was an event, an event that was also clearly invoked by Pope Francis in the document published that day and which would be impossible to ignore if we want to understand something about the traditional Catholic world: the Second Vatican Council.

In this sense, the message was crystal clear. *Traditionis Custodes* reinforced the view that Vatican II constituted, essentially, the foundational event of a new Church. But this was not the intention of the majority of the Council Fathers, as it was not the intention of the one who convoked Vatican II. This strategy, unfortunately, can be observed in the strange haste to canonize all the Popes of the Council, while those before them all seemed filthy and bad. Now, I do not wish to discuss the personal sanctity of every Pope ... but all this haste?

Furthermore, had it not been repeated that the traditional Mass could have and ought to have been reformed? But we knew this: changes and additions have always occurred. The problem is that a distortion took place. No one can convince me that the passage from Palestrina to *Le tue mani son piene di fiori* (a popular song used inappropriately in the liturgy of the Italian Church) is part of the organic development of the rite. And yet, in 2017, Pope Francis said to the representatives of the Center of Liturgical Action, "After this magisterium, after this long path we can affirm with certainty and with magisterial authority that the liturgical reform is irreversible." One struggles to understand how the traditional rite can be reversible while this liturgical reform, "with magisterial authority," is not. What strategy does all of this point to, and who are the interested parties? Why all this negative attention to traditional Catholics and openness toward non-Catholics, non-Christians, nonbelievers? Now we will consider the question that so many in the Church are now asking: *Why?*

CHAPTER 2

The Age of the Good Pope

VATICAN II

THE POPE ACCEPTED THE help of two cardinals as he put on the amice and alb, tied with a cincture, together with the rest of the pontifical habit. Angelo Giuseppe Roncalli, John XXIII, was burdened by thought. That day was like no other in his pontificate. An enormous weight had been placed on his shoulders when he was already quite old. And yet he, the son of a peasant farmer, with the appearance of a peasant, had stunned the world when just a few years earlier, on January 25, 1959, he had announced to the cardinals present in the chapter hall of the canons in St. Peter's the calling of an ecumenical council. An ecumenical council! Rome had not seen a council for nearly one hundred years, when the First Vatican Council was interrupted in 1870 by the events that led to the end of the Popes' temporal power.

The Pope seemed absent as he reviewed in his mind those words pronounced on that January 25 before the speechless onlookers:

> Venerable Brothers and Beloved Sons of Ours!
> We pronounce before you, certainly trembling a
> bit with emotion, but together with humble reso-
> lution in our aims, the name and the proposal of
> this double celebration: of a Diocesan Synod for
> the Urbe, and of an Ecumenical Council for the
> universal Church.... For today, this communica-
> tion suffices, made to the assembled Sacred
> College here gathered, imploring you to transmit
> this message to the other Lord Cardinals already
> returned to the various episcopal seats entrusted
> to them throughout the entire world.

Certainly, that was more than enough, seeing that the announcement had profoundly shaken those present. Later
rhetoric would represent that idea as a sort of "sudden il-
lumination," but in reality the Pope had been thinking of
it for some time, and he had spoken a few days after his
election to his faithful secretary, Loris Capovilla, who remembered long after:

> When the Pope spoke to me about it for the first
> time, he had been Pope for just five days. He
> made a vague gesture and said, "On my table
> there are many problems, questions and con-
> cerns. It would take something singular and
> new, not only a Holy Year." In the Code of
> Canon Law, which had been reformed not long
> before, there is a chapter called "*De Concilio
> Ecumenico*."

So it is obvious that the idea did not come to him spontaneously but had already been running through his head for some time—perhaps even before he was elected Pope.

There was no doubt that there were forces in the Church pushing for a renewal. It was, according to some, a dangerous renewal. It would undermine the foundations of the Church. Yet John XXIII was not afraid of being considered a progressive. He had promulgated documents that bore witness to his solicitude for the deposit of Tradition, such as *Aeterna Dei Sapientia* of November 11, 1961, to celebrate the centenary of St. Leo the Great, in which he had forcefully reiterated the role of the Pontifex Maximus: "Center, therefore, and fulcrum of all the visible unity of the Catholic Church is the bishop of Rome, as the successor of Peter and Vicar of Jesus Christ. The affirmations of St. Leo are simply the most faithful echo of the Gospel texts and of the perennial Catholic tradition." He also recalled in the same document that it was his deep desire to witness the return of those who were separated. But he also specified what was, according to him, the objective of that Council he had just convoked:

> It is precisely with the aim of rendering the Church more capable of carrying out in our time that sublime mission, that we proposed to convoke the Second Ecumenical Vatican Council, in the confidence that the impressive gathering of Catholic hierarchy, shall not only reinforce the bonds of unity in faith, in worship and in governance, which are the prerogative of the true

> Church, but also shall attract the attention of
> innumerable believers in Christ and shall invite
> them to gather around the "great Pastor of the
> flock" (Heb 13:20), whose perennial guardian-
> ship he entrusted to Peter and to his successors
> (cf. Jn 21:15-17).

Indeed, this was an invitation to return to the Church of Rome
under the jurisdiction of the Supreme Pastor, the Pope. That
this did not please many Protestants was not hard to imagine.
What had happened to the ecumenical movement?

There was another document that certainly could not
have been promulgated by a progressive Pope, the Apostolic
Constitution *Veterum Sapientia* of February 1962, just weeks
before the start of the Council. What was the topic of this
document? Nothing less than the study of Latin! Just
months before the Council, on which some had placed their
hopes that the vernacular languages would be introduced
into the liturgy, the Pope wrote a document defending Latin,
and he did so in noble and lofty words that would surely
have traditionalists trembling with emotion even in our day:

> It is necessary that the Church use language that
> is not only universal, but also unchanging. If, in
> fact, the truth of the Catholic Church were en-
> trusted to some or many of the modern languages
> that are subject to continual mutation, none of
> which having greater authority or prestige than
> the other, due to their variety, it would not be
> manifest to many with sufficient precision and

clarity the sense of these truths, nor would there be a common and stable language with which to compare the meaning of the others.

The document also said:

> The same bishops and superiors general of religious orders, moved by paternal solicitude, shall be vigilant that none of their subjects, itching for novelty, should write against the use of the Latin language in teaching the sacred disciplines and in the sacred rites of the liturgy and, with preconceived opinions, permit themselves to exasperate the will of the Holy See in this matter and to interpret it erroneously.

Pope John XXIII a progressive? Who could have thought that?

While the rite of his investiture continued, he looked around the beautiful and sumptuous Hall of the Vestments. That October 11 was the feast of the Divine Maternity of the Blessed Virgin Mary, and he placed under her protection the Council that was about to begin. He had risen quite early as was his habit, before five o'clock, and looking out the window, he noticed that it was raining. Raining! Today? The Pope feared that the weather might ruin the solemn procession in St. Peter's Square, a truly historic event for the Church with such a large number of bishops gathered. But the rain subsided a few hours later. The master of ceremonies was surely nervous because of this, but then they decided to proceed with the original program.

That day, as the Pope was carried upon the gestatorial chair in the solemn procession that led to the basilica, he did not appear as jovial as usual. Rather he was aloof, lost in thought, perhaps aware of the great responsibility he had assumed. He was the Pope; it was fully within his rights to convoke a council, but this event was not a light matter. It was a shock that could put into motion good as well as bad things. For this reason, he had spent a week preparing the discourse for the Mass of Inauguration, a discourse that was not without controversy. The journalist Ignazio Ingrao, in *The Secret Council*, says that the Italian version was manipulated:

> If we reread what *L'Osservatore Romano* wrote, "The substance of the ancient doctrine of the *depositum fidei* is one thing; the formulation of its covering is another." While the Pope had said in Latin, "One thing is the deposit of the faith, namely the truths that are contained in our venerable doctrine, another is the way by which they are announced, always in the same sense and in the same meaning." (*Est enim aliud ipsum depositum Fidei, seu veritates, quae veneranda doctrina nostra continentur, aliud modus, quo eaedem enuntiantur, eodem tamen sensu eademque sententia.*)

We can already see here that someone is trying to stick a wrench in the spokes! However, the same Ingrao also said this: "The historian Alberto Melloni, director of the John

XXIII Foundation for Religious Sciences in Bologna, who has studied Vatican II and the *Gaudet Mater Ecclesia* [the Pope's convocation address] his whole life, turns the question on its head: it was not the Italian version that was manipulated but rather the Latin version."

Really? Well, the Council becomes a mystery novel right from its opening, and reasons for concern were not few. Pope John himself would try to clarify the aim of the Council in a discourse in December of the same year, in which he said,

> From the renewed, serene and tranquil adhesion to all that the Church teaches in its entirety and precision, as it radiates still today in the documents of the Councils of Trent and Vatican I, the Christian, Catholic and Apostolic spirit of the entire world awaits a leap forward towards a doctrinal penetration and a more lively formation of consciences, in perfect fidelity to the authentic doctrine; but this must be studied and elucidated by means of the modes of inquiry and literary formulation of modern thought ... all measured in the modes and proportions of a magisterium predominantly pastoral in character.

Yet this would not avoid numerous problems that would come out of the Council, and which, as we shall see, would continue for many decades to come.

The Pope knew well that there were new ideas, that the various currents of thought that agitated the intellectual scene (biblical, ecumenical, liturgical) were influencing high-ranking members of the clergy and yet did not align with traditional Catholic doctrine. Was it perhaps for this reason that Pius XII had considered a council but then gave up the idea? Pope John thought about his predecessor, sage and learned, and about his prudence. Why did he not convoke a council? It is said for reasons linked to his age, but John was in the same condition as well. Others held that he did not because Pius XII had understood that it was better not to tempt fate, seeing the agitated times in Catholic thought. Was he afraid that a certain progressive current would take the reins and direct the Church where she ought not to go? This thought must have agitated the Pope's mind on that fateful day, October 11, 1962. In his mind he went back in time, many decades earlier. It was August 10, 1904.

A Young Priest and the Embattled Church

That August day in 1904, at the Basilica of St. Mary in Montesanto, seminarian Angelo Giuseppe Roncalli was surrounded by a bustle of people busily preparing a liturgical ceremony which was to begin shortly. Roncalli was particularly emotional because he was about to be ordained to the priesthood. This was to bring to fulfillment a path that had begun with so much difficulty, but also with great zeal. He would celebrate his first Mass at St. Peter's, the day after his ordination — the same place where he would later be elevated to the supreme dignity of the pontificate. He remembered that first Mass in St. Peter's, because he was to be received at midday by Pope Pius X. In his *Giornale dell'anima* (*Journal of a Soul*) he remembered the event thus:

When the Pope reached me and the vice-rector presented me to him, he smiled and bent over to listen to me. I spoke to him kneeling and told him I was glad to humble myself at his feet, sharing the sentiments I had placed during my first Mass at the tomb of St. Peter, and I presented them briefly as best I could. Then the Pope, still bent over me, placed his hand on my head, and almost speaking into my ear, said to me, "Good, good, my son … that is pleasing to me. And I shall pray the Lord that he bless in a special way these good intentions and that you are truly a priest according to his heart."

These were certainly beautiful memories for Angelo, the new priest.

But we return now to St. Mary's in Montesanto, the beautiful church in Piazza del Popolo, where one of the most important streets in Rome passes. Assisting at that Mass was a priest who would become quite famous, Ernesto Buonaiuti (1881–1946). Buonaiuti was to become one of the protagonists of that reform movement in the Catholic Church that took the name of Modernism, the attempt to accommodate Catholicism to the mentality of the modern world.

Historians place the Modernist movement between the last decades of the nineteenth century and the death of St. Pius X in 1914. The unrelenting battle against Modernism was carried out thanks to this Pope, who defined this error in his most important document concerning this fight, *Pascendi* (1907), as the "synthesis of all heresies." This was so because Modernism did not have just one manifestation but appeared in many fields: philosophical, theological, social, and biblical. Among its most resolute protagonists were the Irish Jesuit George Tyrrell (1861–1909) and the French priest Alfred Loisy (1857–1940). Together with Buonaiuti, these three were to become the reference points of Modernism, and due to their affirmations they were reduced to the lay state and excommunicated (Buonaiuti three times!). And not merely a simple excommunication, but rather what was called *vitando*, the gravest of punishments, which obliged others to avoid the excommunicated person and to reconsecrate places of worship if the person was seen to enter there.

Effectively, Pius X's battle against Modernism was one of the distinguishing elements of his pontificate. In *Pascendi*, he says, "What urges us to action above all is the fact that the agents of error are no longer to be found among declared enemies; but what gives us such great remorse and trepidation, is that they hide in the very bosom of the Church, all the more pernicious as they are more hidden from view."

The document confronted this muddle of heresies with great forcefulness, because it clearly intuited that behind Modernism lurked the currents of thought that spanned from Luther to Jansen, from Kant to Hegel, and on through modern philosophy. A current of thought that, according to Catholic doctrine, could not be allowed if one wanted to see the world with the eyes of authentic faith.

Furthermore, Modernists were astute and understood that victory might not be had in their lifetime. The repression under Pius X was not light; vigilance toward all that reeked of Modernism was intense—at times one could say obsessive. One of the most well-known Modernists was Antonio Fogazzaro (1842–1911), and his novel *Il Santo* (*The Saint*) became a manifesto for Modernists. Dripping with ideas of religious reform and the desire to accommodate to the world, there is a famous passage which refers to a meeting of "Catholic reformers" who are planning what to do. Giovanni Selva, one of the band leaders, says,

> Look, there are a lot of us Catholics in Italy and abroad, ecclesiastics and laymen, who want reform in the Church. We want it without rebellion, carried through by legitimate authority. We want reforms in religious teaching, reforms in worship, reforms in the discipline of clergy, reforms even in the supreme governance of the Church. For this reason, we need to create an opinion that would induce the legitimate authority to act accordingly even in twenty, thirty, or fifty years. Now, we who think in this way are in fact dispersed. We know nothing of each other, except for the few who publish articles and books. Most likely, there is in the Catholic world a great quantity of people, religious and educated, who think like us. I thought it might be useful, in order to spread our ideas, at least to get to know each other. This evening a few of us will meet to come to an agreement.

The plan being hatched through this literary fiction was impressive, and for some was to become reality. Buonaiuti too had said, in the anonymous documents he had written, that they needed to conquer Rome with the help of Rome. *The Modernist Program*, a pamphlet he had helped to write, explained the purpose of Modernism, saying, "We must defend the entire critical foundation and the factual presupposition of all our thought; we must show that if Modernism is not a simple or unambiguous name, it is a method, or better it is the critical method applied as a duty to religious forms of humanity in general and to Catholicism in particular."

That is, it was religion investigated with the always-changing methods of science. Not that these cannot or should not be used in certain settings! But to reduce all of faith to an object of human investigation and pure rational comprehension means condemning it to irrelevance. St. Augustine said that if we understood God, he would not be God.

Now, Modernism is a complex phenomenon, and an extremely pervasive one. Pius X's battle against all its manifestations was truly intense. But did he defeat it? It is true, historians declare its end to be in 1914 with the death of the great Pontiff. But when the Pope was praised for having defeated Modernism, it seems he was offended. He understood that he had won a battle, but had not won the war.

In fact, Modernism had an important social manifestation, well represented by the priest Romolo Murri (1870–1944) — he too reduced to the lay state and excommunicated. He sought to reconcile Catholicism, democracy, and socialism and was at the origin of what then became the political party *Democrazia Cristiana* (Christian Democrats), witness to the labors of another priest, Luigi Sturzo

(1871–1959). The Christian Democrat Party, after the fall of Benito Mussolini's fascism, dominated Italy's political life for many decades.

Then, at the beginning of the century, the Liturgical Movement began, seeking the renewal and deepening of the rites of the Church. The movement had a strong impulse, thanks to intellectuals of centuries past such as Mabillon and Muratori, and especially thanks to the work of Dom Prosper Guéranger (1805–1875), abbot of Solesmes. It was quickly infiltrated by several currents of thought which aligned with those of certain fringe Modernist groups. This was due above all to the work of another Benedictine monk, Lambert Beauduin (1873–1960), founder of the Monastery of Chevetogne. His work for the reform of the liturgy was inspired by a passage of an important document by Pius X on the restoration of sacred music, *Inter pastoralis officii sollicitudines*, his motu proprio of November 22, 1903. This passage stated,

> It being, in fact, Our intense desire that the true Christian spirit blossoms once again in every way and is maintained in all the faithful, it is necessary to provide for the sanctity and dignity of the temple before every other thing, there where the faithful gather to draw that spirit from its first and indispensable source, which is the active participation in the sacrosanct mysteries and in the public and solemn prayer of the Church.

This passage led Dom Beauduin to work unsparingly in favor of a liturgical reform encouraging greater participation of the people in the sacred rites. Obviously, no one could object to this desire; everyone was sympathetic to greater participation by the faithful in a more intense manner in the rites of the Church. But at what price? At a certain point it seemed that to foster this participation one had to dismember the rite. It would be like inviting someone to visit a beautiful house but then making a mess of it to render it more acceptable. If the house is no longer beautiful, why would anyone want to come and visit?

The passage of Pius X should be reconsidered, as it was to become a banner for future causes. In this regard, the scholar Carol Byrne, in a book published in 2020 on the liturgical movement called *Born of a Revolution*, says the following:

> It is only in the Italian version (which lacks the authoritative status of the Latin version) that the expression "active participation" made its sudden and unexpected irruption. One theory of how the Italian phrase "*partecipazione attiva*" found its way into TLS [*Tra le sollecitudini*] is that it could have been inserted by the person who actually drew up the text, the Vatican musicologist Fr. Angelo de Santi SJ, who had been closely associated with the Pope's musical reforms when the latter was Bishop of Mantua and Patriarch of Venice. This is a distinct possibility, considering that Fr. de Santi was known to have used this expression in articles he had written on sacred music even before the 1903 motu proprio.

Whatever might be the true interpretation of the phrase, and whether or not that little word had truly been added, we know that the idea of "participation" was much discussed at the time, as it is today, seeing that this concept would be at the center of the liturgical reform of Vatican II.

This participation did not only have liturgical implications, however, but also political ones, as we have seen. We recall the matter of Marc Sangnier (1873–1950) and of his journal *Sillon*. He was inspired by Leo XIII's social teaching and proposed the involvement of Catholics in social issues, but at a certain point, he was condemned by Pius X under suspicion of political Modernism. But whether political or liturgical, the appeals brought forth by Modernists continued to spread, and new generations of theologians took the baton and raced forward with these ideas. Some of the important old guard exponents of Modernism, such as Loisy and Buonaiuti, were still alive in the 1940s, and thus still capable of influencing the new generations, despite their excommunicated status.

In the political sphere, there were attempts to bring together socialism, communism, and Christianity, an effort that the hierarchy had always condemned. However, we recall a text by Buonaiuti, precisely at the end of his life, in 1945, which he begins thus: "Christianity was born Communist, and Communism was born Christian."

THE NEW THEOLOGY

All these currents of thought spreading out from Modernism continued to be present in the Church like subterranean rivers, and soon enough they were incarnated in important theologies whose ideas were to have great relevance at the Second Vatican Council. The Church realized this and faced the question in various ways. Here we remember above all an important document by Pius XII, the encyclical *Humani Generis* of 1950, in which the Pontiff attempted to confront this new theology. But was it truly new? It was certainly formulated in a new way, but for the most part it recycled well-known ideas that, in part, had already been condemned.

Pius XII's encyclical confronted the problem on its own terms. It suffices to read several sentences at the beginning of the document: "Disagreement and error among men on moral and religious matters have always been a cause of profound sorrow to all good men, but above all to the true and loyal sons of the Church, especially today, when we see the principles of Christian culture being attacked on all sides."

Further on, the Pope deals with the ideas which were undermining the intellectual foundations of the Church. The citation is a bit long, but it is worth the effort to read.

> How deplorable it is then that this philosophy, received and honored by the Church, is scorned by some, who shamelessly call it outmoded in form and rationalistic, as they say, in its method of thought. They say that this philosophy upholds the erroneous notion that there can be a metaphysic that is absolutely true; whereas in fact, they say, reality, especially transcendent reality, cannot better be expressed than by disparate teachings, which mutually complete each other, although they are in a way mutually opposed. Our

traditional philosophy, then, with its clear exposition and solution of questions, its accurate definition of terms, its clear-cut distinctions, can be, they concede, useful as a preparation for scholastic theology, a preparation quite in accord with medieval mentality; but this philosophy hardly offers a method of philosophizing suited to the needs of our modern culture. They allege, finally, that our perennial philosophy is only a philosophy of immutable essences, while the contemporary mind must look to the existence of things and to life, which is ever in flux. While scorning our philosophy, they extol other philosophies of all kinds, ancient and modern, oriental and occidental, by which they seem to imply that any kind of philosophy or theory, with a few additions and corrections if need be, can be reconciled with Catholic dogma. No Catholic can doubt how false this is, especially where there is question of those fictitious theories they call immanentism, or idealism or materialism, whether historic or dialectic, or even existentialism, whether atheistic or simply the type that denies the validity of the reason in the field of metaphysics.

The Pontiff had understood that something was returning from the past, a past that he too, as a young priest, had experienced. Modernism, with its immanentism and its rationalism, had not been defeated but only weakened. Now its strength was recovered, and it effectively took advantage of an opening to continue to influence the life of the Church.

When this encyclical was written, Buonaiuti and Loisy had been dead for several years. Despite the judgment the Catholic Church had given them, it cannot be denied that they were men of great intellectual stature, as were many of the protagonists of the Modernist movement. These intellectual gifts only made them even more dangerous. Now a new group of theologians was arising, they too men of great intellectual stature who considered renewal in the Church to be necessary, but who seemed to take it in a less than prudent direction, assuming great risks. Who were these intellectuals?

THE *NOUVELLE VAGUE* IN THEOLOGY

I shall begin with the French Jesuit Teilhard de Chardin (1881–1955), who had one of the greatest influences on theological thought in the previous century. Precisely because of his influence, seven years before his death the Holy Office published a *monitum*, a warning to alert him to the presence in his works of elements problematic for Catholic orthodoxy. A text by Gianandrea de Antonellis for the journal *Radici Cristiane* (*Christian Roots*) discussed these elements in the French Jesuit's work:

> Teilhard was a pantheistic and evolutionist theologian, considered one of the masters of Modernism.... Teilhard fascinates both heterodox and orthodox believers. Yet, one must acknowledge the curious fact that Freemasonry has claimed the rights to publish and sell his posthumous books, insofar as they are devoid of Catholic Doctrine.... The

> evanescencies of Teilhard, of a pantheistic type, are
> most harmful for the necessary concreteness of the
> ascetic path and of Christian life and destroy the
> "originality of Christianity," which is the intimate,
> personal relationship with the concrete and most
> amiable Man-God.

And yet, Teilhard has become popular once more in our time. Even during his life, he had his defenders. He is without a doubt one of the authorities of a change of mentality in the Catholic world. This man with an almost demure appearance was to be one of the strongest voices in Catholicism in the twentieth century.

Another important Jesuit comes to mind: Henri de Lubac (1896–1991), a figure of great importance in the theological panorama of the past century. He was a peritus at Vatican II and was also made a cardinal. Cardinal Angelo Scola called him "the heir and father of Vatican II" (*Avvenire*). Francesco Lamendola comments on de Lubac's career in this way:

> After the promulgation of the encyclical *Humani Generis* of Pius XII, which harshly condemned the "new theology," accusing it of being a new form of Modernism, the Jesuits removed his teaching position and his books were removed from Catholic faculties. De Lubac left Lyon and moved to Paris for several years. His rehabilitation and the remarkable recovery of his career smack of the prodigious but can be explained by the death of Pius XII.

After a period of suffering in the Church of Pacelli, de Lubac was able to enjoy full rehabilitation in the conciliar Church. He was certainly an important author, and many of his works reflect great profundity. Don Ennio Innocenti, an expert on Gnosticism, wrote in 2000 of the judgment of the cardinal of Genoa, Giuseppe Siri, on de Lubac's work, saying that it was "subversive." Then Innocenti continues, "We thought it necessary to indicate in Henri de Lubac a source of theological contamination particularly insidious because it is masked." He was, then, a theologian whose ideas were seen with suspicion but who found rebirth. According to father Andrea Mancinella, in his book *Surnaturel* of 1946,

> De Lubac presented his thought on the relationship between supernatural grace and human nature: despite the usual ambiguities and posturing as a misunderstood victim, supernatural grace was considered as necessarily due to man by God, as a constitutive element of man's nature. For those who did not capture the gravity of the question, we recall that from this affirmation, postulating a humanity that remained *de facto* in a state of grace and therefore also "self-sufficient" in the order of knowledge of God and eternal salvation, the demolition of the dogma of original sin necessarily followed, in the sense understood by the Church, and the complete stultification of Revelation, of Redemption and of the mission of the Church itself, which was relegated to being an accessory reality, entirely relative.

Here as well, ideas which once would have been accepted only with great difficulty due to their contrast with traditional theology now seemed to be in vogue.

If we can pass easily from Teilhard to de Lubac, it is also simple to pass from de Lubac to another Jesuit, Hans Urs von Balthasar (1905–1988). He too was announced to become a cardinal, but he died before he could be donned in purple. This Swiss thinker was unique and even tormented, particularly active in the field of aesthetical theology, in which he was hailed as a great master. He was the author of voluminous reflections and was also the propagator of theories not exactly in line with traditional Catholic doctrine, such as the idea that Hell might be empty.

In his critical analysis of von Balthasar's thought, Fr. Curzio Nitoglia, a former member of the Society of St. Pius X and the current director of the journal *Sì Sì No No* (*Yes Yes No No*), founded by Fr. Francesco Maria Putti in 1975, affirms:

> Although he was not called to the Council as a peritus, "he made his influence strongly felt: his ideas of reform and aggiornamento found vast consensus there and entered into the conciliar texts...." According to von Balthasar, revelation "cannot be set aside and preserved," because "today it is fresh, tomorrow it rots." It should be "reconsidered from the top," including "language ..., concepts," otherwise "it gets dusty, it rusts and crumbles."

These quotes from Fr. Nitoglia's study furnish us with an idea of the dangerous thought, however fascinating, of von Balthasar.

We continue to talk about Jesuits by introducing the one who was considered the diamond tip of progressive thought in the period before and after the Council, who in a poll taken at Gregorian University was judged the most recognized theologian by students, even more than St. Thomas Aquinas: Karl Rahner (1904–1984). With Karl Rahner we are considering one of the key names of the theological renewal of the Council. If on one side he was idolized by progressive theologians, on the other he was harshly condemned by those who sought to defend Catholic orthodoxy. He was a particularly cryptic author in the way he expressed his thought; in a text recalling the ferocious criticism of Rahner's thought by the theologian Cornelio Fabro, Silvio Andreucci writes,

> In *The Anthropological Shift of Karl Rahner*, Fr. Cornelio Fabro denounces the misrepresentation carried out by the Jesuit regarding healthy Thomistic doctrine. This was a clear mystification and manipulation of the Thomistic texts, despite the often-declared intention to reproduce doctrine faithfully, effectively a downright unhinging of fundamental Thomistic principles.

Having said this, it comes perhaps as no surprise that he too was a peritus at Vatican II, an expert theologian to Cardinal Franz König. There is no need to hide the immense influence he had there.

Then there is John Courtney Murray (1904–1967). He was also invited as an expert to the Council and was very influential in the drafting of *Dignitatis Humanae*, on religious freedom. Piergiorgio Grassi (rivistadialoghi.it) portrays his experience at the Council in this way:

> The news that John Courtney Murray, professor at Woodstock College in Maryland, the oldest Jesuit college in the United States, had been called to take part in the work at the beginning of the second session of Vatican II (1963), took many Council Fathers by surprise.... The greatest obstacle lay in the fact that religious liberty as an essential principle to the civil and international legal system seemed not to find an echo in the interpretation of the magisterium of the Popes of the nineteenth century. To the contrary, the structure that had supported the argumentation in favor of a certain solution to relations between Church and State resisted the renewed interpretation that sought a complete reorganization of the entire question. As some qualified scholars noted, when they were still discussing the first draft presented in the assembly by the Belgian Bishop Emiel-Joseph De Smedt, the content seemed to "go beyond the previous doctrine of the Catholic Church, not in a gradual manner, but starkly as a matter of principle."

The perception that they were going beyond traditional doctrine was naturally not only felt in that assembly, but had repercussions in the reactions of traditionalists, such that this document was to be one of the most important, as we shall see, for understanding the following ones.

I would like to say that I have finished with the Jesuits at this point, but this would not be true. It is peculiar how they represented the strongest resistance to Modernism at the beginning of the twentieth century, while later in that same century they mounted the barricades of progressivism. Now we shall consider another Jesuit who was also a peritus at the Council and then made a cardinal: Jean Daniélou (1904–1974). While not as famous as some of his brother Jesuits, he nevertheless had considerable importance. To understand his attitude toward the Council, we entrust ourselves once more to the analysis of Silvio Andreucci: "The highly acceptable '*destruens*' work of Catholic progressivism which Fr. Daniélou carried out in the first section of his work *Objectionable Objections* risks being, at least for the most part, frustrated by his naively positive evaluation of the Second Vatican Council, in which he is led to recognize a 'hermeneutic of continuity in the tradition.' "

There is also Michel de Certau (1925–1986), who was perhaps a more ambiguous intellectual figure compared to his Jesuit brethren, but who was quite active in the postconciliar period, especially in his attention to psychoanalysis.

Moving on now from the Jesuits, we move to the Dominicans.

First we cite Marie-Dominique Chenu (1895–1990), a distinguished medievalist. His fellow Dominican Gerardo Cioffari remembers his difficulties with the Pacelli Church, due to his less than orthodox ideas, in this way:

Chenu must have suffered a nasty surprise through his Augustinian shift together with the thesis of the necessity of renewing theological language. In 1927, he had even used the term "rationalism" to emphasize the centrality of reason in St. Thomas and was thus seen as a theologian who did not sufficiently appreciate the autonomy of philosophy and reason. According to Donneaud, therefore, his theological evolution might have been caused by criticism from ecclesiastical circles.

Fr. Chenu contributed especially to the constitution *Gaudium et Spes*. Reading his appraisal of the days of the Council, one notes his anxiousness for renewal and his disdain for the structures and rites of the preconciliar Church. It is enlightening reading.

One of the pivotal names of the theology of that time was another Dominican, Yves Congar (1904–1995), another figure of highest visibility at the Council. He too was awarded with the cardinalate toward the end of his life. There is no doubt that Congar was one of the most important names in theology in the previous century, not only because of the volume of his work, but also due to the influence he had on many theologians to come. His career is, effectively, similar to that of the other theologians we have already considered; namely. one of suffering hostility in the preconciliar Church due to his positions judged not entirely orthodox, only to be rehabilitated and valorized following Vatican II. He investigated oriental and Protestant spirituality, attempting to recover elements from these systems in the

Catholic tradition. Fr. Luigi Villa, director of the bellicose journal *Chiesa viva* (*Church Alive*), published a booklet on Congar, in which he gave this judgment:

> In the Pauline journal *Jesus* of October 1990, which together with *Famiglia Cristiana*, sow doctrinal corruption in every parish, one had the audacity to call Congar "a giant among theologians" and "a great one for whom we feel so much nostalgia." If this be true, one need only read the text of the person interviewed to come to terms with the theological stature of that "giant," who presents erroneous judgments on Luther, on the state of theology in France, on reconciliation with the Anglicans, to arrive at the denial even of the existence of Hell, of which he affirms "he does not believe in the least," providing as explanation that "the eternal punishment of Hell is not possible, because God revealed himself as Love; therefore, if there is a Hell what does this mean? And what does eternal mean?... That there are no longer days nor time. In our life, we cannot in the least way represent the other life. St. Paul, moreover, says it quite well, 'those things which eye has not seen, and ear has not heard, which have never entered the heart of man, these God has prepared for those who love him' (1 Cor 2:9). We have no experience of it and, therefore, no idea of the afterlife."

Now, as I said, the polemical style of Fr. Villa can certainly be criticized, and not all that he says should be believed without reflection. But his rancor toward Congar and toward other theologians of the *Nouvelle theologie* can be explained by the enormous impact they have had on the Church. I am lingering over them because without them the Council cannot be explained, and without the Council, present-day traditionalism cannot be clarified. They too must be explained without losing sight of Modernism, which is an important harbinger of all that I am narrating.

Continuing with the Dominicans, we must speak now about Edward Schillebeeckx (1914–2009), a Belgian theologian of the University of Nijmegen. He had many problems with authorities in Rome, although he was never formally condemned by them. He was certainly influenced by modern theology and was a standard-bearer for it in his country. Fr. Giovanni Cavalcoli, also a Dominican and beyond suspicion of traditionalist sympathies, offers this judgment in a text from 2016:

> Clearly, I limit myself here to signaling the errors, without downplaying the merits of Schillebeeckx, and I do so because these errors have not yet been sufficiently highlighted, with the consequence that they do damage to the Church. The errors are more numerous than I point out here. I limit myself to the main ones, referring to the interventions of the Congregation for the Doctrine of the Faith: after the first reprimands in 1969, 1976, and 1978, the Letter of November 20, 1980, that of June 13, 1984, and the Notification of September 15, 1986. The fundamental accusation made

against him was that of having carried out in an erroneous and misleading way the task assigned to theologians at the Second Vatican Council of advancing theology, offering the Church a reinterpretation of Catholic doctrine obtained from a critical comparison with modern thought, faithful to the Magisterium of the Church, and to the doctrine of St. Thomas Aquinas. In fact, Schillebeeckx, basing himself on an erroneous notion of rational knowledge and of faith, fell into numerous grave errors in the conception of dogma, Christology, ecclesiology, sacramental and moral theology and eschatology, and in the comparison of Christianity with other religions. The underlying vice of Schillebeeckx's thought is of having built his house on the sand (Matt. 7:26). It is, therefore, an unreliable thought, which, in the light of modernity and freedom of opinion, never gives security and never persuades, due to the lack of solid arguments and fidelity to the Magisterium of the Church.

I repeat, although Cavalcoli is certainly not a traditionalist and is a fellow Dominican, he offers a very harsh judgment of Schillebeeckx.

We now recall that he discussed another star of progressive theology, recently deceased, the Swiss Hans Küng (1928–2021), for decades at the center of a media firestorm—and he knew how to handle the press. Fr. Cavalcoli wrote in 2021,

> Küng was a disciple of Rahner and with him was
> one of the principal creators of the Modernist
> interpretation of the Council, which sparked as
> a reaction the rise of the Priestly Society of St.
> Pius X, it too believing the Modernist character
> of the Council doctrine, with the difference that
> while for Küng he delighted in the fact, the
> Lefebvrians regretted it.

Fr. Cavalcoli's analysis is sufficiently clear to see on one side the importance of Küng in the development of postconciliar thought, but also to see the dangers that derived from it, on the other.

There are certainly other theologians to mention, but this would lead us too far from our topic. Yet I cannot omit alluding to another intellectual who had a great influence over the Council and who would continue to have great influence afterward: Joseph Ratzinger. For obvious reasons, we shall discuss him extensively as our narrative continues.

One might think that the influence of these theologians and their progressive ideas were in the end not as important as it seems. But this would surely be a deception. Their influence was very important—and not only in the ecclesial setting but also in social and political settings. This is confirmed by one of the most well-known activists of the protest movement of those years, Mario Capanna, a student at the Catholic University of Milan. In his important book *Formidabili quegli anni* (*Those Tremendous Years*), he recalls the following:

We studied day and night. But not only the sub-
jects in which we were preparing for exams. We
read Marx and other Marxist authors, practically
prohibited in the official syllabi. And we read
theologians, at the time innovators on the frontiers, like Karl Rahner, Edward Schillebeeckx,
Hans Urs von Balthasar. We often discussed one
or the other of them until dawn. Precisely there,
Catholic dissent, growing in the country, was
nourished by rational and solid arguments. It was
the signal of an unrest that was branching out
and becoming profound. It was the forewarning
of politics.

THE HOLY WEEK REFORM

Returning to 1962, many thoughts doubtless rushed through
John XXIII's mind. When he convoked the Council, he took
upon himself a great responsibility. And he was certainly aware
of this. He had succeeded Pacelli, a long-serving Pope who was
admired by the people for his great culture and wisdom. And
yet, in the final years of the pontificate of Pius XII, some noticed
creaking in the works: the aging Pope was taken advantage of
by some prelates who ushered in ideas which a more vigorous
Pius XII would probably have stopped. As we have said, a
privileged field for progressive ideas was in the liturgy, and so
behold the reform of Holy Week, which gave space to those
who desired to reform the liturgy and occupied the last phase
of the Pope's life. Stefano Carusi (unavoce-ve.it) describes the
work of the Piana Commission instituted for this aim:

The Commission worked in secret and acted under the pressure of the episcopates of Central Europe, although it was not clear whether to block it or to indulge it. The secret was so well kept that the sudden and unexpected publication of the *Ordo Sabbati Sancti instaurati* in early March of 1951 "took by surprise even the officials of the Congregation for Rites," as a member of the Commission, Annibale Bugnini relates. It was the same Fr. Bugnini who tells us of the singular way by which the results of the work of the Commission on Holy Week were informing the Pope: he was "kept up to date by Msgr. Montini, and, weekly by Fr. Bea, the confessor to Pius XII. Thanks to this method they were able to attain remarkable results, even in the periods when the Pope's illness impeded most from drawing near to him." The Pope was afflicted by a serious stomach illness which required a long convalescence, and it was not the Cardinal Prefect of Rites, head of the commission, who informed him, but rather Msgr. Montini and the future Cardinal Bea, who had such a great role in later reforms.

Here there are names of colossal importance in what was to be the path of the conciliar Church, such as that of the liturgist Annibale Bugnini (1912–1982), the architect of the reform; the Jesuit Cardinal Agostino Bea (1881–1968), architect of ecumenical dialogue and in a special way of Jewish-Christian dialogue; but above all Giovanni Battista Montini

(1897–1978), who will occupy a place of honor in the story we are narrating, as we shall shortly see.

As concerns the Holy Week Reform, it was seen by some under a less than favorable light and interpreted as a sign of weakness on the part of Pius XII. This was reflected in a phrase from a discourse of September 22, 1956, to the participants at the International Congress on Pastoral Liturgy:

> Le mouvement liturgique est apparu ainsi comme un signe des dispositions providentielles de Dieu sur le temps présent, comme un passage du Saint-Esprit dans son Église, pour rapprocher davantage les hommes des mystères de la foi et des richesses de la grâce, qui découlent de la participation active des fidèles à la vie liturgique. [The liturgical movement thus appeared as a sign of God's providential provision for the present time, as a passage of the Holy Spirit in His Church, to bring men closer to the mysteries of faith and the riches of grace, which flow from the active participation of the faithful in the liturgical life.]

It seemed a clear encouragement for the Liturgical Movement, but in reality, Pius XII also said something quite different in that discourse. Was it not good that the Pope would encourage the Liturgical Movement? It was, had it not been for the fact that the direction of the Liturgical Movement no longer seemed that of Dom Guéranger and St. Pius X, but had assumed a different significance. It encouraged an idea of change in liturgy relating to the role of the priest, the use of Latin, and the preference for Gregorian chant, among other matters. Thus, the tendency was no longer one of deepening the venerable liturgy that had been received but of pushing for major changes—radical even, according to some. All of this was knocking at the doors of St. Peter's that October day in 1962. And John XXIII could certainly not ignore it.

GAUDET MATER ECCLESIA

In his opening discourse, John seemed to want to give a clear signal that would encourage those whom, according to some, he ought to have feared. We recall some of his words:

> Mother Church rejoices because, thanks to a special gift of Divine Providence, the long-awaited day has now come in which here, next to the tomb of St. Peter, under the auspices of the Virgin Mother of God, whose maternal dignity we celebrate today with joy, the Second Ecumenical Vatican Council solemnly begins.... It often occurs, as we have experienced in performing the daily apostolic ministry, that, not without offense to our ears, voices are referred to us which, although burning with zeal for religion, evaluate facts without sufficient objectivity or prudential judgment. In the current condition of human society, these are incapable of seeing anything but ruin and woe; they say our times, when compared to centuries past, seem to have worsened; and reach the point of behaving as if they had nothing to learn from history, which is a

master of life, and as if in the times of previous Councils all proceeded happily in terms of Christian doctrine, morals, and the proper liberty of the Church. To Us it seems a duty resolutely to dissent from such prophets of doom, who always announce what is worse, as if the end of the world were at hand.... In these our times, however, it is needful that the whole of Christian teaching be subjected by all to a new examination, with a serene and placid soul, without taking anything from it, in that thorough manner of thinking and of formulating words that stand out especially in the acts of the Councils of Trent and Vatican I.

These sentences seem to synthesize the message of John XXIII. The Council was to present doctrine in a new way, adapted to the times, preferring not to condemn but rather to exercise mercy, wary of prophets of doom who see disaster everywhere they look. But to whom was he referring?

Some think the Pope was referring to Cardinal Ottaviani, or perhaps to a French priest, who in fact was to comment on the Pope's words thus:

Above all, Jesus was, in line with his Precursor, a prophet of doom ... a doom which came about, but not entirely. There are still some disasters in the Gospels that are awaiting their time, a fact which gives a possibility to all prophets of doom ... until the end of time. Among the disasters and curses of Jesus, I choose this divine word: "Woe to you when all speak well of you! This is the way in which their fathers treated the false prophets" (Lk. 6:26). The entire life of John XXIII is revealed in this line. Then, I would fill a large notebook of inspired accusations, taken either from Sacred Scripture or from the works of the saints, Fathers of the Church, Pontiffs, those sent by God and miracle workers, without forgetting the Mother and Teacher of Wisdom of them all, the Virgin Mary in all of her apparitions ... up to La Salette and Fatima: all of them denounce the prophets of happiness as impostors, inspired by the devil, and corruptor of their people. Damned by God. All of them!

These are the words of Abbé Georges de Nantes (1924–2010) as reported by his disciple and successor, Brother Bruno. Abbé de Nantes was one of the great protagonists in the contestation of the Council on the traditionalist front. In reality, when the Council was announced, he was favorably surprised. In fact, he rejoiced because he thought that through it the errors that were threatening Catholic doctrine would finally be condemned. But very soon he was disabused of this hope and became one of the most ferocious critics of the Council. To this we shall return later.

John XXIII was probably soon to realize that the Council would not be a simple matter. We all remember a sort of mythologized version, like the celebrated "moon discourse" made on the evening of that same opening day, October 11, in response to the invitation of pilgrims gathered in St. Peter's Square after a torchlight procession. Who does not remember those words?

Dear children, I hear your voices. Mine is but one voice, but it gathers together the voice of the entire world; here the whole world is represented. One could say that even the moon made haste to be here this evening—look at it up there!—watching this spectacle.... Let us continue, then, to love one another, to love one another in this way, meeting each other like this, taking what unites us, leaving aside whatever, if anything, creates difficulties between us.... This morning was a spectacle which not even St. Peter's Basilica, which has four hundred years of history, has ever contemplated.... Returning to your homes, find your children; give a caress to your children and say: "This is the caress of the Pope." You might find a tear to dry. Do something, say a good word. The Pope is with you especially in the hour of sadness and bitterness. And then, all together, let us love each other, singing, sighing, crying, but always, always full of trust in Christ who helps us and listens to us, go on and take up again our path. Thus, you await the blessing that I will give you and the Good Night that you will allow me to wish you. With the prayer, though, that we are not only beginning. The Council begins and we do not know when it will end. That it might end before Christmas..."

Before Christmas? Certainly, the Pontiff was a bit too optimistic, but everyone remembers only the goodheartedness of the Pope in that discourse, that peasant's manner of winning everyone's trust, as if he had been speaking to each person individually.

Pope John was certainly a beloved Pope, but I also believe he was misunderstood to some extent. In his gestures and ways, he was definitely not a progressive. To the contrary, as a French journalist remarked in the days before the Council, he was fond of the ceremonial decorum that surrounded his function, even though he maintained great humility as far as his person was concerned. This difference between the function (the papacy) and the person (the Pope) is very important, though not every pope has understood this. The honors given to him were not for Angelo Giuseppe Roncalli but for John XXIII. I remember what my maestro, Domenico Bartolucci, told me, who directed the Sistine Chapel's Pontifical Musical Cappella in John XXIII's time. He told me how Pope John was a great benefactor of that choir, furnishing it in the best of ways so as to perform its role in the liturgy to the best of its abilities. As concerns the Council, John XXIII was audacious, especially considering his age, but perhaps this audacity revealed itself to be imprudence.

At any rate, why was he elected Pope? We should not forget that he was already seventy-seven years old at that time, and many considered him merely a transitional Pope. Perhaps some would have preferred Giovanni Battista Montini to become Pope, whom Pius XII had sent as archbishop to Milan in 1954 without making him a cardinal. Strange, it was said, seeing that Montini was one of the closest collaborators of Pius XII and had carried out a high-visibility role in the Curia. To remedy this, John XXIII made him a cardinal immediately after he was elected.

When accepting the mandate of his pontificate, John XXIII opened with these words, in which he made reference to the name chosen, John XXIII, which had also been the name of an antipope. I will quote them in Latin just as they were pronounced:

> Vocabor Ioannes. Nomen Nobis dulce, quia nomen patris Nostri: nomen Nobis suave, quia titulare est humilis paroeciae in qua baptismum accepimus: nomen sollemne innumerabilium Cathedralium, quae in toto orbe terrarum habentur, imprimisque sacrosanctae Lateranensis ecclesiae, Cathedralis Nostrae: nomen, quod in serie pervetusta Romano- rum Pontificum gaudet de maximo primatu pluralitatis. Sunt enim enumerati Summi Ponti- fices, quibus nomen Ioannes, viginti duo. Fere omnes breviter in Pontificatu vixerunt. Malumus obtegere parvitatem nominis Nostri hac magnifica Romanorum Pontificum successione. [I will be called John. A name sweet to us because it is the name of our father, dear to us because it is the name of the humble parish church where we were bap- tized, the solemn name of numberless cathedrals scattered throughout the world, including our own basilica. Twenty-two Johns of indisputable legiti- macy have [been Pope], and almost all had a brief pontificate. We have preferred to hide the smallness of our name behind this magnificent succession.]

A brief pontificate, but one that would have much longer consequences for the life of the Church.

As was needed, outlines (schemata) were prepared for the documents of the Council, outlines prepared by Roman theologians. Perhaps the Pope thought that these documents, full of robust doctrine, would gladly be accepted by the nearly 2,500 bishops gathered for the Council. The outlines had been prepared under the responsibility of the Holy Office, for some years presided over by Cardinal Alfredo Ottaviani (1890–1979), universally judged the standard-bearer of the conservative front. In reality, he truly had much in common with Angelo Giuseppe Roncalli—like himself, a son of the people.

Ottaviani came from a neighborhood in Rome associated with the most genuine people: Trastevere. I can testify to this because I too share the same origins as the illustrious cardinal and have the good fortune of living still in this celebrated part of Rome. So, coming from a family that was probably similar to that in which Ottaviani was raised, I am aware of the imprint this might have left on his character: an obstinate attitude, at times strident, but also capable of recognizing what is essential.

It is said that the short-statured Ottaviani dressed in altar boy's garb when walking through the streets of his neighborhood on the occasion of a patronal feast or the traditional procession in which the statue of the Madonna of Carmel is taken through the streets in July. The intense devotion these people are known for, and which I saw in my mother, would mark him for his entire life. This is certainly not a bad thing; on the contrary.

Like Abbé de Nantes, he probably saw in the Council an occasion for reaffirming important truths of the faith and condemning errors that threatened the purity of doctrine, such as communism. He was doubtless surprised, as was also the Pope perhaps, when two days after the opening of the Council, a first significant setback occurred.

WINDS OF REBELLION AT THE COUNCIL

In his famous discourse of the moon on October 11, John XXIII expressed his hope that the Council would close by December of 1963. Perhaps it was naïvete, but his hope was immediately extinguished from the beginning.

The day was October 13. We follow the narrative given by the journalist Ignazio Ingrao:

> The assembly entered into the heart of the debate, and it immediately became intense. It was not the best of days from many points of view. A torrential rain awaited the 2,500 council fathers at 9:00 a.m., as they hastened to enter St. Peter's Basilica for the first general congregation.... The choice to submit to the fathers the list of names found in the preconciliar commissions was not by chance: it was a trick of the Curia, with Cardinal Alfredo Ottaviani at the head (Secretary of the Holy Office), Carlo Confalonieri (Secretary of the Sacred Consistorial Congregation, the current Congregation of Bishops), and Msgr. Pericle Felici (Secretary General of the Council). The objective was to persuade the fathers, who were poorly acquainted, to choose the members of the

preceding commissions. In this way, the documents provided to them would be confirmed
and the assembly would proceed briskly, without reserving any surprises.

This might very well have been a sleight of hand, but it made
good sense. In this way, the Council could proceed quickly
and might even have finished by December, as the Pope had
hoped. But this did not happen. Let us not forget that the
Council had just begun two days earlier with a lavish ceremony
in which all the bishops participated, a ceremony whose music
and rites demonstrated the splendor of the Catholic liturgy.
The Jesuit liturgist Josef Jungmann described the opening of
the Council with a pinch of fiendishness, saying, "It was carried out correctly: good sacred music, excellent sound system,
but overall, it followed the style of Leo XIII."

There were evidently voices of dissent. In a letter of
Cardinal Giacomo Lercaro, who was to become one of the
architects of the liturgical reform, the opening of the Council was spoken of with enthusiasm:

> Never before as today have I felt so immersed in
> the Church of God: the presence of the Pope, of
> almost all the Sacred College, of the Bishops
> from the entire world, around the altar which
> was in the center and on which the sacrifice was
> celebrated and then the Gospel was enthroned;
> the gaze of the entire world was fixed on what
> was happening, as was clear from the delegations
> of many nations and from the presence of the

separated Churches.... All of this made me feel
the vitality of the Church, both its unity and its
diversity, its humanity and its divinity; and I believed in myself, that I felt part of this, invested
with special functions and powers, a profound
feeling of joy and gratitude to the Lord.

Lercaro continued, then, with a mention of the election of the
members of the commissions, confessing that it was a concern
of some of the Council Fathers. This was to become quite clear
on the thirteenth. We continue with Ingrao's narration:

In reality, already the previous day the awkward-
ness and irritation caused by this attempt at
stacking the cards by Ottaviani, Confalonieri and
Felici was spreading among various episcopates.
The French devised a countermeasure in secret:
the night of October 12, after a reception at the
French Embassy, a small group of bishops from
beyond the Alps met at the seminary of San Luigi
de'Francesi in Largo Toniolo and prepared the
text of a motion to submit to Cardinal Achille
Liénart, Archbishop of Lille and member of the
President's Council. The document asked for the
postponement of the elections of the commissions, to leave more time for the council fathers
to get to know each other. His countryman
Eugène Tisserant, who guided the President's
Council, although not having participated in that
meeting, was favorable and postponed the voting. But he had to deal with Secretary General

Felici, who was ready to do anything for the sake of concluding rapidly the election of the commission members according to the indications of Ottaviani.

Thus, from its first steps, the antagonism in the leadership of the Council was delineated between these two esteemed and influential figures, on whom the development of the work carried out in the four sessions would depend; they were both experienced Curia prelates but extremely different from each other.

The two parties that would direct the fate of the Council (with the clear prevalence of one of them, as we shall see) began to clash almost immediately. An important role among the progressives was played precisely by Cardinal Achille Liénart (1884–1973), who had much to do with one of the most significant protagonists of Catholic traditionalism, Marcel Lefebvre, having ordained him priest in 1929 and consecrated him bishop in 1947.

Staying on that day, October 13, we see how matters played out, according to Ingrao:

> The Presiding Council sat at a long table before the empty papal throne. Tisserant, before the session began, tried in vain to convince Felici to postpone the voting. The dean of the College of Cardinals asked the opinion of the Secretary of State Amleto Cicognani, who sided with Felici, however, refusing the postponement. In the

meantime, at the entrance to the basilica, Cardinal Joseph-Charles Lefebvre (Archbishop of Bourges, in no way related to the traditionalist bishop Marcel) was able to give Liénart the text of the motion to be read in the hall.

Felici opened the session and illustrated how the voting would work. At the end of the brief intervention of the secretary general, the Archbishop of Lille asked to take the floor. But Cardinal Tisserant was forced to deny him the request: "I cannot give you the floor ... because the program for this session does not allow for discussion."

Liénart then stood up and spoke without permission. The murmur in the hall gave way to an icy silence. The Cardinal read the text of the motion in Latin: it asked that the vote be postponed for several days to allow the fathers time to get to know each other and to permit the episcopal conferences to elaborate their own lists to propose to the assembly. Those present broke in with a prolonged applause that forced Liénart to pause. At the end of the reading of the motion, another long applause reiterated the general approval of the French cardinal's words. Ottaviani, Confalonieri, Felici and Cicognani were paralyzed: the reaction of the assembly, swayed by the French delegation, took them completely by surprise.

The Dominican Marie Dominique Chenu recorded the event in his diary as follows:

At 9:00 a.m., the general assembly in St. Peter's for the elections. The session concluded in twenty minutes: after the invitation to the assembly and the indications of Msgr. Felici, an intervention by Cardinal Liénart asked for a postponement (applause); it was seconded by Cardinal Frings on behalf of the German cardinals (applause). After a brief discussion among the presiding council, the elections were postponed to Tuesday October 16 (applause). The unanimous and spontaneous expression of the freedom of the bishops to evade the "regimentation" (règlement) created an uproar among the bishops themselves and everyone around them.

Thus, what was to be defined as the "European Alliance," the progressive wing of the bishops—above all from France, Belgium, Germany, and Holland—began to consolidate its position. It is interesting to note that the Council, which today demands blind obedience, was given its direction by a gesture of supreme and solemn disobedience.

We must not forget that in those days there was great tension on the international level with the Cuban Missile Crisis between the United States and the Soviet Union. John XXIII was to offer the Soviet Union gestures of *rapprochement* by receiving Kruschev's daughter and a Russian general on March 7, 1963. But in the days when the ecumenical council was getting underway, tensions were rising, bringing the two superpowers to the brink of armed conflict.

At the center of the conflict at that moment was the island of Cuba, whose leader was the revolutionary Fidel Castro (1926–2016). Already in 1961, the United States had attempted to overthrow Castro's government with the failed Bay of Pigs invasion. Now the tension rose even higher, and President Kennedy had to warn the public that they were on the verge of a possible conflict. Then, on October 25, John XXIII gave a radio message to avert the possible catastrophe, appealing to the powers in conflict and to their sense of responsibility. That message seemed to have a positive effect, avoiding a nuclear war that for nearly two weeks kept the world holding its breath.

Although of a different magnitude, tensions continued even at the Council, and the muscular maneuverings of the European Alliance made their weight felt. For example, on October 30, there was an episode in which Cardinal Ottaviani was interrupted while giving a discourse in the hall. He was intent on protesting the changes which were being proposed for the liturgy and he exceeded the time limit for his discourse. Cardinal Eugène Tisserant (1884–1972), who at that time presided over the Sacred College, instructed the Dutch Cardinal Bernard Jan Alfrink (1900–1987), archbishop of Utrecht and one of the most conspicuous red hats of the progressive wing, to have Ottoviani's microphone turned off. Aware that he could no longer be heard and that he had been humiliated, Ottaviani returned to his chair, while some of the Fathers openly applauded the episode disrespectfully.

In reality, we should not think of the Council Fathers as all inclined either to progressivism or conservatism. As the historian Roberto de Mattei noted in *The Second Vatican Council: An Unwritten Story*, there existed in the Council two minority factions which fought each other actively, one progressive and one conservative (which we shall consider), while the majority of the Fathers simply oscillated between the progressive and traditionalist camps.

Pope John XXIII certainly knew what was being unleashed and, according to some, was quite pleased. It is difficult to say how much of this is true and if this could be part of a type of naïvete that, at bottom, was an integral part of the "Good Pope." His guilelessness would lead one cardinal to quip that while John XXIII was the Good Pope, he was not a good pope. This recalls the age-old question of the "goodness of the Pope" in general. Must a Pope be good? It seems an odd question referring to a Pontiff, but in reality, it has an important meaning. We certainly would not want the Pope to be bad, for this would compromise his very soul, but the Pope is also a head of state and pastor of the universal Church. Precisely in this role he is often called to make unpopular decisions, to judge when necessary, and to be obeyed. At times this goodness leads one to seek compromises which do not always work, especially when one exercises this type of role. Therefore, although we might wish for goodness on a personal level, it still requires great discipline for the Pope to exercise his authority at the level of his role so that the Church does not fall sway to forces that can easily lead it where it should not go.

Returning to our narrative, the skirmishes at the first session continued, and certainly Pope John XXIII must have felt relief at its conclusion on December 8, 1963. In his discourse, the Pope summarized what had been done in that session:

> On that memorable October 11, the mutual and collective work of the Fathers began. Now that the first session of the Ecumenical Council has been celebrated, we do well to reflect a moment on what has been done. The first session opened the doors, so to speak, with a certain slow and solemn style, to the great work of the Council: it was, that is, a beginning in which the Fathers, with swift resolve, could become fully involved in the cause and in the intimate logic of this endeavor, namely the divine plan. It was necessary that the brothers convening from distant regions and congregated in this ancient setting should get to know one another; it was necessary that they become acquainted with each other to ascertain their reciprocal tendencies; it was necessary that each one rationally and fruitfully communicate to each other his experience matured through apostolic activity, carried out in different places and with different groups of people. One readily understands that in an assembly this vast it was necessary to allow ample time to arrive at agreement upon that which, with respect to charity, had offered motive for disagreement, which must not surprise in the least, but rather stimulate the soul. This too has come about through the providential will of God, that the truth be brought to light and before the entire human community

the holy freedom of the children of God which is
active in the Church be made manifest. Not by
chance did we begin by examining the outline on
the Scared Liturgy, because it deals with the relations that run between man and God.

Nothing had been approved yet, but the Pope almost seemed
to approve of the sleight of hand which we described, as a
providential incident allowing the Council Fathers better ac-
quaintance. Then the Pope mentioned the schema on the
liturgy, which was the only schema not to be rejected. The
others were seen as too Scholastic, too influenced by the immobilism of the Curia; they were too "Roman." It was precisely
over the liturgy that the bloodiest battles were fought.

Speaking then of the fruit which he hoped to harvest
from the Council, the Pope stated, "This shall be the duty of
all: that the faithful correspond with dynamic and loyal will
to the labors of this Ecumenical Council. Then without a
doubt, the desired new Pentecost will shine, and abundantly
enrich the Church with spiritual energy and extend her ma-
ternal spirit and her salutary power in all environments of
human activity." These are beautiful words, certainly, and
there is no reason to doubt that Roncalli strongly believed
that this "New Pentecost" would renew the life of the
Church. But for many this was not the case. And the signs
of disintegration were certainly visible.

That same year, a book with the provocative title *The
Plot Against the Church* was published. The author was a
certain Maurice Pinay, who did not actually exist. This was

the pseudonym behind which a number of authors hid. Among them was a Jesuit named Joaquin Saenz y Arriaga (1899–1976), who would go on to become a pioneer of the sedevacantist movement, which claims that the Apostolic See is vacant due to the lack of a validly reigning Pontiff.

The Plot Against the Church, recently republished in Italy, is a continuation of certain theories present in Catholicism around the time of Modernism and before as well, on secret conspiracies to destroy the Church. Fr. Curzio Nitoglia, in his guide to the reading of the recent edition of this work, says:

> Maurice Pinay wrote in 1962: "The most perverse conspiracy against the Holy Church [the Second Vatican Council] is being carried out.... It shall seem ... incredible to those who ignore this conspiracy that such anti-Christian forces continue to have, within the hierarchy of the Church, a true "fifth column" of agents controlled by Freemasonry, by Communism and by the occult powers that govern them. These agents are among those Cardinals, Archbishops and Bishops who form a type of progressive wing at the Council.
>
> Already in 1824, the leader of [the masonic lodge] "Suprema Vendita," Nubius wrote the following to Volpe: "We have to reach with small, gradual means ... the triumph of the revolutionary idea through a Pope." What the sect desired was not a Freemason Pope.... What did it want? The Instructions tell you: "a Pope who fits our needs."

What exactly does that mean, "a Pope who fits our needs"? The answer is simple: a Pope who, though not a member of the Freemasons, adheres to the sect's beliefs: pantheism, naturalism, rationalism, liberalism, and pluralism.

This string of ideas will also become important in certain sectors of traditionalism and can be found in some literature that attracts many readers passionate about conspiracies and intrigues. While the book's claims must be weighed prudently, not all of them are false.

The 1960s were, in reality, complicated years in many ways. There was much ferment agitating souls, undermining society and consolidated habits and customs. It was a time of profound and significant changes, especially as concerns mentalities and customs.

For example, on January 13, 1963, an article appeared in the *Giornale del Mattino* with the title "The Church and the Fatherland." In this article, the author took a strong position in favor of conscientious objection (i.e., refusing to fulfill mandatory military service on religious or ethical grounds), which is not mandated by Church teaching. The author was a priest, a member of the Congregation of the Scolopi. His name was Fr. Ernesto Balducci (1922–1992). He was one of the most influential minds of Catholic progressivism, and one of the most active agitators in Italy and beyond. A synthesis of his thought can be deduced from a collection of his writings in honor of Don Lorenzo Milani (whom we shall discuss shortly):

> Bonhoeffer said we have reached the end of the
> age of the sacred, the religious epoch has ended;

nonetheless, the end of the religious epoch does
not at all mean the end of faith in Christ, because
religion is one thing, whereas the faith is another.... The salvation of God is the salvation of
this world, and the reign of God, even if it is not
of this world, is realized in this world. The final
point of salvation will not be another world, but
will be this world transfigured by his power and
assimilated to the glory of the Resurrection.
Thus, the believer must fulfill in this world his
worldly task, must be nothing more than a
human; not a human and, moreover, a Christian;
a human, because there is no other possibility to
be totally human than that of receiving fully the
project of fullness of the world that was manifested in Jesus Christ.

It is not difficult to see in Fr. Balducci (who was always protected by Cardinal Montini) a line of thought that led him
to disdain the sacred, tradition, and all preceding ecclesial
practice.

Fr. Balducci was also the founder of an important journal at that time, *Testimonianze* (*Testimonies*), founded in
1958. This periodical is still in print and is heavily involved
in the environmentalist movement. In that period, Fr. Balducci's articles obviously focused, among other things, on
the Council which had just begun and on which he counted
heavily to champion his struggles.

We remember at this point that 1963 was also an important year in the world of music. On March 22 in England,

the album *Please Please Me* came out, produced by a band that was destined to revolutionize the pop music scene for decades to come: the Beatles. It is undeniable that this would be the most important band of the twentieth century and that their musical and cultural influence (fully 1960s, topped off with drugs, oriental cults, the Sexual Revolution, and so forth) would far surpass their career together (which ended in 1970). Having said this, it cannot be denied that in their genre they were protagonists and that some of their songs, such as "Yesterday," certainly have become part of collective memory, and rightly so.

Early that same year, the superior of the Holy Ghost Fathers sent a letter to the members of his institute on the use of the priest's cassock. Evidently, the winds of revolt had crashed against this important priestly discipline. In his letter of February 11, the superior recalled to the members of his congregation the importance of wearing the cassock: "The priestly collar alone, although sufficient, is nonetheless more ambiguous. It does not indicate clearly the Catholic priest." Later he states,

> The priest is a living sermon thanks to his apparel, thanks to his faith. The apparent absence of priests, above all in big cities, constitutes a serious regression in the preaching of the Gospel. It is the continuation of the nefarious work of Revolution that has plundered the churches, of the laws of separation that have chased consecrated men and women out, and which has laicized the schools.

These words were written by the most important figure in the history of Catholic traditionalism: Archbishop Marcel Lefebvre (1905–1991).

MARCEL LEFEBVRE

Born in Tourcoing into a large family steeped in Catholic traditions that would offer many of its members to the Catholic Church as priests and religious, Lefebvre studied in Rome at the French Seminary in Via Santa Chiara from 1923 to 1929. His superior was Fr. Henri Le Floch (1862–1950), whom some deemed very close to *Action Française*, a reactionary, royalist political party. Fr. Le Floch taught his students respect for the tradition of the Church and for her theological and spiritual disciplines. Lefebvre was also influenced by Jean Ousset (1914–1994) and by proximity to the counterrevolutionary association *La Cité Catholique*. We recall that Jean Ousset was the author of a book that was fundamental to the counterrevolutionary battle, *Pour qu'il règne*, published in 1959, the same year as *Rivoluzione e controrivoluzione* (*Revolution and Counterrevolution*), which we shall consider shortly.

Feeling he had a missionary vocation, Marcel Lefebvre entered the Congregation of the Holy Ghost to go to Africa, where he would spend himself untiringly as a missionary for nearly thirty years. He served first in Gabon; then Pius XII named him apostolic vicar of Senegal in 1947. He then became the apostolic delegate to all of French colonial Africa, becoming the metropolitan archbishop of Dakar, Senegal. His work in Africa was meritorious and recognized as such even by those who later were not to follow him. In 1962 he was recalled to France as archbishop in a secondary diocese, that of Tulle, but in July of that year he was elected superior of his congregation. In this role, he was to participate in the Council, taking as his peritus the priest Victor Berto (1900–1968), oddly not a member of his congregation, but who had also studied at the French Seminary under Fr. Le Floch. At this point, we begin to follow his story, the story of one of the main protagonists of this book.

Now, we have seen his battle for the priestly cassock. But what were his impressions of the Council? On March 25, he sent a letter to his confreres to comment on the first session of the ecumenical assembly. He sought to explain how the reform of the liturgy, which he did not reject (although at that time, the conciliar document had not yet been promulgated), was a good thing if this meant a deepening of the same, that the liturgy might increasingly occupy its due place in the lives of men. Archbishop Lefebvre tried to explain that the liturgical reform ought to be done with prudence and due respect for the venerable rite. Speaking then of the liturgical language, he added,

> Another consideration that has its value: the in-telligence of the texts is not the final end of prayer, nor is it the only means of placing the soul in prayer, that is, in a state of union with God, which is the aim of prayer. The proper object of prayer is God. The soul that draws near to God and unites spiritually to Him is in prayer and drinks from the well of life. It would, there-fore, be contrary to the very goal of the liturgical

> action to focus the attention of the intelligence
> on texts such that it hinders union with God. On
> the other hand, the simple soul, not necessarily
> educated, but truly Christian, will find its union
> with God either in virtue of heavenly, religious
> song, or in the general atmosphere of the liturgi-
> cal action, in the piety and recollection of the
> place, in the architectural beauty, in the fervor of
> the Christian community, in the nobility and
> piety of the celebrant, in the symbolic decora-
> tion, in the fragrance of the incense, etc.

It is interesting how Archbishop Lefebvre gives importance
to the nonverbal language of the liturgy, a language that was
in fact sacrificed in the postconciliar period in favor of a nearly
one-way verbalism.

JOHN XXIII AT THE END OF THE LINE

In the meantime, John XXIII presented to the world on April
11, 1963, one of his most important documents, the encyclical *Pacem in Terris*. It begins thus: "Peace on earth, profound
longing of human beings of all times, can be established and
consolidated only in the complete respect for the order established by God."

The encyclical was praised by many, and it was essentially the Pope's swan song. In 2016, Hans Küng would say
of him that "the old 'transitional pope' transformed into the
pope of the great transition." In fact, one must admit that in
five years, he transformed the Church profoundly, although
they were the last moments of his life. He was already ill at

that time, and was to die just two months later, on June 3, 1963. He died amidst the consternation of so many who were struck by his good nature and humility. Now, with a Council underway, they had to choose a new Pope.

Chapter 3

The Age of Paul VI

Paul VI and Modernity

In conclave, the cardinal-electors elected the popular and influential Giovanni Battista Montini to succeed John XXIII. He took the regnal name Paul VI.

Born September 30, 1897, Giovanni Battista Montini's father, Giorgio, was a leading representative of social and political Catholicism. He had exercised a decisive influence on Giovanni Battista, who was, after his priestly ordination, for many years a leading figure of the Roman Curia. At a certain point, as has been mentioned, Pius XII had sent then-Bishop Montini to Milan without making him a cardinal—as a punishment, according to rumors. Montini was an intellectual quite taken by modern culture.

Paul VI was elected June 21, 1963. In his message "to the entire human family" of June 22, he made the following announcement:

The preeminent part of Our Pontificate will be concerned with the continuation of the Second Ecumenical Vatican Council, to which the gaze of all men of good will is fixed. This shall be the main work, for which we intend to exert all of our energies which the Lord has given Us, that the Catholic Church, which shines in the world as the *standard raised for the distant nations* (cf. Is 5:26), can attract men to itself with the majesty of its organism, with the youth of its spirit, with the renewal of its structures, with the multiplicity of its strengths, coming *from every tribe, language, people and nation* (Rev 5:9): this shall be the first thought of the pontifical ministry, that it be proclaimed always more loudly before the world, that only in the Gospel of Jesus is the awaited and desired salvation: *because there is no other name under heaven given to men by which we must be saved* (Acts 4:12).

He affirms above all that the Council would continue; it would not be interrupted as the First Vatican Council had been a century earlier. And there were important themes to discuss.

Take, for example, the theme of social inequality caused by racism. This was a particularly sensitive topic in those years of the sixties—especially in the United States, but also in South Africa, thanks to the witness of Nelson Mandela (1918–2013), who had already been sentenced to life in prison for his fight against apartheid. On August 28 of that year, the Protestant pastor and activist Martin Luther King Jr., gave his famous "I Have a Dream" speech in Washington, D.C., after having marched in the defense of civil rights. Everyone remembers his famous words: "I have a dream that one day this nation will rise up and live out the true meaning of its creed: 'We hold these truths to be self-evident, that all men are created equal.' I have a dream that one day on the red hills of Georgia, the sons of former slaves and the sons of former slave owners will be able to sit down together at the table of brotherhood."

At the end of that year, the political activist Malcolm Little (1925–1965), called Malcom X, made another famous speech on the racial issue, his "Message to the Grass Roots" (November 10), in which he said,

> So, we're all black people, so-called Negroes, second class citizens, ex-slaves. You're nothing but an ex-slave. You don't like to be told that. But what else are you? You are ex-slaves. You didn't come here on the "Mayflower," you were brought here by the so-called Pilgrims, or Founding Fathers. They were the ones who brought you here. We have a common enemy. We have this in common: We have a common oppressor, a common exploiter, and a common discriminator. But once we all realize that we have a common enemy then we unite—on the basis of what we have in common. And what we have foremost in common is that enemy—the white man. He's an enemy to all of us. I know some of you all think that some of them aren't enemies. Time will tell.

The terms of the racial struggle were truly explosive, and this threatened social peace at various levels. But just a few days later, on November 22, the unthinkable occurred: the American president John Fitzgerald Kennedy was assassinated in Dallas.

We cannot omit the theme to which we shall return later, namely feminism, which was at the center of attention as well in 1963, thanks to the publication of the book *The Feminine Mystique* on February 19, written by the American writer Betty Friedan. Elena Magalotti explained the importance of this essay as follows:

> In this study, the author interviewed a large number of women who had, like her, finished their studies some fifteen years earlier, beginning with her former classmates. At the same time, the author began a study investigating specifically the condition of women, her contemporaries, with the objective of finding the causes of female frustration and depression within the context of the family.

Thus, they began to challenge the role of women as homemakers.

Here in Italy, as well, people began to examine the theme of poverty and inequality. That year, at the end of January, the film called *Gli ultimi* (*The Last Ones*) came out, adapted from a novel by a religious brother who had become famous as a preacher and above all a poet, David Maria Turoldo (1916–1992). The expression of peasant Italy, he was an overflowing personality, as he defined himself, certainly a poet of renown. Yet he was also definitely a Catholic, albeit one of a progressive stamp. In the *Dizionario elementare del pensiero pericoloso* (*Elementary Dictionary of Dangerous Thought*), Nicolò Tarquini speaks of him in these terms:

> As a young man, he entered the Order of the Servants of Maria (Servites) and was ordained a priest in 1940. He transferred to Milan where, appointed by Cardinal Ildefonso Schuster (1880–1954), he assumed the role of Sunday preacher in the Cathedral. With his confrere Br. Camillo de Piaz (1918–2010) he founded the Cultural Center Corsia of the Servites, where they discussed questions of national and international importance and themes concerning the Lombard capital. Under pressure from the Holy Office, suspected of having positions that were considered too "liberal," he was sent abroad in 1953 by his superiors and sojourned in the houses of his Order in Austria, Bavaria, England, the United States and Canada. Returning to Italy after his roaming about, he transferred in 1964 to the Monastery of the Servites in Sotto il Monte, the birthplace of Pope John XXIII. Socially and politically active, he adhered to the Resistance with the group *"L'uomo"* (The Man), in a "choice for humanity against inhumanity."

The attitude of Fr. Turoldo toward the Council was also interesting. He left us his feelings about the convocation of the Council in the form of a poem: "Forgive me and read no further / no more of whatever / I have written you before / I have just got news of the Council!" It is evident that for Fr. Turoldo the Council could be considered a wellspring moment, the advent of much-desired change in the Church. In that 1963 which we are discussing, his collection of poems *Se tu non riappari* (*If You Do Not Reappear*) came out.

In the meantime, the so-called European Alliance forged ahead with its agenda, especially in regard to ecumenism and religious liberty. An important moment in this process occurred on August 26, when the so-called Conference of Fulda took place, at which bishops and theologians met to elaborate a strategy in light of the continuation of the Council. We should not consider this meeting as a sort of conspiracy, for other episcopates were meeting to elaborate strategies as well, such as that of the Italian episcopate at the same time and that of the American episcopate shortly before.

The group that met in Fulda was certainly one of the most important forces at the Council. Now, this suspicion of a sort of conspiratorial meeting had already appeared in the press in those days; I am not promoting it here. One reason might be found in the fact that in this case the encounter was not that of just one episcopal conference (the German conference was to meet a few days later), but of a group, a lobby we could say, within the world episcopate. This too, was nothing unusual. The conservatives were also to create a "lobby" of their own. But the fact is that the Secretary of State was forced to deny the conspiratorial nature of the event.

On September 29, the second session of the Council opened. Theologians made strident appeals for episcopal "collegiality" and ecumenicalism, including Yves Congar's hugely influential *Sainte Eglise* and *La Tradition et la vie de l'Eglise*. Of course, these efforts were met with a certain amount of conservative resistance. Among the resisters was Brazilian Archbishop Geraldo de Proença Sigaud (1909–1999), who on October 9 protested in the hall against this collegiality. He was very attentive to the harm caused by these egalitarian ideas on Church government, as he was to narrate later in his *Anti-Communist Catechism*, in which he states:

> The communist sect affirms that the ideal society, once the inevitable phase in which the horrors of the "dictatorship of the proletariat" are manifested has ended, there will come a communist society without classes or property, and in which all will be equal, all will work each according to his abilities, and all will receive what is necessary to live. This will be the true paradise on earth.

Archbishop Proença Sigaud was an important figure because he was one of the souls in that group of resistance to the European alliance which took the name *Coetus Internationalis Patrum*. This is how Ignazio Ingrao remembers them:

> Beyond the official conciliar organisms, the most well-structured and organized group was the traditionalist organization *Coetus Internationalis Patrum* founded by Geraldo de Proença Sigaud, bishop of Jacarezinho and the archbishop of Diamantina in Brazil, a religious with the Society of

the Divine Word (Verbiti). With him from the very beginning was Msgr. Marcel Lefebvre, who was destined to become the leader of the traditionalists who would unite around the Priestly Society of St. Pius X. It was Antonio de Castro Mayer, bishop of Campos in Brazil, who put Lefebvre in contact with Sigaud. Thus, from the first session of the Council, in October of 1962, the two Brazilian bishops and their French confrere met in Rome at the generalate of the Holy Ghost Fathers, to organize meetings and conferences for the council fathers.

PLINIO CORRÊA DE OLIVEIRA AND THE TFP

An important part of the organization of the *Coetus* was the presence of the Brazilian professor Plinio Corrêa de Oliveira (1908–1995). Though a layman, he had the ears of Bishop Castro Mayer and Archbishop Proença Sigaud. Just a few years earlier he had founded the Brazilian Society for the Defense of Tradition, Family, and Property (TFP).

Plinio Corrêa de Oliveira explained the significance of the name of this group, making reference to a critical passage from the same publication by another author:

> Superficial observers might be surprised by the triple name "Tradition—Family—Property," as if it were a question of an artificial amalgamation. In reality, the union of these three terms is not due to chance, nor was it an arbitrary choice to place them together to provide a name to a particularly

formidable far-right movement (sic). As is understood in most cases, tradition, family, and property constitute de facto three alienations (sic) fundamental to man, which coexist one next to the other, sustaining one another continually through an extremely complex fabric of relations and interdependences of an economical, psychological, and juridical nature. It would be quite easy to demonstrate how, for example, access to private property has been possible only in union with the particularity of the family, and how its conservation can be guaranteed only thanks to a system that secures the familiar nucleus in its individualism. One could also demonstrate in what way a certain tradition, made of habits that have solidified in institutions of every type, can be the adequate instrument of this immobilism, etc. "Tradition—Family—Property" constitutes a coherent block which can be accepted or denied, but whose elements cannot be separated. (Max Delespesse, *Jésus et la triple contestation—Tradition, Famille, Proprieté* [Paris/Ottawa: Fluerus, Novalis, 1972], pp. 7–8.)

The TFP is one of the most important traditionalist movements and is present today in many countries. They are involved in battles in the social field. Their action has influenced similar associations around the world, collaborating with them and encouraging them in their fight against revolutionary ideas. The most important work, or at least the most well-known, of Professor de Oliveira is *Revolution and Counterrevolution*. Therein he identifies the ideas and actions throughout history which have militated against Christian civilization: "From the French Revolution was born the communist movement of Babeuf. And later, from the evermore active spirit of Revolution, arose the schools of utopian communism of the nineteenth century and the so-called scientific communism of Marx."

Revolution and Counterrevolution, like Jean Ousset's (1914–1994) book *Pour qu'il reigne*, appeared in the same period, and both are considered classics in the counterrevolutionary battle. Professor Roberto de Mattei has dedicated two books to reconstructing de Oliveira's biography (see bibliography, de Mattei 1996, 2017).

We may recall another author aligned with TFP, Arnaldo Vidigal Xavier da Silveira (1929–2018), who wrote an important volume entitled *Considerations on the Ordo Missae of Paul VI*, which contains an important section on the hypothesis of a heretical Pope. This work, disseminated by the TFP, was very influential in Catholic settings.

At the death of its founder in 1995, there was a major split in the TFP, which led to the creation of a religious congregation inspired by the thought of Corrêa de Oliveira and called Heralds of the Gospel. This division was to be quite painful, and the consequences have still not been healed today. One must say that today, in the Church of Pope Francis, the new congregation is in troubled waters, considering that it was recently put under external administration.

Plinio Corrêa de Oliveira was certainly a person of enormous influence in the Catholic traditionalist sphere, not only for his role as founder of the TFP, but also for the intellectual impact he had on vast sectors of this sphere which, through his ideas, has been able to adopt a vision of the things of the world which they felt to be more coherent and truer.

SACROSANCTUM CONCILIUM

We have discussed how the alliances within the two opposed fronts were being consolidated and how the *Coetus* was trying to gather consensus to slow the advance of the European Alliance.

The second session will be remembered for having approved the Constitution on the Sacred Liturgy *Sacrosanctum Concilium*, on December 4, 1963. This important document, as we have seen, had fewer problems compared to the outlines proposed for other topics. Yet this too was a controversial document. For example, a very well-known traditionalist Catholic author, Michael Davies (1936–2004), in his work *Liturgical Time Bombs in Vatican II*, stated:

> The Modernist heresy at the beginning of the twentieth century was driven underground by St. Pius X. Father Bonneterre claims that Modernist theologians who could no longer propagate their theories in public saw in the Liturgical Movement the ideal Trojan Horse for their revolution and that, from the 1920s onward, it became clear that the Liturgical Movement had been diverted from its original admirable aims....
>
> The Bugnini *schema* received the almost unanimous approval of the Council Fathers on December 7, 1962, and became Vatican II's

"Constitution on the Sacred Liturgy" (CSL). But the Constitution contained no more than general guidelines; therefore, to achieve total victory, Father Bugnini and his cohorts needed to obtain the power to interpret and implement it....

The liturgical principles of Pistoia ... have been imposed throughout the Roman Rite as part of the conciliar reform, even though not specifically ordered by the Council. The CSL provided the door through which they entered.

Once more, the name of Annibale Bugnini appears. Davies also mentions the Synod of Pistoia from the eighteenth century, at which there was an attempt to implement Jansenist principles in the Roman liturgy.

Sacrosanctum Concilium, however, offered a foothold to conservatives as well:

"The use of the Latin language, except for particular privileges, should be preserved in the Latin Rites." But then it specifies that there could be concessions for a more ample use of national languages. It seems to offer footholds for sacred music also:

The musical tradition of the universal Church is a treasure of inestimable value, greater even than that of any other art. The main reason for this pre-eminence is that, as sacred song united to the words, it forms a necessary or integral part of the solemn liturgy.

Holy Scripture, indeed, has bestowed praise upon sacred song, and the same may be said of the fathers of the Church and of the Roman pontiffs who in recent times, led by St. Pius X, have explained more precisely the ministerial function supplied by sacred music in the service of the Lord.

Therefore sacred music is to be considered the more holy in proportion as it is more closely connected with the liturgical action, whether it adds delight to prayer, fosters unity of minds, or confers greater solemnity upon the sacred rites....

The treasure of sacred music is to be preserved and fostered with great care. Choirs must be diligently promoted, especially in cathedral churches; but bishops and other pastors of souls must be at pains to ensure that, whenever the sacred action is to be celebrated with song, the whole body of the faithful may be able to contribute that active participation which is rightly theirs, as laid down in Art. 28 and 30.

Great importance is to be attached to the teaching and practice of music in seminaries, in the novitiates and houses of study of religious of both sexes, and also in other Catholic institutions and schools. To impart this instruction, teachers are to be carefully trained and put in charge of the teaching of sacred music.

It is desirable also to found higher institutes of sacred music whenever this can be done.

Composers and singers, especially boys, must also be given a genuine liturgical training.

The Church acknowledges Gregorian chant as specially suited to the Roman liturgy: therefore, other things being equal, it should be given pride of place in liturgical services.

But other kinds of sacred music, especially polyphony, are by no means excluded from liturgical celebrations, so long as they accord with the spirit of the liturgical action, as laid down in Art. 30....

In the Latin Church the pipe organ is to be held in high esteem, for it is the traditional musical instrument which adds a wonderful splendor to the Church's ceremonies and powerfully lifts up man's mind to God and to higher things.

But other instruments also may be admitted for use in divine worship, with the knowledge and consent of the competent territorial authority, as laid down in Art. 22, 52, 37, and 40. This may be done, however, only on condition that the instruments are suitable, or can be made suitable, for sacred use, accord with the dignity of the temple, and truly contribute to the edification of the faithful.

Thus, all things considered, it seemed that what could be salvaged had been salvaged, despite the emphasis on the "full, conscious, and active participation in the liturgical celebrations." The concept of participation reappears twenty-three times throughout the document, which is not long.

The importance being given to it, therefore, was quite clear. And we cannot blame Michael Davies when he states that the anguished question would be about interpretations, because these were to orient the law in one direction or another. And as we shall see, that is what happened. The second session closed with this document. Obviously, this was to be at the center of much successive controversy.

In the meantime, on January 5, 1964, Pope Paul VI encountered Ecumenical Patriarch Athenagoras of Constantinople during the Holy Father's journey in the Holy Land. Domenico Agasso Jr., in an article in *La Stampa* in 2014, reconsidered some passages from the dialogue between the two religious leaders. Here is a fragment:

> "I know this is difficult; I know there are susceptibilities, a mentality," said the Pontiff, "that there is a psychology."
>
> "On both sides," admitted Athenagoras.
>
> "But I also know," continued Montini, "that there is great rectitude and the desire to love God, to serve the cause of Jesus Christ. And in this I place my confidence."
>
> And the Patriarch as well places "my confidence. Together, together."
>
> Then Paul VI begins to deal with the questions: "I do not know if this is the moment. But I see what must be done, namely to study together or to delegate to someone who..."
>
> "On both sides," adds Athenagoras.

And the Pope would like "to know what is the mind of Your Holiness, of your Church, about the Constitution on the Church. It is the first step..."

Athenagoras responds, "We will follow your opinions."

"We will discuss," foresees the Pope, "we will try to find the truth."

Athenagoras: "The same for our part, and I am sure that we shall always remain together."

Paul VI: "I hope this will perhaps be easier than we think."

Athenagoras: "We shall do everything possible."

The strategy of dialogue, at any rate so central to the pastoral efforts of Paul VI, is thus fully in action, a strategy that will also be an element of controversy with the traditional world, which will accuse him of sacrificing the truth to dialogue and of rendering it not a means but an end.

In the meantime, Archbishop Lefebvre sent his Congregation of the Holy Ghost another letter of comment on the second session of the Council, just days after Paul VI's journey to the Holy Land.

The archbishop comments in a very respectful manner on the declarations of Paul VI, especially concerning the liturgy. Archbishop Lefebvre had already dealt at length with the way this reform was to be interpreted, not rejecting cautious openings but placing any precocious advancement under scrutiny. Then, the prelate confronted the issue of episcopal collegiality and the danger that certain ideas might undermine the constitution of the Church, which rests on the Petrine primacy and not on a type of democratic government. That such democratist tendencies existed was known to the French prelate, who feared the desire to impose on the Pope a type of episcopal council to carry out the governance of the Church. What is certain is that Archbishop Lefebvre on one hand tried to raise caution about precocious advances by the progressive wing, while on the other hand attempted to help the Pontiff save face—for instance, by referring to Paul's closing discourse to the second session as "memorable."

On March 12, a new bishop was named for Olinda and Recife in Brazil, Hélder Câmara (1909–1999), who would be one of the most representative figures of Catholic progressivism. As a young man, Bishop Câmara had been an exponent of counterrevolutionary Catholicism. Yet he then underwent a change that led him to declare he had become a Communist. Reviewing a volume that Bishop Câmara dedicated to the Council on the website of the Center for Studies of New Religions (cesnur.org), the sociologist Massimo Introvigne shows us how this prelate had ideas which were quite far from those of Catholic doctrine—for example, on the matter of contraception:

> The mother of all defeats for Dom Helder and his friends was nevertheless the refusal of Pope Paul VI to have the Council make a pronouncement on the theme of contraception, a refusal which forewarned of *Humanae Vitae*, the doctrine concerning which Câmara, already three years before the

encyclical in 1968 by Paul VI, had judged harshly as an "error" destined "to torture spouses, to disturb the peace of many homes," "in its own way, another condemnation of Galileo [Galilei, 1564–1642]" (p. 363); to the contrary, even, it represented "the death of the Council," "the practical negation of collegiality," "the practical annihilation of ecumenism" (p. 461). A poet. Dom Hélder Câmara lampoons also the children which women—"victims" of the doctrine of the Church on contraceptives—are forced to generate, with expressions that are born of emotion regarding a specific, atrocious episode (a "child that, in my Recife, had part of his face devoured by rats"), but which leave many perplexed about its agreement with Catholic theology on the value of every human life: "Children, children, children. If it's pleasure you want (and what else do you have, poor woman?), you have to procreate, you have to procreate! Even if your child will be a skeleton, will be a horrendous little rat that not even the rats will welcome (they are attractive, enchanting little rats). Children, children, children... If it's your coitus that you want (But do you know what volition is?), you have to procreate, you have to procreate! Even if your child is born without bowels, with little stick legs, a head like a balloon, ugly as death" (pp. 390–391). This "poetic" newsletter closes with an invocation to the Virgin Mary that she ask the Heavenly Father "not to collaborate in the birth of Little Monsters!" (p. 392).

These expressions were not taken lightly, and
they confirm how the question discussed in *Humanae Vitae* was targeted already during the
Council for dissent, which struck at the very
foundations of papal authority. The target would
widen from contraceptives to abortion, and one
even spoke openly of explicit approval of divorce,
adopting the position of the Orthodox Church
that did not "preclude the possibility of another
religious marriage to someone abandoned" by a
spouse (p. 377).

This reflection is not extraneous to the matters we have seen
in the descriptions of Rahner, Teilhard de Chardin, Balducci,
Milani, Turoldo, Câmara and so on, for it is important to
remember that these figures were true heroes to many in
postconciliar Catholicism.

The Secretariat for Non-Christians was created May 19.
It was one of the most urgent requests of the progressive
wing of the Council Fathers, who were already using the
Secretariat for Christian Unity, created four years before by
John XXIII and headed by Cardinal Bea, to spearhead their
cause in the heart of the Council as well.

On August 6, Paul VI published the encyclical *Ecclesiam
Suam*. Among other things, the Pope stated in this encyclical,

As we all know, the Church is deeply rooted in
the world. It exists in the world and draws its
members from the world. It derives from it a
wealth of human culture. It shares its vicissitudes

and promotes its prosperity. But we also know that the modern world is in the grip of change and upheaval. It is undergoing developments which are having a profound influence on its outward way of life and habits of thought. The great advances made in science, technology, and social life, and the various currents of philosophical and political thought pervading modern society, are greatly influencing men's opinions and their spiritual and cultural pursuits.

The Church itself is being engulfed and shaken by this tidal wave of change, for however much men may be committed to the Church, they are deeply affected by the climate of the world. They run the risk of becoming confused, bewildered and alarmed, and this is a state of affairs which strikes at the very roots of the Church. It drives many people to adopt the most outlandish views. They imagine that the Church should abdicate its proper role, and adopt an entirely new and unprecedented mode of existence. Modernism might be cited as an example. This is an error which is still making its appearance under various new guises, wholly inconsistent with any genuine religious expression. It is surely an attempt on the part of secular philosophies and secular trends to vitiate the true teaching and discipline of the Church of Christ.

Several months after its publication, the Argentinian traditionalist Fr. Julio Meinvielle (1905–1973) was to offer a critical commentary on this encyclical. He was also the author of many other texts on (and against) Catholic progressivism.

In the meantime, on September 14, the feast of the Exaltation of the Cross, the third session of the Council opened. In his opening discourse, Paul VI said,

> In the third session of the Ecumenical Council, among the various questions to be discussed, the problem regarding the clarification and explanation of the doctrine on the nature and mission of the Church shall be preeminent. Thus, the development begun in the first two sessions shall be renewed and integrally completed, that this solemn Assembly General should become the logical continuation and extension of the First Ecumenical Vatican Council. The Church finally wants to contemplate itself, or better, seek itself in the mind of Jesus Christ, its Divine Founder. This is surely the equivalent of rendering honor to the wisdom and charity of its Founder and, while with continual compliance professes faith and fidelity to him, rendering herself more suitable for carrying out the mission of salvation for which she was instituted.

He also greeted the female auditors present for the first time:

> We extend greetings to the Auditors present, whose noble sentiments and illustrious merits are known to Us. Thus, with joy we greet Our beloved daughters in Christ, namely the so-called Lady

> Auditors, to whom the authority was given for the
> first time to participate in some of the assemblies
> of the Council. All, whether men or women Audi-
> tors, from this access to the Council granted them,
> can without a doubt understand the paternal atti-
> tude with which We gaze upon all classes of the
> people of God and how We desire to give to Chris-
> tian society an ever-greater abundance of concord,
> mutual harmony, and action.

In those very hours in America, something quite important
was moving that would have enormous repercussions over the
following years. America was involved in the Vietnam War
which was having domestic repercussions as well. At the University of California Berkeley, a group of students insisted upon
their right to carry out political demonstrations which had been
denied by the university administration. This gave rise to a
protest march, and among the leaders there was a student of
Italian Catholic background, Mario Savio (1942–1996). With
him and other students, the Free Speech Movement was born,
which was an anticipation of what would become known as
"1968." In a discourse in early December of that year (the
original to be found at don-onde.blogspot.com), Savio said,

> The university and many segments of industry
> are growing increasingly similar. As the university
> ties itself to the working world, professors (at
> least those in natural sciences and some in social
> sciences) acquire the characteristics of business-
> men.... The two worlds are blending together,

physically and psychologically.... The campus and society are blending with some reluctance and caution, but the fusion has already occurred and is in an advanced stage. And if President Kerr is the manager [of this large company], then I tell you one thing, the professors are a bunch of workers, employees! And we are the raw material! But we're a mass of raw material that has no intention of working, of being transformed into a product, of being bought by customers of the university, whether they're government, or industry, or unions, or whoever! We're human beings!

Such ideas were enflaming other universities in America, and then around the world.

The themes of civil rights, racism, and inequality were very present, together with that of religious freedom, in the world and in the Church in those days. On September 18, Paul VI received Martin Luther King Jr. This encounter was described by Michela Beatrice Ferri in this way:

The testimony of the Reverend King regarding this private audience, which lasted twenty-five minutes (in the presence of Archbishop Paul C. Marcinkus, who acted as interpreter during the colloquy), is still with us today. He explains that Pope Paul VI promised to make a public denunciation of racial segregation. A few days after the audience with the Holy Father, Martin Luther King communicated to the press the following words: "Pope Paul was very open and forthright

in his statements on the situation. He said he was
a friend of the Negro people and that he was following our struggle in the United States." The
Holy Father had reassured the Reverend King,
explaining to him that the Catholic world would
support the nonviolent struggle against racism.

At the Council, on September 23, the debate opened on what
was to be one of the central topics of division between traditionalists and the Vatican establishment, the theme of religious
liberty. There had already been sparks over the draft on the
Church and the role which the Virgin Mary has in the Church.
Religious liberty would only further excite passions. Cardinal
Ottaviani was among those opposing this text, while among
its supporters were above all the American bishops.

The draft prepared by Cardinal Bea was not to have an
easy time, and after its revision was returned modified. On
September 29, Cardinal Rufino Jiao Santos (1908–1973),
archbishop of Manila, became the spokesman of *Coetus*.
This was a good turn of events, because it gave *Coetus* the
possibility of becoming better organized and of imposing its
weight during votes at the Council.

On November 13, Paul VI carried out one of the gestures which made him famous: he renounced the tiara. We
read how the *L'Osservatore Romano*, in 2019, remembered
the deed:

On November 13, 1964, in the Council Hall, an
important step in recent Church history was
made. On that day in St. Peter's, the Melchite

patriarch Maximos IV Saigh of Antioch, in full communion with the Holy See, celebrated in the presence of the Pope, together with the bishops and archimandrites, the Mass according to the rite of his Church. At the end of the liturgy, the Secretary General of the Council, Archbishop Pericle Felici, informed the Council Fathers and the faithful present of an important, very particular decision of the Pope. He reminded them that during the Council hunger and world poverty were often spoken of with great concern, adding that the Church has always demonstrated its love for the poor. It has always followed the example of its divine Founder, and for this reason is called the Mother of the poor, of the oppressed, of the disinherited, of the needy and of the unfortunate. The Pope now desired to give a new sign of this love and mercy and thus would donate to the poor his personal tiara. Paul VI then approached the Altar of the Confession in the Basilica of St. Peter's and deposed his tiara on it, which had been the gift of artisans of his former diocese of Milan. In the hall one heard a loud and prolonged applause from the Council Fathers.

Don Thierry Gaudray of the Society of St. Pius X read this gesture thus: "That November 13, 1964, was symbolic, when Paul VI deposed the tiara, the sign of the fullness of his powers!" He was not the only one to understand the gesture in this way, and it would not be the only gesture of Paul VI's to be criticized. As they say, the worst was yet to come.

A few days later, on November 16, Paul VI read the explanatory note to the conciliar Constitution on the Church, what would be called *Lumen Gentium*. This explanatory note served to limit possible erroneous interpretations of the important document.

On November 21, the third session of the Council closed. The Virgin Mary was declared Mother of the Church and *Lumen Gentium* was approved. This document was to have strong ecumenical repercussions but would also be subject to heavy criticism. We shall consider this immediately.

THE QUESTION OF THE *SUBSISTIT IN*

One of the words most pronounced in ecclesiastical settings is ecumenism. Ecumenism, or the relationship of the Church with other Christian confessions and with other faiths outside of Christianity, was one of the central themes discussed and had an influence not only on theology but also on the Church's liturgy. Not everyone was happy with the emphasis placed on the theme of ecumenism. In fact, some have serious doubts about it. Prolonged debate occurred over one particular definition of the true Church, which "subsists" in the Catholic Church, but which "is" not the Catholic Church. The declaration on religious freedom of Vatican II, *Dignitatis Humanae*, says the following:

> First, the council professes its belief that God Himself has made known to mankind the way in which men are to serve Him, and thus be saved in Christ and come to blessedness. We believe that this one true religion subsists in the Catholic and Apostolic

Church, to which the Lord Jesus committed the duty of spreading it abroad among all men. Thus He spoke to the Apostles: "Go, therefore, and make disciples of all nations, baptizing them in the name of the Father and of the Son and of the Holy Spirit, teaching them to observe all things whatsoever I have enjoined upon you" (Matt. 28:19–20).

In *Lumen Gentium* we find the following affirmation:

> This is the one Church of Christ which in the Creed is professed as one, holy, catholic and apostolic, which our Saviour, after His Resurrection, commissioned Peter to shepherd (Jn 21:17), and him and the other apostles to extend and direct with authority (cf. Mt 28:18), which He erected for all ages as "the pillar and mainstay of the truth" (1 Tm 3:15). This Church constituted and organized in the world as a society, subsists in the Catholic Church, which is governed by the successor of Peter and by the Bishops in communion with him, although many elements of sanctification and of truth are found outside of its visible structure. These elements, as gifts belonging to the Church of Christ, are forces impelling toward catholic unity. (*Haec Ecclesia, in hoc mundo ut societas constituta et ordinata, subsistit in Ecclesia catholica, a successore Petri et Episcopis in eius communione gubernata.*)

Romano Amerio, in his *Iota Unum*, made the following observations:

But despite the papal declarations, the decree *Unitatis Redintegratio* rejects the *reditus* of those separated and professes the thesis of the conversion of all Christians. Unity does not necessarily come through the return of separated brethren to the Catholic Church, but rather by the conversion of all the Churches into the total Christ, who does not subsist in any of them, but is to be reintegrated by means of the convergence of all into one. Where the preparatory drafts defined that the Church of Christ is the Catholic Church, the Council conceded only that the Church of Christ subsists in the Catholic Church, adopting the theory that also in the other Christian Churches the Church of Christ subsists and that all must become aware of this common subsistence in Christ. The separated Churches, as a professor at the Gregorian University wrote in *L'Osservatore Romano* on October 14, are recognized by the Council as "instruments of which the Holy Spirit makes use to carry out the salvation of their adherents." Catholicism, in this peer vision of all the Churches, no longer has a preeminent or exclusivist character.

If this interpretation by Amerio were considered, it would be a clear distancing from traditional doctrine. That this was a clear problem is evident by the fact that the Congregation for the Doctrine of the Faith examined the matter in an article of commentary to the *Responsa ad quaestiones de aliquibus sententiis ad doctrinam de Ecclesia pertinentibus* in 2007, which had to respond precisely to the question of why *subsistit* was used and not *est*. This is what they said:

> It was precisely this change of terminology in describing the relationship between the Church of Christ and the Catholic Church that gave access to the sundry conjectures, above all in the field of ecumenism. In reality, the Council Fathers simply wanted to recognize the presence, in non-Catholic Christian communities, of ecclesial elements proper to the Church of Christ. It follows that the identification of the Church of Christ with the Catholic Church is not to be understood as if outside the Catholic Church there were an "ecclesial vacuum".... Hence, the substitution of "est" with "subsistit in," contrary to many unfounded interpretations, does not mean that the Catholic Church has given up the conviction that it is the only true Church of Christ, but simply signifies a greater opening to the particular request of ecumenism to recognize truly *ecclesial* dispositions and dimensions of the Christian Communities not in full communion with the Catholic Church, thanks to the *"plura elementa sanctificationis et veritatis"* present within them. Consequently, although the Church is only one and "subsists" in a unique historical subject, even outside of this visible subject there exist true ecclesial realities.

In my opinion—and I say this with profound respect for the Congregation (now Dicastery) for the Doctrine of the Faith—this seems to be an elegant way of running with the hares and hunting with the hounds. If these ecclesial communities not in communion with Rome have elements proper to the Church of Christ, to what degree of properness can we refer? Because if everything is left indeterminate, the slippage that occurs from having "some elements of the true Church of Christ" to having "the elements of the Church of Christ" is not inconceivable. For example, in Pope Francis's famous Declaration of Abu Dhabi of 2019 we read:

> Freedom is a right of every person: each individual enjoys the freedom of belief, thought, expression and action. The pluralism and the diversity of religions, colour, sex, race and language are willed by God in His wisdom, through which He created human beings. This divine wisdom is the source from which the right to freedom of belief and the freedom to be different derives. Therefore, the fact that people are forced to adhere to a certain religion or culture must be rejected, as too the imposition of a cultural way of life that others do not accept.

Therefore, the diversity of religion (not even of Christian confessions only) is the fruit of a divine will that is also wise. But can this be harmonized with what the Congregation said; namely, that the Church as willed by Christ is the Catholic Church? It seems the Son wants only the Catholic Church, but the Father wants many religions. And where does the Holy Spirit fit into all of this?

The scholar Corrado Gnerre also contests the use of *subsistit in* and denounces it as ambiguous, "because it compromises the affirmation '*Extra Ecclesiam nulla salus.*'" He continues:

> This affirmation is "definitive." In fact, Pius XII said, "Now among the things that the Church has always preached and shall never cease to teach, there is this infallible declaration that says that there is no salvation outside of the Church" (Letter to the Holy Office, November 11, 1949). This affirmation establishes that in the other confessions one can be saved not thanks to, but despite one's belonging to them. The man who was to become the Pope of the Council, John XXIII, said in the homily on the day of his coronation, November 4, 1958: "Men can certainly attain salvation only when they are joined to him (the Roman Pontiff), because the Roman Pontiff is the Vicar of Christ and represents his person on earth."

Father Angelo, a Dominican priest and contributor to amicidomenicani.it, responds to the lingering question "*subsistit* or *est?*" in this way:

> The classic apologetical tracts on the Church aimed mostly at establishing above all that Christ founded one Church, which he entrusted to the College of the Apostles with Peter at its head as its Pastor, Guide, and Supreme Teacher.

Their intention was to demonstrate that the one, true Church of Christ existing today is the Catholic Church. Doubtless, by this demonstration they did not intend to negate the existence of Christian values and of ecclesial realities among the Orthodox, Protestants, Anglicans, or other Christians. But the apologetical preoccupation forced them to underline the points of differentiation among the various churches and non-Catholic denominations.

This response recalls the attitude assumed by some in the missionary field, according to which the objective of the missions is that of appreciating the cultures of non-Christians rather than bringing them to Christianity. It would seem that our efforts are aimed at rejoicing in the good things present in other religions more than promoting the greater good in our own.

Returning to our initial question, we appreciate the comment by Benedict XVI during a conversation with his former students on this theme:

> As concerns *subsistit*, I must add two aspects. The proposal to utilize the term *"subsistit"* came from Fr. Tromp. This is interesting in itself. I would say … on one side it is broader and on the other more restricted than the term *"est."* *Subsistit*, certainly, is a concept of Scholastic philosophy. Subsistence is the way in which a subject exists as such. In this sense, the Catholic Church says that in her the

Church of Christ subsists and, as a subject, is concretely present in history and therefore does not remain a Platonic idea. In this sense, it renders Christ in the Church very concrete. The Catholic Church is the subsistence of the Church itself. On the other hand, it is at the same time a greater expanse because it does not exclude the existence of ecclesial reality outside of this subsistence. For this reason, the plural "Churches" was created next to the singular. (gliscritti.it)

The Forces of the Tradition Get Organized: *Una Voce*

We return to the end of the year 1964, in which the conciliar documents on the liturgy and on the Church caused those who clung to tradition to foresee somber horizons. On December 19 in Paris, the *Foederatio Internationalis Una Voce* was founded. The primary aim of this association was the defense of the Latin language, and then the aims widened to the defense of the liturgy and of Gregorian chant. This association was to have an important role in the resistance to the liturgical reforms that were being announced and that prefigured rough times to come, as we shall see.

In the cultural world, many things were moving in a manner not in conformity with Christian culture. Also in 1964—the same year *Una Voce* was founded—German sociologist and philosopher Herbert Marcuse (1898–1979), published *One-Dimensional Man*. In the text, he instigated revolt against the social mechanisms that had held man captive:

> The totalitarian tendencies of one-dimensional society render inefficacious the traditional ways and means of protest, and perhaps even dangerous because they maintain the illusion of popular sovereignty. This illusion contains some truth: "the people," once the leaven of social change, has "risen" to the point of becoming the leaven of social cohesion. It is here and not in the redistribution of wealth or in progressive equality of the classes that we need to see the new stratification characteristic of advanced industrial society.

This book was to have a great impact on the protest movement.

Fr. Congar in that same year came out with *Chrétiens en dialogue*, "Catholic contributions to ecumenism." The theme of ecumenism, as we have seen, was at the center of everyone's attention at the Council as well, and in that context Fr. Congar's voice was given great attention.

A text that is particularly important in our study is *Les Nouveaux Prêtres*, by the French writer Michel de Saint Pierre (1916–1987). Remembering the writer in 2016, Raimondo Gatto, Italian intellectual and blogger, states:

> Monarchist and Catholic, Michel de Saint Pierre was a tenacious defender of the traditional Mass suppressed by Paul VI. He plunged vigorously

into the great debates opened in France and in the Catholic world after the announced opening of the Second Vatican Council. In 1964, his novel *Les Nouveaux Prêtres* (*The New Priests*) came out, expressing the distress of many Catholics surprised by the liturgical reforms and by the pastoral approach of Vatican II. The tale is set in a suburb of Paris, where the abbot Barrè, full of admiration for communism, spent himself tirelessly for the working classes from whom, he holds, Christians have much to learn. Because the working-class world is totally impermeable to the religious idea, the only means is to find a compromise with the communist city administration and to associate himself with all of its undertakings. The two vicars of the Abbot Barrè are also of the same opinion. Only the intervention of Fr. Florian will bring back the doubters to meditate on the truths of the Catholic Faith.

We shall have to discuss the long-underway encounter between Catholicism and communism.

Before this, I would like to cite a passage from the Christmas message of Paul VI in which he stated, "The barriers of egoism must fall; and the affirmation of particular, legitimate interests must never be an offense to others, nor a negation of reasonable sociality. Democracy, to which human coexistence makes appeal today, must open to a universal conception that transcends the limits and obstacles to effective brotherhood."

He gave a clear affirmation of his predilection for democratic ideas, which could have been seen as a contradiction, given that the Church was not in the least democratic but had a structure rigidly monarchical—and not by caprice, but because the Lord Himself commanded Peter (and not all of the apostles) to strengthen the brothers and to sustain the Church in His name. But democratic ideas would find a welcome hold in the Church as well, as we see in Paul VI.

CATHOLICISM AND COMMUNISM

A mistake of perspective which I would like to spare those who read this text is that of thinking that the errors ascribed to the postconciliar period arose at the Council. This would be a grave intellectual error. The postconciliar period gave rise to errors that had already begun beforehand, as we have already seen with Modernism.

Communism, for example, had already been abundantly condemned by the Magisterium, even before the publication of Karl Marx's *Manifesto*, by Pius IX in 1846. In his *Qui Pluribus*, he wrote,

> Gregory XVI of holy memory, whom though with lesser merit we have succeeded, emulating the examples of his Predecessors, in his apostolic letter reprimanded these societies [the encyclical *Inter praecipuas machinationes*], and We likewise want them to be condemned. We say of that system that disgusts the light of natural reason, that it is the indifference of Religion with which they, removing every distinction between virtue

and vice, between truth and error, between honesty and depravation, teach that any religion would be equally fit for attaining eternal salvation, as if between justice and the passions, between light and darkness, between Christ and Belial there could ever be agreement or commonality. The vile conspiracy against the sacred celibacy of the clergy aims at the same objective, fomented, O what dolor! even by some men of the Church, miserably forgetful of their proper dignity, and yielding to the enticements of voluptuousness. To this end as well, tends the perverse institution of teaching in the philosophical disciplines, with which incautious youth is corrupted, foisting upon them the bile of the dragon in the chalice of Babylon. To this the nefarious doctrine of *Communism* aims, as they say, especially adverse to natural law; once this is permitted, the rights of all, objects, property, even human society would be subverted from the foundations.

And this was 1846!

Nor did the Church cease to condemn these doctrines. Consider Pius XI in *Divini Redemptoris* of 1937, an encyclical directed precisely against atheistic communism:

In the beginning Communism showed itself for what it was in all its perversity; but very soon it realized that it was thus alienating the people. It has therefore changed its tactics, and strives to entice the multitudes by trickery of various forms, hiding its real designs behind ideas that in themselves are good and attractive. Thus, aware of the universal desire for peace, the leaders of Communism pretend to be the most zealous promoters and propagandists in the movement for world amity. Yet at the same time they stir up a class-warfare which causes rivers of blood to flow, and, realizing that their system offers no internal guarantee of peace, they have recourse to unlimited armaments.

These words display great clarity, and if this was not enough, on July 1, 1949, Pope Pius XII excommunicated all Communists *en masse*. The persecution of Christians by the Soviets was well known. Three months after the excommunications were issued, the Chinese Communist Party took power in China, opening another front of suffering for the "Church of Silence." The Church would confront it with the controversial strategy considered a failure by many, *Ostpolitik*.

And yet, despite all this, the fascination with communism in the Christian context has still not faded. We can see this in an article that appeared in the journal *Adista* by Luca Kocci, also a collaborator with the communist newspaper *Il Manifesto*. The article's title was "Catholics and Communists: A Dialogue with Ancient Roots," which was published on March 6, 2021. It summarized the fascination of certain Catholics with Marxist and communist ideology, favored as well by the political opening of the "Party of the Catholics," namely, Christian Democrats (heir of the Popular Party and of the ideas of Don Romolo Murri and Don Luigi Sturzo), political openings that leaned to the left. On February 22, 1962, the first central-left government in Italy began. We follow the narrative of Luca Kocci's article:

> During the resistance and in the first years of the Republic, movements and political parties were developed by Catholics and Communists, either left-leaning (the movement of Catholic Communists, then the Party of the Christian Left, of Rodano and Ossicini; the Christian Social Party of Gerardo Bruni; the Christian Movement for Peace). Within the Christian Democrats, important were the careers of Giuseppe Dossetti, a partigiano, elected deputy-secretary of the party by the constituents of and an exponent of the internal left, inspiring the current of the "Dossettians"—though not formally organized—which published the journal *Social Chronicles* together with the "little professors" Giorgio La Pira, Giuseppe Lazzati, and Amintore Fanfani. In 1952, dissenting with the moderate, liberal, Atlanticist line of De Gasperi, Dossetti left the Christian Democrats, considering them unreformable. The archbishop of Bologna, Cardinal Giacomo Lercaro, then convinced him to run for mayor of the city in 1956 against the Communist Giuseppe Dozza. Dozza won the election, and two years later Dossetti retired from politics and embraced the religious life. At the Second Vatican Council he was Lercaro's closest collaborator, a leader of the progressive wing. After being removed by the cardinal of Bologna, he retreated to monastic life.

In this article appear names we are already familiar with and some that we shall encounter again later, like Fr. La Pira, Dossetti, Cardinal Lercaro, and so forth — all names representing the progressive shift in the Church.

The link between the Catholic political world and Modernism must not be forgotten, as we have already discussed. In 1945, Ernesto Buonaiuti published a text we have already mentioned on the Church and communism. In this, he says:

> Who knows if, from the propaganda of those without God, a handful of idealists might appear tomorrow who show men how to bring justice and peace into the world. Not through propaganda would they lay the foundations on miserly and precarious daily life, but only through spiritual preaching that instills in man the sense of those higher ideals for the sake of which alone it is worth living and dying. On that day it will be possible to evaluate the opportune function of Catholic communists.

I do not know if Bonaiuti's hopes were ever realized, but clearly to be able to read the path of the Church through the previous century and in this one, it is important to keep in mind the fascination that Marxist ideology would have on so many, and how, as we shall see, it would soon guide some of the theological developments which were to have notable consequences. If we fail to understand this, we will not be able to understand the various reactions of Catholic traditionalism.

The Last Session of the Council

In the meantime, 1965 began, the year in which the final session of the Council would be celebrated. The factions were by now ever more divided. The year began with an event that certainly did not usher in calm and an easing of tensions in the effervescent world of social revolt in the United States: on February 21, before he was to give a speech in New York, Malcolm X was assassinated.

On March 7, *Sacrosanctum Concilium* became effective. This document was to have very important repercussions in the traditionalist world as well. Divergent and often contrary interpretations gave rise to what in the United States would be called the "Liturgy Wars." Paul VI celebrated Mass in Italian in the Roman parish of All Saints. It was the first Sunday of Lent. The new missal had not yet come into effect, so this became a prototype of what would come later. In his homily, the Pope said,

> What are we doing? This is the moment for reflection, and it is inserted into the sacred Rite to arouse the considerations that must accompany it. We are actualizing a reality, which, already as such, is presented as solemn and has two aspects: an extraordinary one, and an ordinary, usual one. Extraordinary is today's new manner of praying, of celebrating the Holy Mass. Today we inaugurate the new form of the Liturgy in all the parishes and churches of the world, for all the Masses followed by the people. It is a great occurrence, which will be remembered as the start of a thriving spiritual

life, as a new commitment to corresponding to the
great dialogue between God and man.

This was truly a historical event, whose consequences we are
still living with today.

CATHOLIC TRADITIONALIST MOVEMENT

Returning to the United States: on March 15 the organization
known as the Catholic Traditionalist Movement was officially
launched. Fr. Gommar A. De Pauw (1918–2005) was its
founder. He was a priest originally from Belgium, who then
transferred to the United States. Father De Pauw was a peritus
at the Council, but entered into conflict with his bishop over
the direction the Council was taking, above all in the matter
of the liturgy. The movement was already active in 1964, but
on March 15 of 1965, the platform was presented, in which
twelve points were formulated:

1. That, calling a halt to any further progress
    of vernacularism, English as now used in
    read Masses be allowed to continue while at
    the same time keeping our sung Masses en-
    tirely in Latin.

2. That in the seminaries where our future
    priests are being trained Latin regain the
    place of honor assigned to it by all the Popes
    of modern times.

3. That ... priests and people be allowed to
    pursue the defense and promotion of the use

of the traditional liturgical language and customs with the same freedom given to the proponents of vernacularism.

4. That the centuries-sanctioned liturgical Latin form of the Mass not be banned, but, if not given full priority, at least be allowed to co-exist with the new vernacular forms.

5. That the new methods of group participation at Mass *not* be made mandatory at all public Masses, but that individuals be allowed to participate silently if they so desire, with such silent participation being recognized as equally fruitful and as praiseworthy as any form of group participation.

6. That in the new methods of community participation and especially in the field of sacred music and of architecture our Catholic heritage be preserved.

7. That special caution be exercised to prevent the secondary social aspects of the Mass from being affected by the error of homocentricity or an exaggerated concept of the so-called lay-priesthood.

8. That the real presence of Christ in our tabernacles continue to be hailed as our greatest and uniquely Catholic possession.

9. That our eminently Catholic devotion to the Blessed Virgin Mary, mother of our

divine Savior and mother of His Church, be
continued and encouraged.

10. That respectfully mature loyalty and filial
obedience to the Supreme Roman Pontiff as
Christ's Vicar on earth and the visible Head
of His Church continue to be preached and
practiced by all Catholics.

11. That our priests continue to live in celibacy
and to wear their distinctive black street
clothing with Roman collar, while our Sisters introduce only those dress changes that
will still allow their uniform to remain indicative of their special dedicated position
among God's people.

12. That, while truly respecting all non-Catholics who follow their conscience into what in
candid honesty we must continue to call objective errors or partial truths, our bishops,
priests, religious and laity alike renew their
truly ecumenical efforts to proclaim the full
unadulterated doctrine of Christ's Catholic
Church in a world that desperately needs it.

*(Excerpted from http://www.latinmass-
ctm.org/about/charter.htm.)*

Effectively, this text sought a certain compromise between
the exigencies of the Council and those of the tradition.
Also important was the work of Gloria Cuneo, with whom
Fr. De Pauw cofounded his movement — a movement which

still exists today, long after both Fr. De Pauw and Mrs. Cuneo have died.

SKIRMISHES

On July 25, 1965, the father of *Coetus* sent a letter to the Pope, with religious freedom as its object. The Pope responded to the letter on August 11 through Cardinal Cicognani as an intermediary. We present here the description of this report in *Documentation Information Catholique Internationales* (DICI), which they in turn obtained from *Nouvelles Certitudes*:

> Cardinal Cicognani, Secretary of State, responds in the name of the Pope to the letter of *Coetus*. He underlines that Paul VI was surprised and disapproved of the existence of an "international group of Fathers who follow the same opinion in theological and pastoral matters," and namely "a particular group in the heart of the Council." He holds that this could deprive the Council Fathers of their decisional freedom, which to the contrary should be safeguarded beyond any individual judgment. Furthermore, he holds that groups of this sort accentuate disagreements and divisions.

In the meantime, on August 13, the members *Coetus* met at Solesmes to deliberate among themselves and on August 20 sent their response to Cardinal Cicognani's letter, which was never answered. The Pope, however, seemed to be sending a message to conservatives in his encyclical *Mysterium Fidei* of

September 3, 1965, in which he attempts to reaffirm the traditional doctrine on the Eucharist against various deviations:

> For We can see that some of those who are dealing with this Most Holy Mystery in speech and writing are disseminating opinions on Masses celebrated in private or on the dogma of transubstantiation that are disturbing the minds of the faithful and causing them no small measure of confusion about matters of faith, just as if it were all right for someone to take doctrine that has already been defined by the Church and consign it to oblivion or else interpret it in such a way as to weaken the genuine meaning of the words or the recognized force of the concepts involved.

On September 14, the fourth and final session of the Council was opened. Paul VI affirmed the following in his opening address:

> In the tumult of contemporary events, in the anticipation of other future upheavals, in the disappointing experience of the continual revival of human discord, and in the irresistible movement of peoples toward their unification, we have need to verify, almost experientially, the unity which makes us all the family and temple of God, the mystical body of Christ; we needed to encounter one another and truly to feel we are brothers, to exchange the kiss of peace, to love each other, in a word, as Christ has loved us.

New concepts found in the conciliar documents were echoed in the discourse of the Holy Father.

On September 29, Msgr. Carli, on behalf of *Coetus*, promulgated a letter asking the Council to condemn communism explicitly. In the outline of the Council's document on the Church in the contemporary world, speaking on atheism, explicit mention of communism is not made. We recall the work behind the scenes of Plinio Côrrea de Oliveira and the members of his group, TFP, on this matter. Oliveira disseminated the Italian translation of one of his writings, *The Liberty of the Church in the Communist State*, in which he cautioned against the dangers inherent in that ideology which he clearly sought to condemn.

On October 9, the letter of Msgr. Carli obtained the support of nearly 450 Council Fathers, but nothing was to come of it. In 1962, in the city of Metz in France, there was a meeting between Cardinal Tisserant, representative of the Vatican, and a representative of the Moscow Patriarchate, in which participation of their representatives at the Council was granted on condition that the it would not condemn communism.

Romano Amerio, one of the greatest Catholic intellectuals of the past century, narrates, in his fundamental work *Iota Unum*, the issue of the Council and communism in the following way:

> The weakening of the logical sense particular to
> the spirit of the age raises fear in the Church as
> well, because of this compromising agreement. In

its inaugural discourse, the Council celebrated the
freedom of the contemporary Church at the very
moment in which it confessed that many bishops
are imprisoned for their fidelity to Christ and in
which, due to an agreement desired by the Pontiff,
the Council finds itself tied to a commitment not
to pronounce its condemnation of communism.
This contradiction, which is great, remains nonetheless minor compared to the foundational
contradiction upon which the renewal of the
Church rests regarding the opening to the world;
and then it liquidates the problem of communism — the principal, essential, and decisive
problem — as one of the problems of the world.

Amerio's prose, which as always goes to the heart of the problem, places us before one of the crucial problems for the
Church at that time (and also for our own) — not only the
attitude of the Church regarding Christians suffering under
Communist regimes (for example in Eastern Europe or China),
to whom the response was given in the form of *Ostpolitik*,
but also the attitude toward those Christians who see in communism the response to the evils of the world and yearn for
an "encounter" between their faith and Marxist ideology. As
we have seen, the temptation was certainly not absent in
previous decades and in just a few years was to take theological
form, especially in Latin America, and would constitute a
powerful, important movement in the Church of the twentieth
century, and to some extent, in the twenty-first.

On October 4, Paul VI gave a historic speech at the United Nations in New York. In this important discourse, the Pope exalted the role of the UN:

> What you are proclaiming here are the basic rights and duties of man, his dignity, his liberty and above all his religious liberty. We feel that you are spokesmen for what is loftiest in human wisdom — we might almost say its sacred character — for it is above all a question of human life, and human life is sacred; no one can dare attack it. It is in your Assembly, even where the matter of the great problem of birth rates is concerned, that respect for life ought to find its loftiest profession and its most reasonable defense. Your task is so to act in such a way that there will be enough bread at the table of mankind and not to support artificial birth control which would be irrational, with the aim of reducing the number of those sharing in the banquet of life.

This discourse might seem a bit strange when one knows how the UN in many of its policies affirms ideas antithetical to Catholic doctrine. This value system is the direct successor to the liberal ideology of the French Revolution. And as many intellectuals have pointed out, there is a grave danger in pursuing such values. To quote Romano Amerio,

> Equality, in fact, when it concerns the nature of man and his redemption, is a philosophical and

theological truth. Liberty, if one intends the liberation of man from every non-divine service, is the very essence of religion. Fraternity, founded not on man's amiability but on the evangelical imperative, whence philanthropy is an extension of love of God, is a *punctum saliens* of Christian ethics. But it is obvious that the specific value of these three principles in the system of 1789 consists precisely in their becoming a value in themselves without reference to God in the scale of values.

This emphasis placed on democracy and on the principles of 1789 is important, because they would become the main charges made against the postconciliar Church, as we shall soon observe.

THE WORKER-PRIESTS

On October 23 the French episcopate, with the permission of Paul VI, authorized once more the activity of "worker-priests" — priests who not only offered pastoral care to workers and their families but who were authorized to share in their work as well. The experiment was begun in France as early as the 1940s, thanks above all to the work of Cardinal Emmanuel Suhard (1874–1949), archbishop of Paris, who recognized the growing dechristianization of his country and considered France to be a mission territory. He felt this was an effective method of (re)evangelization in the twentieth century. The worker-priest movement arrived in Italy in 1950 under the leadership of Don Bruno Borghi. But between

1953 and 1954 this way of life was prohibited by the Holy Office. Fr. Congar and Fr. Chenu, whom we have already encountered, wrote of this movement of worker-priests:

> The condition of the proletariat is such that it is inseparable from the struggle for its liberation. Is it therefore possible to be its advocate, even as a Church, without accompanying it in a fight that concerns the exigencies of the Gospel and liberation—transcendent, no doubt, and total, but real and concrete—which Jesus Christ produces? We cannot refrain from proposing the problem of the Christian meaning of history and of transposing this problem from the merely personal and spiritual level of salvation to the collective level of earthly history. It is likewise impossible to avoid the encounter with Marxism, not only as a theory, but as the concrete ferment of the workers' struggle, daily present and active.

The experience was prohibited for an obvious reason as well: a man cannot work as a priest and a factory worker at the same time; the demands of a vocation interfere with those of the profession. Then there was the concrete risk that it would not be the priest who converted the workers, but the workers (communists) converting the priests.

Non-Christian Religions

Just a few days after the declaration of the French episcopate on worker-priests, the Council promulgated an important document, the Declaration on the Relation of the Church to Non-Christian Religions *Nostra Aetate* (October 28). Particularly important were the words on Judaism:

> Since the spiritual patrimony common to Christians and Jews is thus so great, this sacred synod wants to foster and recommend that mutual understanding and respect which is the fruit, above all, of biblical and theological studies as well as of fraternal dialogues.
>
> True, the Jewish authorities and those who followed their lead pressed for the death of Christ; still, what happened in His passion cannot be charged against all the Jews, without distinction, then alive, nor against the Jews of today. Although the Church is the new people of God, the Jews should not be presented as rejected or accursed by God, as if this followed from the Holy Scriptures.

At the beginning of the document, the following was stated as concerns other religions:

> The Catholic Church rejects nothing that is true and holy in these religions. She regards with sincere reverence those ways of conduct and of life, those precepts and teachings which, though differing in many aspects from the ones she holds and sets forth, nonetheless often reflect a ray of that Truth which enlightens all men. Indeed, she proclaims, and ever must proclaim Christ "the way,

the truth, and the life" (John 14:6), in whom men
may find the fullness of religious life, in whom
God has reconciled all things to Himself.

The Church, therefore, exhorts her sons, that
through dialogue and collaboration with the followers of other religions, carried out with prudence
and love and in witness to the Christian faith and
life, they recognize, preserve and promote the
good things, spiritual and moral, as well as the
socio-cultural values found among these men.

Certainly, this text might offer room for ambiguous interpretations. What does it mean to promote the "good things,
spiritual and moral" of other religions? Romano Amerio did
not hide his perplexity:

The conciliar declaration *Nostra Aetate*, 2, cites
the renowned text from John on the "light that
enlightens every man," which would constitute
the foundation of every religion. But the Council
is silent about what, according to John Paul II, is
the parallel mystery of the Incarnation, namely
that light was rejected by men. It is thus impossible that it constitutes the foundation of all
religions (*L'Osservatore Romano*, December 26,
1981). The Pope says that in Christmas we believe in the mystery of the birth of the man-God
and there is the unresolved mystery of the non-
acceptance of him by the world and by his own.
The council does not speak of a supernatural
light but of "fullness of light." The naturalism

that characterizes both *Ad Gentes* and *Nostra Aetate* is patent in their terminology as well, since the word "supernatural" never occurs.

The Declaration opened, therefore, more questions than it resolved. Ecumenism was to become one of the important debates after the Council, as all well know.

On November 18, the Dogmatic Constitution on Divine Revelation *Dei Verbum* was promulgated. On December 6, there occurred a significant name change for the important Vatican dicastery: the Holy Office became the Sacred Congregation for the Doctrine of the Faith. On December 7, two more important documents were promulgated: *Gaudium et Spes* on the Church in the contemporary world and the declaration *Dignitatis Humanae* on religious liberty. These documents were to have enormous repercussions on the postconciliar Church and on the movement of Catholic traditionalism, as we shall see below.

In his closing allocution to the Council, Paul VI said the following:

> Secular humanism, revealing itself in its horrible anti-clerical reality has, in a certain sense, defied the council. The religion of the God who became man has met the religion (for such it is) of man who makes himself God. And what happened? Was there a clash, a battle, a condemnation? There could have been, but there was none. The old story of the Samaritan has been the model of the spirituality of the council. A feeling of boundless

> sympathy has permeated the whole of it. The at-
> tention of our council has been absorbed by the
> discovery of human needs (and these needs grow
> in proportion to the greatness which the son of the
> earth claims for himself). But we call upon those
> who term themselves modern humanists, and who
> have renounced the transcendent value of the
> highest realities, to give the council credit at least
> for one quality and to recognize our own new type
> of humanism: we, too, in fact, we more than any
> others, honor mankind.

These intense words caused much discussion, seeing in these statements a sort of anthropological shift in the Church that set man in the place reserved for God. Certainly, one can think that this was not the intention of Paul VI, but many theologians did follow this path. This ceremony, in its rite and in its music, displayed a marked difference with respect to the opening ceremony. The Church no longer seemed the same.

An Infinite Postconciliar Period

Thus began the period which everyone defines as "postconciliar," and in which, apparently, we still find ourselves, a time that never seems to end. Obviously, from here onward we shall consider the many open questions the Council has left us, with special attention to the object of our study, the world of Catholic traditionalism, seen always in the backlight of what was happening in the world, in the Church, and in particular, in the progressive wing of the Church. For this reason, we must emphasize that already since 1965, an important editorial project came to life, a journal called *Concilium*. It was founded July 20, 1963, but started publishing in 1965. Among its founders were Karl Rahner, Hans Küng, and Yves Congar, a fact that makes abundantly clear what direction this influential journal was to take in the theological debates that followed.

We are confronted, at the beginning of 1966, with political and social events of great importance. On January 24, the sociology faculty in Trent was occupied by students. The journalist Ugo Maria Tassinari described what was in the air: "The setting of Trent was chosen also considering its 'decentralized and tranquil' geographical position, for the broad political and cultural hegemony exercised by Catholics there, and with the not secondary objective of bringing provincial realities into the national limelight."

At the University of Trent, what would become the head of one of the most important terrorist groups of the 1970s and 1980s, the Red Brigade (*Brigate Rosse* or BR) was forming. Catholic Trent was to become one of the laboratories not only of student protests but also of leftist sedition.

On February 4, the Congregation for the Doctrine of the Faith abolished the Index of Prohibited Books. Many exulted at what they defined as the end of ecclesiastical censorship. In reality, the Index, and the idea it represented, was that of keeping texts harmful to the soul at a distance from the Catholic faithful, whose salvation is the supreme good. Seen from the Catholic perspective, the Index was not something wrong per se, even though it might have been used at times in an erroneous manner.

On February 15, Camillo Torres was killed in an ambush. This would have an important role in the progressive Catholic imagination for decades to come. The journal of *Pax Christi*, a movement inspired by Catholic progressives, described it in this manner: "Camillo Torres Restrepo was a Colombian priest, guerrilla, and revolutionary and had a fundamental role in the promotion of dialogue between revolutionary Marxism and Catholicism." As we can see, this theme of encounter between Christianity and Marxism was increasingly felt—and in particular the Latin American experiences of this encounter.

We cannot forget that precisely that year a book appeared, published by *Cittadella di Assisi*, under the title *Marxism and Christianity* (in that order), written by the Salesian Giulio Girardi (1926–2012), who passed from strict orthodoxy to Christians for Socialism, a movement that intended to reconcile socialist ideas with Christian doctrine. Girardi's book was an important text for understanding that season. At his death, the Italian daily *La Stampa* remembered him this way:

> Despite his academic commitments and his participation in the work of the Second Vatican Council as a peritus, his choice to work with the grassroots movements and his position in favor of Marxism caused him, in 1969, to be expelled from the Salesian University due to "ideological divergencies." He then transferred to Paris, where he taught anthropology at the philosophy department of the Catholic University as well as

Introduction to Marxism at the Institute of Sciences and Theology of Religions.

His is a name to keep in mind when remembering those difficult years.

But the new ideas, which the Council had never promoted, made headway in other fields as well, especially in that of liturgy. Consider the April 27 event that made a profound impression, at the beautiful Sala Borromini in Rome, where a Beat Mass was conducted. The songs for this Mass were accompanied by a band like those playing for children's birthday parties or folk music festivals, with rhythms and melodies imitating those of commercial music. But how could they have passed from Gregorian chant to this? The fact that there were priests — liturgists from pontifical institutes — among the promoters of this initiative shows that it was part of a larger project of liturgical reform. There were many protests against the event in Sala Borromini, but that was only the beginning, because commercial music was to invade the Church more and more, profaning (literally) the most sacred act of worship for a Christian. They were no longer promoting the reform; they wanted a revolution.

I use this word *revolution* intentionally, because in that very year the Cultural Revolution was to begin in China, by which Mao Zedong (1893–1976) sought to consolidate his power in the great Chinese nation. He urged the Chinese people to stamp out the "Four Olds" — old ways of thinking, old culture, old customs, and old traditions — because they undermined the transformation of China into a socialist country. The beginning of the Cultural Revolution is traditionally indicated as May 16, and it is important to keep this event in mind, because both Mao and the Cultural Revolution itself would exercise a strong fascination over youth, and not only communists.

On June 7, the Italian section of *Una Voce* was formed, an association for the defense of Latin and Gregorian chant. One of its great protagonists, the art historian Carlo Belli (1903–1991) recalls:

> "*Una Voce*," in Italy as around the world, immediately opposed such an amazing theft of the age-old institutions of the Tradition with action aimed at the containment of the levees and the recovery of what was being lost. It began its battle above all against the new conformism, aimed at removing the supernatural sentiment in divine worship, and at shaping it into the form of a positivistic Protestantism, to indulge on one side triumphant materialism, and on the other a sort of amateur ecumenism, of which the new clergy was particularly fond.

Then Belli speaks of the genesis of one of the most well-known documents opposing the liturgical reform:

> With the generous contribution of some sympathizers and the sums immediately paid by many adherents, we were able to set up our office in a luxurious apartment on Corso Vittorio [Rome].

> There, the "Brief Critical Examination" of the
> new *Ordo Missae* was edited, compiled with long,
> attentive studies by a team of recognized experts,
> and presented to the Pope by Cardinals Bacci and
> Ottaviani; a compilation that was, is, and re-
> mains the document containing the prologues to
> any future criticism of the religious reform. Dis-
> seminated throughout the entire Catholic world,
> it is still today taken as an illuminating text in
> studies on this topic. (unavoceitalia.org)

Later we shall refer to several things the author discusses.
The president of *Una Voce* from 1979 to 1988 was Count
Neri Capponi (1925–2018). He represented the part of the
aristocracy still tied to the values of tradition. We also recall
Princess Elvira Pallavicini (1914–2004), who sided with
Archbishop Lefebvre, and the Marquise Luigi Coda Nunziante (1930–2015), whom I had the pleasure of meeting
and whom I remember as a man of profound kindness toward
all. I also met Princess Eliane Radziwill, whom I remember
with great tenderness, for despite her noble status, she did
not disdain performing the role of a sort of secretary for the
Roman office of *Una Voce* and was always very courteous
with all who approached her.

In the meantime, Paul VI tried to govern the barque of
Peter, which sailed in troubled waters. He seemed to try to
satisfy first one group and then another. On one side, he
promoted the new Mass in Italian, but on the other side he
issued documents that seemed to put on the brakes, as the
apostolic letter of August 15, *Sacrificium Laudis*, shows. In

it, he asked religious communities to maintain the prayer of the Divine Office in Latin:

> In fact, this is not only a matter of preserving the choral Office in Latin, undoubtedly worthy, not a small matter, to be given great care, being in the Latin Church the most fecund source of Christian civilization and a most rich treasure of piety, but also of preserving unharmed the quality, the beauty, and the original vigor of those prayers and chants: it is a matter of the choral Office expressed "with the voices of the Church that sweetly sing" (cf. St. Augustine, *Confessions*, 9,6: PL 32, 769), and which your founders and masters and saints in Heaven, luminaries of your religious Families, passed on to you.

It seems quite odd to read this text written by a Pontiff who was among the protagonists of one of the most momentous liturgical changes in the history of the Church. And yet, the Pope continued in the document in the same vein: "What language, what chant would seem capable in the present situation of substituting those forms of Catholic piety that you have used until now? Serious reflection must be given that things are not made worse after having refused this glorious inheritance."

From this letter, we can presume that Paul VI had set up a liturgical Church on two levels: the traditional one preserved for religious, and the renewed one for the simple faithful. It is not clear how novices, drawn from the simple faithful, could have willingly accepted a sense of liturgical dignity in which they had never been educated. A mystery of the faith!

We must now return to the issue of Abbé de Nantes, of whom we have already spoken. On August 25, he was suspended *a divinis* (prohibition to celebrate Mass) by the bishop of Troyes. This did not discourage him much, given that he started another journal, *The Catholic Counter Reformation of the 20th Century*, in addition to his *Letters to Friends*. There were various attempts to bring back into the sheepfold Abbé de Nantes, who protested ever more vehemently against the deviations in the Church and against the Council.

On October 9, the Dutch Catechism was published, one of the most representative documents of the progressive deviation in the Church. This catechism was also a very strong signal of the progressive aberration in the heart of the Church of Holland, which would lead in the coming years to an enormous exodus of the faithful, which still today has no end in sight.

On December 20, Archbishop Lefebvre sent a letter to Cardinal Ottaviani. In it, he stated:

> I would gladly have followed the order of truths listed in Your letter, but allow me to say that the current evil seems to be much worse than the negation or the placing up for discussion of some truths of our faith. Today, it manifests itself in an extreme confusion of ideas, in a breakdown of the institutions of the Church, of religious

foundations, of seminaries, of Catholic schools, in short, of what was the permanent support of the Church. And this is nothing but the logical continuation of the heresies and errors that have undermined the Church in recent centuries; above all, liberalism in the previous century, that sought at any cost to reconcile the Church with the ideas that brought about the French Revolution.

This affirmation that the principles of the French Revolution had already entered the Church would be one of the battle cries of Archbishop Lefebvre in the years to come. This assertion would also have great impact on the way his movement would develop.

Before we leave 1966 behind, we must remember an important text, *The Peasant of the Garonne* by the philosopher Jacques Maritain (1882–1973). An important intellectual, he had enormous influence, especially on the pontificate of Paul VI. In this text, Maritain seems to caution against the excesses found in the postconciliar period: "Today's unrestrained Modernism is irremediably ambivalent. It tends to ruin Christian faith, although it denies doing so, busying itself as well as it can with emptying it of its content."

Looking into 1967, on January 8 the *International Federation Una Voce* was formally constituted in Zurich. As mentioned, this was to become one of the most influential resistance associations in the coming years. Yet even the Pontiff must have intuited that something was moving in a dangerous direction, and in this we can see what some observers defined as Paul VI's ambiguity, that on one side he encouraged the innovators, while on the other he seemed to want to slow them down.

On March 26, Paul VI promulgated one of his most well-known documents, the encyclical *Popolorum Progressio*. Nevertheless, the traditionalist front represented by the Abbé de Nantes was not very impressed by this encyclical. To the contrary, in one of his letters to friends he criticized it harshly:

> This analysis of the social situation in the world is extraneous to the Latin mind and is not even explicitly Catholic. Paul VI borrowed it from the French progressive school of thought. It is materialist in its complete lack of evaluation of political realities; it is dialectic in its exclusive concern for opposing the aspirations of indigenous populations to oppression by capitalist forces; it is atheistic in its Modernist reduction of religious phenomena to mere superstructures inherited from the past; it is anti-Christian in its all too evident diminution of the Christian miracle and of the incomparable civilizing power of the Church in the world. On the basis of this analysis, how can a program of salvation be different from that of a Communist Revolution? This is truly the essential ambition of the Pope. Substantially in agreement with the Marxist analysis of the crisis in the world, he intends to propose to Christian peoples a synthesis of a new Christianity, capable of satisfying the aspirations of men better than communism and beyond.

Meanwhile, on June 26, Don Lorenzo Milani died. A complex personality, he had just published *Letter to a Professor*, while a few years earlier he had published *Obedience is No Longer a Virtue*, authoritative reference texts for all progressive Catholics. Don Balducci, having known and frequently visited him, interpreted Don Milani's proposal thus:

> Don Milani had that purity of opinion that came from not having had a background in Catholic education. He had the ability of straightforward gestures, immediate and a free language, which for those of us who have passed through the gates of the seminary is always a difficult language. For this reason, Don Milani was immediately able to detect the ambiguity of a presence of the Church in which the entire apparatus rested, as if out of spontaneous gravitation, on the moribund peasant civilization. The new problems emerging from the industrial world had archaic, generic, moralistic solutions, insufficiently dosed for the severity of the problem posed by class struggle.

I believe this is a very important text, because it gives us the hermeneutical key for understanding how a certain type of progressive Catholicism viewed the world, and still views the world: how the Church struggles to adjust to contemporary reality interpreted according to Marxist categories of the class struggle. Father Turoldo defined Don Milani as "a man more concrete and incarnated in matters of faith than we can even imagine."

Not everyone is aligned with this exaltation of Don Milani. Mario A. Iannaccone, for example, observed the following:

> What was new in Don Milani was his claim of class warfare, perfectly in line with the times. A commentator wrote, "After *Letter to a Professor*, which was the 'red book' of 1968, a position of mass conscience of a privileged character, of a certain way of doing school, of doing culture at school, the strategy of massive and brutal selection entered into crisis" (Tullio de Mauro). The letter was addressed to an actual professor who had failed two students at the school *Barbiana*. In it, he defends a type of collective study in which the teacher would be a non-authoritarian guide. The letter holds that schools tend to expel the poorest children (it is "classist"), that the use of grades is counterproductive, that abstract notions are not needed.

Don Milani's text raises real problems, such as the disparity between rich and poor, but does not seem to offer the most useful answers for resolving the questions in a Catholic way. On the contrary, he seems to confine himself to the ideology of class struggle, as Iannaccone observes:

> A physical clash was drawing near, in his estimation, in the mid-1950s, and when it would come no one had the right to complain. Don Milani's disciple, Michele Gesauldi, president of the Province of Florence and president of the Don Milani Foundation, asked Pope Francis to rehabilitate

his master's *Pastoral Experiences*, which contained incendiary words. When publishing the revolutionary words of his master (in 1970, but also in a more recent edition in 2008), Gesauldi did not seem to notice how dangerous they were, or if he was aware, was not cautious.

Just days after the death of Don Milani (June 26), Paul VI promulgated another encyclical which would raise protests, his *Sacerdotalis Caelibatus*, in which the Pope reaffirmed the importance of celibacy in the life of priests: "Priestly celibacy, which the Church has guarded for centuries as a radiant jewel, preserves all of its value even in our time characterized by a profound transformation of mentality and structures." The theme of priestly celibacy and its defense would continue to be, in the coming years, an embattled terrain where traditionalists and progressives would clash.

THE ROLE OF PROTESTANTS IN THE LITURGICAL REFORM

The day after Don Milani's death, June 27, an interview appeared in the *Detroit News* with Fr. William Wakefield Baum (1926–2015), a former peritus at the Council, later to be made a cardinal. His statements about the role of Protestants in the Council and in the liturgical reform caused an uproar. "They were not only present as observers," he wrote, "but also as consultants, and participated fully in the discussions on the Catholic liturgical renewal. It would not have meant much had they limited themselves to listening, but they contributed." It's an interesting claim, and one which contrasts with the attempts on the Vatican's part of minimizing this influence. Romano Amerio spoke of this:

> Also regarding the meeting of non-Catholic Christians, the voice was heard of those who equated Protestants—without the priesthood, without the hierarchy, without apostolic succession, and without or almost without the sacraments—to the Orthodox, who instead have everything in common with Catholics, except the primacy and infallibility. Pius IX had made a clear distinction: he sent apostolic envoys to deliver letters of invitation to the oriental patriarchs (who all declared they could not attend the Council), but did not recognize as Churches the various Protestant confessions, considering them mere associations, and sent an appeal *ad omnes protestantes*, not so that they might intervene at the Council, but that they would return to the unity from which they had departed. The latitudinarian stance emerging in the preparation rests on an implicit partial equality between Catholics and non-Catholics, and turned out to be a minority in the preparatory phase, but then succeeded in inviting Protestants as observers, indistinct from the Orthodox, and then explained their influence in the decree *de oecumenismo* (§245–7).

Later, referring to the Eucharist, Amerio adds:

> Indeed, there are numerous Protestants who claim they find the new Mass to be in conformity

with their beliefs and acceptable for the celebration of the Eucharist in the heart of their communities. Max Thurian, of the Community of Taizé, in the journal *La Croix* of May 30, 1969, declared one of the fruits of the new Mass to be, "*que des communités non catholiques pourront célébrer la Sainte Cène avec les mêmes prières que l'Eglise catholique: théologiquement c'est possible.*" ["that non catholic communities could celebrate the holy banquet with the same prayers of the Catholic Church theologically is possible]." It must, therefore, be recognized that the reform changed a Catholic Mass that was inacceptable for Protestants into an acceptable Catholic Mass. And the judgment of acceptability implies that a profound variation occurred: of the variation then, those who are judges are precisely those who alone have competence. The testimonies in this sense have by now been numberless, and the celebrations, by priests and ministers, of the same promiscuous Eucharist confirm the doctrinal variation, despite the weak opposition by the hierarchy.

Michael Davies concurs with Amerio:

> On 3 May 1970 *Documentation Catholique* published the text of a speech made by Pope Paul VI to the members of the *Consilium.* ...
>
> The cover of this issue of *Documentation Catholique* was devoted to a picture of Pope Paul

VI posing with the six Protestant Observers who had been invited to participate in the work of the *Consilium*. This photograph proved to be a source of astonishment and even scandal to large numbers of the faithful who had had no idea that Protestants had played any part in the compilation of the new Catholic rites.

In the July/August 1974 issue of *Notitiae*, official journal of the *Consilium*, Archbishop Bugnini (its secretary) claimed that the Observers confined their role simply to observing (pp. 249/50). Here are his exact words: "What role did the 'Observers' play in the *Consilium*? Nothing more than that of 'Observers.' First of all, they only took part in the study meetings. In the second place, they behaved with impeccable discretion. They never intervened in the discussions and never asked to speak."

In sum, the role of Protestants in the reforms following the Council is not clear.

Incendiary Books

In the meantime, editorial production certainly did not stop, and many books would consolidate the faith on both sides of the theological spectrum.

That year, Fr. de Lubac published *Paradox and Mystery of the Church*, in which he critically confronted the ferment deriving from the Council, especially that concerning *Lumen Gentium*, the constitution on the Church. Not long after, Michel de Saint Pierre responded on behalf of the traditionalists with his *Ces qui souffrent* (Those who suffer). But the book that decidedly caused the most uproar was written by a Florentine author, a layman with a biting tongue. I am speaking of Tito Casini (1897–1987), who wrote *The Torn Tunic*. Cardinal Antonio Bacci, in his introduction, stated:

> I have been invited to make a brief presentation of this little volume by Tito Casini. I cannot, nor do I wish to refuse; to the contrary, I do so gladly, though with some reservations, both because I have known Tito Casini from his early youth and I appreciate him as one of the premier Catholic writers in Italy for his fresh style, caustic and sincere, which reminds me of the pure mountain air of my Firenzuola, but also because he is an upright Christian and can say what an ancient sacred writer said of himself, *"Christianus mihi nomen, catholicus cognomen"*; and also finally because, if his writing seems to some not reverent enough, all will recognize however that it issues from an ardent love for the Church and her liturgical décor.... I trust therefore that those interested will generously pardon the Author certain phrases that might seem to them less respectful, reflecting that they were not written to offend, but only because the heart was exacerbated by certain innovations that seem and are true profanations. At any rate, there is always something to learn for everyone; even from the

voice of laymen, especially from those laymen
who are, as is Tito Casini, perfect Catholics.

But it is certainly quite enjoyable to read how Tito Casini
mourns for what he was losing (and this was 1967, before
the new missal had even been promulgated!). In the book,
Casini has it out with Cardinal Giacomo Lercaro (1891–1976),
who was responsible for the liturgical reform, was sustained
by bishops of the European Alliance, and was a candidate for
the papacy in the conclave that would see, with his support,
the election of Paul VI. In the book, Tito Casini "inveighs"
in this way:

> You mitered pastors, you have thus flattered and
> promoted us, we who have been up to now sim-
> ple "lambs" in the flock entrusted to Peter there
> on the beach of Tiberius.... To some it even
> seemed excessive and there arose the joke of an
> updated encyclopedia in which the entry "laity"
> was explained with a reference to the entry
> "clergy" and "clergy" with a reference to "laity."
> Jokes aside, you have, I repeat, attributed to us so
> much importance in conducting the Church,
> and I appeal Eminence, to your own words trans-
> mitted to us on TV three days before that March
> 7: "Certainly this Council we can also call the
> Council of the laity because" etc., etc.; so much
> you have said to us that you have inebriated us on
> "freedom," and it no longer seems irreverent to
> speak in church, that is, to address you.

The text is truly enjoyable, as much as it is bitter, seeing the author's love of the traditional liturgy.

After the brouhaha raised over his book, Tito Casini had to defend himself later that year against various accusations that rained down on him. He did so in another book, *Dicebamus Heri*, in which the author, always with his ironic Tuscan language, attempts to refute the attacks:

> A trial, then, in which I am the accused, and behold, in a worthy style, the accusation: "What did this Tito Casini do? He wrote a book, *The Torn Tunic*, in the form of an open letter to the Most Excellent Msgr. Bishop President of the Liturgical Commission, namely Cardinal Lercaro Archbishop of Bologna, guilty of having too rashly insisted on the abolition of Latin in the liturgical usage, preferring the vernacular." And addressing, with ironic courtesy, the accused: "Allow us, illustrious Casini, to tell you that if you consider the sacrality of Catholic worship to be essentially the fact of using Latin and that the Italian vernacular does not allow the individual to communicate with God, you have understood nothing of religiosity and continue to remain stubbornly in your ignorance. But we are serious, illustrious writer, that perhaps God might not understand Italian, or would be horrified by the abolition of Latin!"

Congregatio Mariae Reginae Immaculatae

On August 5, 1967, in the United States, whose ferment we have already observed, a young man named Francis Schuckardt (1937–2006), devoted to Mary and interested in the message of Fatima, founded the *Congregatio Mariae Reginae Immaculatae* (CMRI), a development of an organization that Schuckardt had created the same year called the Crusaders of Fatima. Seeing that some of its members desired a more intense religious experience, he thought of founding this congregation, which according to Schuckardt represented the "true Catholic Church."

The positions of Schuckardt and his congregation were quite strong toward the official Church and can be summarized in three points: Paul VI is a false Pope, the new Mass is invalid, and the ecumenism of Vatican II is erroneous.

Unsurprisingly, these views obviously did not please the official Church. According to a website run by Schuckardt's followers:

> As part of their efforts to denigrate Bishop Schuckardt, some in the post-Vatican II Catholic Church condemn him and declare him to be schismatic and excommunicated. But because Bishop Schuckardt does not recognize the post-Vatican II Catholic Church officially or unofficially, he rejects any accusation of schism or excommunication on their behalf. Because he considers it a new and different Church, and not the Catholic Church founded by Christ that has existed for nearly 2,000 years, he rejects the idea that they have the

authority to excommunicate him or to declare him a schismatic from the "true" Catholic Church. Insofar as he has been excommunicated or declared schismatic by their "new Church," he finds these affirmations ridiculous because he was never part of the post-Vatican II Catholic Church.

This idea of not recognizing the excommunication because he does not recognize the authority of the one imposing it will turn up later and will be one means of defense adopted in the fringe traditionalist camp to continue its protest against the deviations of the Church in recent decades. But now we shall continue with this new congregation.

On the official website of the CMRI, their theological position is explained in the following way:

> The Catholic priests of the Religious Congregation of Mary Immaculate Queen profess their adherence to Catholic Faith, which was intended and taught throughout the centuries since the time of Christ. With the death of Pope Pius XII and the convocation of the Second Vatican Council, the Church has been swept by an unprecedented situation that threatens her doctrine and worship.

In November 1971, Francis Schuckardt was ordained priest and bishop. This gave a new impulse to his congregation. Later, in the early 1980s, he was arrested for drug possession, and then accused of sexual abuse. This led to a division within the CMRI: Schuckardt was expelled and continued his activity outside the congregation. The CMRI is still active today, with over ninety centers for celebrating Mass and various schools, above all in the United States but also abroad.

FATIMA CRUSADER

The *Fatima Crusader* movement must also be mentioned. Founded by Fr. Nicholas Gruner (1942–2015), it made a name for itself through the journal of the same name, which carried out its battle against progressivism. Through this journal they also led a campaign to consecrate Russia to the Immaculate Heart of Mary.

The initiatives of Fr. Gruner created not a few problems for him and his group, to the point that various bishops warned the faithful not to participate in his events. Eventually he was suspended from the priesthood.

THE LITURGICAL REFORM CONTINUES

Before continuing to speak about the ecclesial situation, we recall that on October 9, 1967, Ernest "Che" Guevara died, one of the most representative figures of the 1960s, entering directly into the mythology of the progressive world. Gianpaolo Barra, in his *Elementary Dictionary of Dangerous Thought*, offers a concise judgment: "Despite his nearly universal fame as a romantic guerrilla, liberator of the poor and oppressed, Che Guevara was a man who professed communist and materialist ideas in clear antithesis to the teachings of the Church. In addition, he was a hard, ferocious, cruel man, a downright assassin."

And yet this did not inhibit many progressive Catholics from considering him a reference point. So much so, that during the World Congress for the Apostolate of the Laity that began on October 10 — the day after Guevara's death — the delegates stood up to pay homage to the guerrilla. In the meantime, in November, Danilo Dolci (1924–1997), known as the "Gandhi of Sicily," organized a march against the Vietnam War. Numerous Catholics took part, including several priests.

We return now to the liturgical reform. On March 5, 1967, an Instruction was promulgated for music in the liturgy, called *Musicam Sacram*. I will use several passages here from my article on this topic published in *The International Church Music Review*. This Instruction had the objective of implementing and bringing to completion the requests made in the conciliar constitution *Sacrosanctum Concilium* in matters concerning sacred music. Given that more than sixty years have passed since the promulgation of this document, we cannot hide the fact that it is a sign of contradiction still today. Reading it even at the distance of sixty years, one notices that, along with things entirely acceptable, there are some problematic issues as well as some foundational misunderstandings that still today influence the situation of liturgical music, a situation one could define without exaggeration as "dramatic."

Where does *Musicam Sacram* stand in this framework? It is interesting to note that this document is of course the object of musicological attention, but can be read no less as an indicator of the current situation in the entire Catholic world, namely of a dramatic distancing not only from *Musicam* but also from *Sacrosanctum*: a hermeneutic of discontinuity with the preceding tradition has now firmly taken over ecclesial thought in recent decades, to the point that measuring the objective facts of the documents against the accepted practice exposes a situation of what should be called "abuse."

Certainly, *Musicam* is not entirely extraneous to all this, and some contradictions that stand in the light of day (for those with eyes to see and who have stopped closing their eyes) cannot be explained but by reference to some of the problematic issues of *Musicam*, issues that have worsened the situation that had already deteriorated at the time (in liturgy, as well as in theology, philosophy, and so forth) and that have brought us to the current situation of objective confusion.

Therefore, these sixty years oblige us to make a difficult assessment which, next to good things, cannot overlook the negative, for the latter have taken root in our liturgies to such an extent that to think of a way out is not only difficult but highly unlikely, given the current state of things.

The document enabled certain problems to come to the fore. I will give an example. At number 32 of *Musicam Sacram*, we find this:

> The custom legitimately in use in certain places and widely confirmed by indults, of substituting other songs for the songs given in the Graduale for the Entrance, Offertory and Communion, can be retained according to the judgment of the competent territorial authority, as long as songs

of this sort are in keeping with the parts of the Mass, with the feast or with the liturgical season. It is for the same territorial authority to approve the texts of these songs.

This was, if I may say, the beginning of the end. To give the go-ahead to the substitution of official liturgical texts with "other texts" made it possible to sweep away in just a few years centuries of liturgical pedagogy that was based on texts sanctioned in the Roman Missal. It is true that, in the past, the antiphons were often recited *recto tono* and were often executed by songs with other texts. But there is a substantial difference, I would say: these texts were almost always taken from the Psalms, from the Scriptures, not like today where freely invented texts are proposed that have a religious character, or perhaps the character of popular song, but not that of liturgical song. The scholars Pio Benedetto Nocilli and Giuseppe Antonio Nocilli have observed:

> Perhaps what one expects of music today is a call to interiority. Phrenetic modern life, with its monotonous work, its tasks that estrange man from his interior world, can provoke in him the desire to return within himself, to recall the sentiments, memories, and aspirations that music can arouse. But only the music that is sweet and attractive to him has in him an emotive resonance that leads him to concentrate all of his interests within him, evoking memories or desires proper to him.

This is an important point, insofar as that interiority to which we must be recalled is that in which we discover the presence of God in us, not that which drowns us in ourselves. Thus, when memories and desires evoked by texts heavily influenced by all the themes that form the crown of anthropologism and personalism enter the ears, with correspondingly adequate music, the aim of liturgical song is not attained. Certainly, one can accept that this happens in religious song, which has its liturgical collocation next to and in submission to liturgical song, not substituting it. The equivocation perpetuated over recent decades between religious song and liturgical song has led to serious consequences in our liturgical action. Unfortunately, the documents applied to it from the liturgical constitution continued an agenda promoted by the progressive wing of scholars, and the path had already been laid down for an even more overwhelming advance. Sacred music would be but one aspect of this march; the other important aspect was language.

An article of September 29, 1967, in *The Catholic Transcript* warned that the canon in English was to be inaugurated on October 22:

> English will appear in the Canon of the Mass in churches throughout the United States on Sunday October 22, stated Archbishop John F. Dearden of Detroit, president of the National Conference of Catholic Bishops. Msgr. Dearden, speaking in Rome where he was participating in the Synod of Bishops, stated that there would be no need of books or missals. The inserts for the

Altar Missal will be sent to priests, he said. The text will be prepared by the International Committee for English in the Liturgy, and will be introduced in the Mass with the consent of the Holy See provisionally and as the only text permitted, he said. The prelate also announced that the Holy See has confirmed the work of the United States hierarchy in approving the translation into English of all the rites of ordination and of the rite of consecration of bishops.

Similarly, in *The Catholic Advocate* of October 19, the priest Joseph B. Ryan explained this historic change, saying, "This admirable project has received due care and study." Obviously, not everyone agreed with this evaluation.

Meanwhile, in September 1967, the first Synod of Bishops took place over the course of a month. Among the relators was Cardinal Lercaro, and among the secretaries, Fr. Bugnini. The historian Yves Chiron, whose studies have been very useful for this book, in one of his texts on Annibale Bugnini, remembers what happened on October 24, the famous "Normative Mass":

The New Mass in its finished structure was presented to nearly 180 cardinals and bishops in a Synod in the Vatican in 1967. This first postconciliar Synod dealt with various themes: the renewal of the code of canon law, the doctrinal questions, and the liturgical reform. On October 21, Cardinal Lercaro presented the united cardinals and bishops a report describing the new structure of the Mass and the modifications introduced, as well as the reform of the Divine Office.

On October 24, Fr. Bugnini celebrated a "normative" Mass before the synodal Fathers in the Sistine Chapel. Paul VI did not participate in this celebration because he was "indisposed," however. Besides the modifications already in force from the *Instructions* of 1964 and 1967 (Mass celebrated in front of the people, in Italian, including the Canon, less genuflecting and signing of the Cross, etc.), the "normative" Mass celebrated by Fr. Bungini with a large choir, added other elements: a longer Liturgy of the Word (three readings in all), a transformed Offertory, a new Eucharistic Prayer (the third), and a great number of hymns. During the four general congregations dedicated to the liturgy (October 21–25), cardinals and bishops expressed many comments on this "normative" Mass and on the liturgical reform in general. In all, sixty-three cardinals, bishops, and religious superiors general commented on the topic and another nineteen presented written comments. There was a divergence of opinion. "Out of sixty-three orators," reports Fr. Caprile, "thirty-six expressed explicitly and in the warmest of terms their unreserved enthusiasm" for the reform underway and for its results.

The reform was progressing nonstop. Certainly, opposition was not lacking, but the determination of those who pushed for innovation was truly powerful, secure in the *de facto* support of Pope Paul VI, who despite seeking to contain the forward thrust, seemed to be of an attitude in this matter which some would judge ambiguous.

It must also be said that, as we have seen, the reforms in the Church occurred in a period of general upheaval, in an agitated atmosphere not conducive to a balanced reform that would avoid subversion. The student protests did not cease, but rather intensified. A few days after the normative Mass which we described, the Catholic University was occupied. In 2017, Marco Roncalli recalled the episode in *Avvenire*:

> The real birth of '68 has a precise date: November 17, 1967, in Milan, at the Catholic University. At that moment, many students at the university founded by Gemelli no longer protested about their classes, the "authoritarian" formation, the "classist" criteria of admissions, and so forth, but pushed further into putting the entire social system up in the air, criticizing institutions, including ecclesial ones.

I am not sure this can be called "the birth of '68," or if it dates back to 1964 and what happened in the United States. In that case, once again, the Catholic component was not irrelevant. Mario Capanna, one of the protagonists in the earlier occupation, recalls in his celebrated book mentioned above:

> The occasion was given by a sudden increase in the enrollment tax at Catholic University. On the

14th, a state of agitation was declared and it continued for three days.... The fight at Catholic,
given its massive size, the way it developed, the
place it was carried out, the situation that it laid
bare, the claims it made, surprised everyone and
immediately assumed an emblematic significance. It made visible, in unimaginable ways and
times, the new cultural and political sensibility
that was making headway in the 1960s.

Certainly, we cannot but agree with what Capanna observes,
the occupation of Catholic University had an emblematic significance because it also shed light on the connection existing
between students and certain intellectuals and also (a fundamental aspect) with a part of the Catholic institutional world.

It was also in that year that *Dieu est mort en Jesus-Christ*
was published by the Dominican Jean Cardonnel (1921–
2009), a figure we shall encounter again in this narrative. He
would be one of the most renowned representatives of ultra-
progressive Catholicism and connived with the Marxist left,
a collaboration that would express itself theologically in a
complete form in the ideas of Liberation Theology.

Mention must also be made of the technological and
scientific progress opening new frontiers to mankind and
permitting a better quality of life. Toward the end of 1967,
a historic event took place when the first heart transplant
was performed by a South African surgeon. Science was taking giant steps forward and new moral and ethical problems
were being raised for humanity.

1968 HAPPENED

As we look to the fatal year, 1968, we must remember where we came from and the ferment and conflicts we have observed in the preceding decade. Aware of the situation, Paul VI raised his heartfelt prayer for peace on January 1st, 1968, inaugurating Peace Day:

"Remember, merciful Father, all those who agonize, are suffering and dying in the birth pains of a more fraternal world. That your Reign of justice, peace and love may come for men of every language. And that the earth be filled with your glory! Amen."

Unfortunately, the Pontiff should not have invoked peace only for those who were outside the Church, but also for the Church herself, which continued to be shaken by terrible winds of rebellion.

The Pope had much to reflect upon in the homily given the same day in Bologna by Cardinal Giacomo Lercaro — as we have seen, the leading exponent of the progressive side — who struck out openly against the war in Vietnam:

> The Church's doctrine of peace (placed in focus by Pope John, by the Council, and by Pope Paul), by the intrinsic power of its coherence, cannot but lead us today to judgment on the precise resolution of the question, on which depends the first initial step toward peace or a further and perhaps irreversible step towards the spreading of this conflict. I refer, as you well know, to the insistence finding a growing choral voice around the world, and of which the Pope recently made echo in his

discourse to the cardinals, that America (beyond any concern for prestige and beyond every strategic justification) would be convinced to desist the air bombardments on North Vietnam.

The atmosphere was tense as never before.

Meanwhile, at the extraordinary chapter of the Holy Ghost Fathers, Archbishop Lefebvre resigned. His relationship with his congregation had deteriorated due to the traditional stance of the French archbishop. The history of the relationship between Archbishop Lefebvre and the Holy Ghost Fathers has been thoroughly narrated by Philippe Béguerie, who was also a Holy Ghost Father and who opposed Archbishop Lefebvre in the congregation, in his book *Vers Écône*. The book is quite interesting because it bears witness to Archbishop Lefebvre's will to resist certain dangers which he identified in the advance of communism, in the challenges brought by Islam, and in the victory of the ideals of the French Revolution in the Church. The rupture between him and his confreres had become too profound, and he was no longer capable of governing it. But he was soon to make his voice heard. In a writing of March 7, for example, he confronted head-on the crisis of the Church and attempted to offer answers to those asking for his help. He was soon forced to undertake a quite different approach, which we shall see later.

The yearning for peace expressed by Pope Paul VI was short-lived. In fact, already on January 5 the so-called Prague Spring began in Czechoslovakia. Alexander Dubcek, head of the government, attempted reforms which would then be suffocated the following August by Soviet tanks.

Things were not going better in Italy, and the Pope had firsthand experience of this when students at the Catholic University protested right in St. Peter's Square. Mario Capanna, protagonist of the events of those years, as we have seen, remembered this occasion:

> Unanimous decision (reckless!) to transfer *en masse* to St. Peter's Square to hold a sit-in that would render our claims more forceful.... The protest seemed (was?) so unbelievable that even the Soviet press spoke about it. We left late in the evening, satisfied by the initiative, but embittered by the news of the catastrophic earthquake that struck the Valley of Belice in Sicily. (The ignominy of power: twenty years later, many of the inhabitants whose homes were devasted by the earthquake are still forced to live in hovels today.)

Capanna is referring to the terrible earthquake in Belice that happened the day before, on January 14. On February 12 in Bologna, Cardinal Giacomo Lercaro resigned, probably in light of his declarations on the Vietnam War. There were doubts whether his resignation was spontaneous or solicited; the fact is, he stepped down.

On March 1 in Rome, one of the most renowned episodes in the social clashes between students and institutions took place, the so-called "Battle of Valle Giulia" in which students attempted to retake the Architecture Department, which the police had already cleared of protestors. This episode would inspire Pier Paolo Pasolini, known Communist exponent, poet, writer, and film director, to write a poem, *Il PCI ai giovani* (*The Italian Communist Party to Youth*), in which he scandalized the students by opposing the young radicals:

> Now the journalist of the whole world (including
> Those in television)
> Kiss (as is still said in the language
> Boheme) your ass. Not me, my dears.
>
> Your silver spoon faces,
> I hate like I hate your parents.
> Good breeding tells no lies.
> You have the same bad eye.
> You're cowards, insecure, desperate
> (great!) but you also know how to be
> Overbearing, extorting, secure and insolent, my
>   dears.
> Yesterday, when it came to blows in Valle Giulia
> With the police,
> I sympathized with the police.
> Because the police are the sons of the poor.
> They come from subtopias, peasants or urban as
>   they are.
> As for me, I know well
> Their way of having been children and boys,
> The precious two pennies, the father still a boy too,
> Due to misery, that gives no authority.

So, for Pasolini, the true proletariat were not the students but the police. The atmosphere of protest and contestation was truly red-hot. On March 26 in the Duomo in Trent, a sociology student interrupted the Lenten service, denouncing its reactionary tone. Contention had by now entered into the Church itself. On March 31, Paul VI spoke words at the Angelus that could not hide his disappointment with what was transpiring at the Catholic University: "The issue of the universities has become delicate and difficult due to the agitations which in this period have been disturbing them beyond the limits of legality and the noble ideals proper to protests worthy of higher education and of the chivalrous forms of thoughtful youth which avoids every form of violence and vulgarity."

Unfortunately, he could do little to stave off the floodwaters swirling in and around the Church, to which traditionalism would be a more or less appropriate response. Many were scrutinizing the role of Paul VI, ranging from the most fervent apologetic to those who openly condemned. Perhaps he honestly wanted the Council to be a time of renewal in the Church but did not expect that the idea of renewal in the air could be so far from his own.

Agitations in France and the Trial of Abbé de Nantes

Meanwhile, in France (soon to be the hotbed of traditionalist reaction) the progressive front was moving with ever-greater courage. We have a recent description of this thanks to the important books by the historian Yves Chiron on the history of traditionalism and the Church during 1968, in which the French scene naturally has a place of honor.

The Franciscan journal *Frères du monde* published in the February/March edition a dossier under the title "Faith and Revolution." It began thus: "With our experience and human understanding as our point of departure we have come to the awareness of the necessity, the urgency, of the breadth and radicality of revolution." The party line was already quite clear and defined. And this was only a moment in the intellectual evolution of the journal, an evolution that was not isolated in Catholic settings.

On April 7, the permanent council of French bishops published a communication which countered a book by Fr. Cardonnel which we cited above, *God is Dead in Jesus Christ*. His purely horizontal (i.e., worldly) vision of the Christ event was rejected. This did not stop Fr. Cardonnel, who on three Fridays in March and April of that year, would center his Lenten conferences on a theme which says it all: "Gospel and Revolution." Also, on March 23 and 24 in Paris, he held a talk on the theme "Christianity and Revolution."

In the meantime, the world was shocked by another event: on April 4, Martin Luther King Jr. was assassinated in Memphis. This incident would leave a profound impression on the last sermon of Fr. Cardonnel the next day and inspired Fr. Georges Mollard to publish a Stations of the Cross (April 12) in which Martin Luther King and Camillo Torres were cited as examples in the meditations. The situation grew very tense and difficult.

On April 25, the trial against Abbé de Nantes began. It is interesting to note that on the same day and just meters away from the Holy Office where the trial was being heard, Paul VI was holding a general audience during which he pronounced these words:

> The matter is not unknown. After the Council, the Church has enjoyed a great and magnificent awakening, which We are pleased to recognize and foster; but the Church has also been suffering due to a whirlwind of ideas and events which are certainly not according to the good Spirit and do not guarantee the vital renewal which the Council promised and promoted. An idea with a double effect has made headway in certain Catholic settings as well: the idea of change which for some has taken the place of aggiornamento foretold by Pope John of venerable memory, attributing in this way, against evidence and against justice, to that most faithful Pastor of the Church criteria no longer innovative but at times even subversive of the teaching and discipline of the Church itself.

Thus, once more the Pope attempted to put the brakes on a tendency to which, according to some, even he had contributed and provoked. He sought to save the Council, but he was well aware that the negative effects were going far beyond what he could have foreseen or hoped.

In this climate, the trial of Abbé de Nantes was taking place, who was at this point the most visible representative of the contestation of the Council and of its effects. He saw in Paul VI's attempts to contain the excesses the same spirit that moved General de Gaulle to impede the degeneration of protest in France. We read his words written in May of 1968:

> From Paul VI to Cardonnel, from General de Gaulle to Cohn-Bendit, the same declared desire for reform is exhibited.... It is a fact that chaos arrives on the tails of Reform, both in the nation and in the Church. This is because chaos draws all of its strength, its legality, and its false justification from Reform. The postconciliar tempest is swollen by the wind of the Council.

While the Pope hastened to pronounce those words in the general audience, at 9:00 a.m. the Abbé de Nantes stood before the Holy Office with clear ideas, perhaps too clear:

> Did I have the Catholic faith? It soon became clear that this was the case. As the days passed, we were forced to recognize the fundamental identity of our doctrines which were in no way ours but those of the Church of all times. I had the impression of frequenting a master of theology, and of going beyond him. The traps were classic and easily overcome. The discussions had their lofty moments.... The decisive question was that on the development of dogma. Was I not affirming that the life and thought of the Church had stopped with Pius IX, Pius X, or Pius XII? It seemed that I had suspended the promise of Jesus

Christ regarding the assistance of the Holy Spirit in a time before the Council. Here too, however, I professed no other doctrine than that of my examiners: the doctrine of St. Vincent Lerins and of Cardinal Newman, but with anti-Modernist distinctions due to the current situation. The doctrine we recognize is the logical development of the Tradition, which proceeds from the implicit to the explicit, but we reject Blondel's theory of a creative, vital evolution entirely sustained and directed by an immanent experience of the divine in the infallible human conscience.

In those days of confrontation between Abbé de Nantes and the examiners of the Holy Office, points of contact between the defensive positions of the monsignors and the offensive ones of the French priest seem to have been found. At a certain point, this evolved to some extent:

From the accused I became the accuser. My examiners were transformed into defenders, or better, they became the accused. In virtue of our exact and firm Catholic Faith, they rebelled against the dogmatic presuppositions of a so-called pastoral Reform. The consultation was not capable of catching me off guard but sought to confute my critiques of their newly reformed religion.

This type of division was now far from any simple resolution, and we shall see how these problems magnified by the Council were to form the script for the entire clash between traditionalism and the official Church.

On May 3 in France, even as the trial of Abbé de Nantes was being carried out, the Sorbonne was occupied. This was the beginning of what is known as the "French May." It would be myopic in this case as well, not to see the important role that the Catholic protest (even among the clergy) had within this protest. Consider, for example, the Center Saint Yves, a chaplaincy in the Departments of Law and Business, run by the Dominicans. The center was transformed into a headquarters for the protests not only against society, but also against the Church. The charged atmosphere and the Catholic component played a primary role. After what we have seen, we cannot consider '68 as something the Catholic Church suffered, but something to whose creation Catholics (including priests, bishops, and cardinals!) contributed.

That May, numerous appeals followed, one after another, on the part of Catholic figures in favor of the students and the demonstrators. Besides Fr. Cardonnel, the Marxist-leaning Dominican Paul Blanquart made a name for himself at this time through social activism.

Meanwhile, on June 29, the trial against Abbé de Nantes resumed. On that same day, the Pope pronounced his profession of faith in St. Peter's, on the occasion of the nineteenth centenary of the martyrdom of the apostles Peter and Paul. With this profession he attempted to rebut the many leaps forward, not least that of the Dutch Catechism. The Pope reiterated in this profession, as he had in *Mysterium Fidei*, the sacrificial nature of the Mass:

> We believe that the Mass, celebrated by the Priest
> who represents the person of Christ in virtue of
> the power received in the Sacrament of Ordina-
> tion, and offered by him in the name of Christ
> and of the members of his mystical Body, is the
> Sacrifice of Calvary made sacramentally present
> on our altars. We believe that, as the bread and
> wine consecrated by the Lord at the Last Supper
> were converted into his Body and his Blood
> which were shortly to be offered for us on the
> Cross, in the same way the bread and wine con-
> secrated by the priest are converted into the Body
> and Blood of Christ gloriously reigning in
> Heaven; and we believe that the mysterious pres-
> ence of the Lord, under that which continues to
> appear as it did before to our sense, is a true, real
> and substantial presence. (cf. Dz-Sch. 1651)

On July 1, Abbé de Nantes was asked to retract his accusations against the Pope, the French bishops, and the Council.
He was given four days to decide. The letters he sent to his
friends evidenced the interior torment he lived in those days
and how he sought refuge in prayer in various churches and
basilicas in Rome. He recalled:

> In my role as accused, in the persecution which
> we traditionalists were suffering, I could not
> submit myself to this Reformation imposed
> from above without at least giving the impres-
> sion of having retracted and thus having
> abandoned my brothers. Thus, in this

contradiction between obedience and faith, in
this contrast of discipline with charity, I decided
once again to refuse the signature they awaited
from my weakness.

But that was not the last of his doubts. At a certain point, it
seemed to him better to go in the other direction:

> I was determined to submit, blindly, entirely,
> and definitively. I saw therein the will of God
> expressed through His Vicar on earth. It seemed
> supernatural to renounce the struggle, renounce
> it unconditionally, in an act of obedience that
> would transcend even my most fully justified
> certainties, leaving to others and to God the
> solicitude for doctrine and for the flock. This
> great act seemed to me pleasant and liberating,
> attracting me by its greatness.

And so, he decided to seek an audience with Archbishop Lefebvre the same day he was due to communicate his decision:

> I have informed my august interlocutor of my firm
> decision to sign. He interrupted me firmly: "You
> cannot do this. You have no right to do so." He
> was clear and formal, and was immediately justi-
> fied by invincible reasons, supported by the
> authorities and by the example of the person I was
> listening to: "We ourselves have written the Pontiff
> in due time that the cause of all these evils is in the
> Acts of the Council. Be firm in the truth."

Abbé de Nantes, once more under the weight of his conscience, went to the Holy Office:

> The morning of July 5, 1968, with my soul in peace, I kissed once more the threshold of the Palace of the Holy Office. I was going there to be informed of my sentence by the Supreme Court of the Faith. Someone assured me that the Pope was praying for my intention and had added that His Holiness had himself attenuated and approved the formula they were to propose to me.

He was presented with a text which he had to sign, retracting all his accusations and opposition to the new reforms in the Church. In conscience, he could not accept signing the four articles and said, *Non vobis licet. Non Possum.* ("You cannot ask this of me. I cannot accept this.") The fathers of the Holy Office were very disappointed by the refusal of Abbé de Nantes, ever more determined to continue his crusade in favor of Church tradition. He was given other ultimatums, even the following year, to sign that declaration, but he would not do so. He was even tempted by some hardline priests to start a schism, but this trap too he resisted.

At this point, Rome was not to remain passive. On August 10, 1969, a notification of reproach was issued:

> At the request of Abbé de Nantes, the Sacred Congregation for the Doctrine of the Faith examined his writings and, after having heard him twice, July 6, 1968, and May 23, 1969, considered it

necessary to ask him to sign a formula retracting his errors and his solemn accusations of heresy against Pope Paul VI and the Council. After Abbé de Nantes' first two refusals of this request, the Sacred Congregation for the Doctrine of the Faith tried one final time, on July 11, 1969, to convince him to submit to the official decision of the Roman Dicastery to which he first made appeal.

Abbé de Nantes responded to this solemn request on July 16, 1969, with a categorical refusal. In it, he contested the right of the Sacred Congregation for the Doctrine of the Faith to exact submission from him and confirmed his earlier positions regarding the Council, the *aggiornamento* of the Church, the episcopate of his country, the "heresies" of Paul VI, and the appeal to the Roman clergy in light of their canonical deposition. The Sacred Congregation for the Doctrine of the Faith was forced to take action on this refusal of its legitimate authority, observing with extreme sadness that, by rebelling against the Magisterium and the Catholic hierarchy in this way, Abbé de Nantes discredited all of his writings and activities by which he sought to serve the Church, giving testimony of rebellion against the episcopate of his country and against the Roman Pontiff. But this did not stop him.

PAUL VI BETWEEN MORAL THEOLOGY AND LIBERATION THEOLOGY

Abbé de Nantes was probably the least of Paul VI's problems, though he did follow the question of the French priest. The atmosphere inside and outside the Church was incredibly tense, as we have seen. The United States was again the center of international attention when, on June 6, Bobby Kennedy was assassinated, as his brother John Fitzgerald Kennedy had been a few years earlier. Bobby Kennedy also had an important political position, as a candidate for president that year, and his assassination caused great turmoil in the Catholic world in particular. Paul VI addressed this tragedy in a discourse in which he remembered the American politician whom he had previously met.

The Pope found himself in one of the most complex impasses of his pontificate. He noticed the requests for substantial innovation in the moral teaching of the Church. Within the Church, above all, there was a push for the abrogation of priestly celibacy, for the use of artificial birth control, and for the emancipation of sexual lifestyles that had always been condemned by the Church. This was not simply an ideology of the world but was now gaining ground within the Church as well, at all levels. Here too, Paul VI applied the brakes to the progressive requests, with the encyclical *Humanae Vitae*, which for many was his moment of greatest isolation within the Church. Not a few, even in the hierarchy and not only among the faithful, would reject this encyclical and saw it as a step backward in the Church's progress:

> We are obliged once more to declare that the direct interruption of the generative process already begun and, above all, all direct abortion, even for therapeutic reasons, are to be absolutely excluded as lawful means of regulating the number of children. Equally to be condemned, as the magisterium

of the Church has affirmed on many occasions, is direct sterilization, whether of the man or of the woman, whether permanent or temporary.

Similarly excluded is any action which either before, at the moment of, or after sexual intercourse, is specifically intended to prevent procreation—whether as an end or as a means.

In this case as well, Paul VI, the Pope of the Council, slammed on the brakes. Romano Amerio discussed this encyclical at length in the work cited above:

> The celebrated encyclical *Humanae Vitae* of July 25, 1968, gave rise to the most widespread, important, and in some ways arrogant expression of internal dissent within the Church. Nearly every Episcopal Conference published documents on it, either nodding or dissenting. Episcopal documents on the occasion of Papal teachings or decisions are nothing new in the Church, and it suffices to remember the many letters of bishops to their dioceses under Pius IX. It was a novelty, however, that these letters would express not a judgment of consensus but a syndicate judgment, as if the principle of *Prima Sedes a nemine iudicatur* [the First See cannot be prosecuted by anyone] had fallen.

This was to be one of the most dramatic points of a pontificate which even Amerio judges at the very least to have been sinusoidal. But this would not be the only low point, as soon the clash with communist ideologies would take shape on various fronts.

We have mentioned the Soviet response to the Prague Spring of August 20, an armored invasion. A few days later, on the twenty-fourth, in another part of the world, in Colombia, Paul VI opened the work of CELAM, the general conference of Latin American bishops. We recall that on November 23, 1965, he had said to the representatives of CELAM:

> Among these forces prevails, in the socio-economic sector, the most harmful and the clearest reference to atheistic Marxism which, in its social "messianism" makes of human progress a myth, and places every hope on economic and temporal goods; establishes doctrinal and practical atheism; advocates and prepares violent revolution as the only means for the solution of problems; declares and exalts the example of countries where it has affirmed its ideologies and its systems.

These words were not able to impede those who sought a point of encounter between Catholicism and atheistic Marxism, who were gaining momentum precisely during this meeting of CELAM in Medellín with Paul VI. The just claim in favor of the most disadvantaged classes was transformed into social hatred, class struggle, and armed revolution. This was elaborated into a current of thought, Liberation Theology, which had as its most important exponents the Brazilian Franciscan Fr. Leonardo Boff (b. 1938) and the Peruvian Dominican Fr. Gustavo Gutiérrez Merino (b. 1928). This theological movement promoted base communities, groups of Christians who sought a new way of living their faith far from what had been the traditional Catholic manner.

The winds of contestation made themselves increasingly felt in Italy as well. On September 14, a group of Catholic dissidents occupied the Cathedral of Parma, only to be forcibly removed later by the police. On December 3, a parish priest in Isolotto, Florence, named Enzo Mazzi (1927–2011) was removed from his responsibilities by his bishop, Cardinal Ermenegildo Florit (1901–1985) due to his ultra-progressive theological positions. He had introduced into his community numerous pastoral innovations and pushed for a more social Catholicism; in essence, along the lines of Liberation Theology. It was the Florence of Fr. Balducci and Don Milani, as we have seen. The following January, he founded the *Comunità Isolotto*, one of the most noteworthy such communities in Italy and still around today. This inspired other similar experiments like those of Oregina in Genoa and St. Paul in Rome, as we shall see.

On December 7, 1968, the Pope gave a famous discourse at the Lombardo Seminary in Rome. In it he recognized the state of enormous confusion the Church found herself in:

> The Church is undergoing today a moment of apprehension. Some exercise self-criticism, one could say even self-demolition. It is a type of

acute and complex interior rewinding which no one would have expected after the Council. One expected a blossoming, a serene expansion of concepts matured in the great conciliar assembly. There is also this aspect in the Church, there is a blossoming. But because "*bonum ex integra causa, malum ex quocumque defectu,*" one notices more readily the painful aspect. The Church is struck even by its members: now We will allow you to see the depths of Our soul and to see the two sentiments most at heart in the face of this tumult which is affecting the Church and, logically, has repercussions above all on the Pope. A sentiment of joy that We have been made worthy to suffer for Jesus. The trials are difficult and often harsh. But the reality of our priesthood leads us to bless the Lord for these trials. The Christian knows the joy that flows from trial. It is the certainty of being with the Lord, of walking in his path, of recognizing in oneself the realization of his predictions and his promises, however exacting for our human nature. Also, a sentiment of great confidence and trust. Many expected of the Pope sensational gestures, energetic and decisive interventions. The Pope does not consider it necessary to follow any direction that is not one of confidence in Jesus Christ who cares for his Church more than anyone else. He is the one who will calm the storm. How often did the Master repeat: "*Confidite in Deum. Creditis in Deum, et in me credite!*" The Pope will be the first to follow this command of the Lord and to abandon himself without oppression or undue anxiety, to the mysterious game of the invisible yet certain assistance of Jesus to his Church.

THE NEW MASS OF PAUL VI

On April 3, 1969, Paul VI promulgated the new missal in the Apostolic Constitution *Missale Romanum*, which entered into force the following November 30. In the apostolic constitution, Paul VI synthesizes the innovations in this way:

> According to the prescription of the Second Vatican Council which prescribes that "a more representative portion of the Holy Scriptures will be read to the people over a set cycle of years," ... the readings for Sunday are divided into a cycle of three years. In addition, for Sunday and feasts, the readings of the Epistle and Gospel are preceded by a reading from the Old Testament or, during Paschaltide, from the Acts of the Apostles....
>
> In this revision of the Roman Missal, in addition to the three changes mentioned above, namely, the Eucharistic Prayer, the Rite for the Mass and the Biblical Reading, other parts also have been reviewed and considerably modified: the Proper of Seasons, the Proper of Saints, the Common of Saints, ritual Masses and votive Masses. In all of these changes, particular care has been taken with the prayers: not only has their number been increased, so that the new texts

might better correspond to new needs, but also their text has been restored on the testimony of the most ancient evidences. For each ferial of the principal liturgical seasons, Advent, Christmas, Lent and Easter, a proper prayer has been provided.

Even though the text of the Roman Gradual, at least that which concerns the singing, has not been changed, still, for a better understanding, the responsorial psalm, which St. Augustine and St. Leo the Great often mention, has been restored, and the Introit and Communion antiphons have been adapted for read Masses.

Certainly, the changes were to be more radical than these few lines seem to suggest, as would become clear.

The question of the new Mass was one of the heated topics of the debate between the Vatican and the traditionalist world. On June 5, a study known as the *Brief Critical Examination of the Novus Ordo Missae* was published. It would have a great impact on the traditionalist world, thanks as well to the introduction by Cardinals Alfredo Ottaviani and Antonio Bacci. They stated that,

> The *Novus Ordo Missae*, considering its new elements, susceptible to differing evaluations, which appear suffused and implicated, represents in its entirety as in its particulars, a tremendous departure from the Catholic theology of the Holy Mass, as formulated in the XXII Session of the Council of Trent, which, definitively establishing

the "canons" of the rite, raised an unbreachable
barrier against any heresy that might impair the
integrity of the Magisterium.

This passage is very well-known in the Catholic traditional
world and is cited constantly, seeing the importance in the
Curia of those who wrote it. Among the editors of this study
was the Dominican Fr. Michel-Louis Guérard De Lauriers,
a distinguished theologian to whom we shall return later.
They tried to obtain a broad consensus among the bishops
on this document but, as one who understands the Vatican
can easily appreciate, many were afraid to sign it. The study
bothered Paul VI, given the caliber of the two who did sign.

In March 1968, a new book by the American traditionalist writer Patrick Henry Omlor (1931–2013) appeared, in
which strong reservations about the new Mass were expressed. In 1969, the author published a new, enlarged
version of his book and became a sedevacantist, doubting
the validity of the papal elections since John XXIII.

A CHANGING WORLD

Toward the end of the 1960s, we witness the extraordinary
progress of science, with the first man on the moon (July 20).
Music was also contributing to social change. Rock, for instance,
and groups like the Beatles and the Rolling Stones were exciting
the youth. On August 15 of 1969, Woodstock began, and
would enter collective memory. The scholar Corrado Gnerre
identifies this well in his 2008 book, in which he emphasizes
the social impact of these developments: "Consider how musical

expressions and films became important vehicles of moral per-version. Our way of acting and especially of thinking suffered variations (undoubtedly!) due above all to the new means of communication which became sound boards for the cultural revolution." The role of music and of the youth culture of that time was enormously important.

All of this was intertwined with the protests against the war in Vietnam. These protests would continue in the fol-lowing months. On October 21, Jack Kerouac died, one of the symbols of American literature of that period and among the most important representatives of the movement known as the Beat Generation. Social and political tensions made no sign of attenuating, and in Italy these tensions came to a climax in the massacre of Piazza Fontana in Milan on De-cember 12, in which seventeen people were killed.

SOMETHING MOVING IN SWITZERLAND

The 1970s began under leaden skies. The situation inside and outside the Church was not simple. Paul VI was certainly aware of this, but his attitude was at times ambiguous. On one side he restrained, on the other he conceded. Perhaps he thought the admonition of Abbé de Nantes would have dis-couraged the traditionalist front. He was quite wrong. The atmosphere in the Church was red-hot. Two books in some ways symbolized 1970. Hans Küng, standard-bearer of the progressive front, published *Infallible? A Question*, in which he placed in doubt the infallibility of the Church. The Con-gregation for the Doctrine of the Faith placed the book on trial together with another book by Küng, *The Church*, and came to the following conclusions in a declaration on February 15, 1975:

> The works of Prof. Hans Küng contain several opinions which, in various degrees, are in opposition to the doctrine of the Catholic Church which must be professed by all the faithful. We note only the following ones of greater notoriety, abstaining for the moment from judgment concerning others which Prof. Küng defends. The opinion which places at least in doubt the very dogma of faith regarding the infallibility of the Church and reduces it to a certain fundamental indefectibility of the Church in truth, with the possibility of erring in sentences which the Magisterium of the Church teaches to be believed in a definitive way, contradicts the defined doctrine of the First Vatican Council, confirmed by the Second Vatican Council.

This would not stop the untiring promotion of an ultra-progressive Catholicism, a work in which Küng was among the great protagonists for more than fifty years.

On the other side, the Belgian philosopher Marcel de Corte (1905–1994), of a clearly traditional Catholic orientation, published *The Great Heresy*, in which he denounced in clear and precise terms the disorientation of the Catholic Church: "Catholicism is undergoing a serious crisis: all observers agree whether they are inside or outside, optimists or pessimists, they magnify it or try to strangle it, whether they describe it as a crisis of development or as a self-demolition, all agree in calling it progressivism."

The book was recently reprinted. In this new edition, Fr. Curzio Nitoglia offered the following reflections as an invitation to readers:

> In this book, de Corte treats Modernism and describes it as a great heresy. I think I can say without exaggerating that it is one of the most interesting books ever written on Modernism. From the very beginning, he distinguishes classic Modernism, condemned by St. Pius X, from neo-Modernism, new theology or "progressivism," condemned by Pius XII. Progressivism, according to de Cort, accentuates the characteristics of Modernism, the "heresy *par excellence*," and can therefore be defined as "radical and total" heresy. Progressivism or neo-Modernism are to classical Modernism as philosophical nihilism or postmodernity is to philosophical idealism or to modernity. Now, philosophical postmodernity not only pretends that God is the product of man's sentimental need, but would even like to "kill" God (Nietzsche, Freud, and 1968). The theological postmodernity of Vatican II tried (especially in the constitution *Gaudium et Spes*) to reconcile the irreconcilable, by means of an "anthropological shift" that seeks to make theocentrism and anthropocentrism coincide and to absorb God into Man, but St. Augustine reminds us, "Either God or the I, *tertium non datur*."

Thus appears a clear condemnation of the innovations which, either by using the Council, or perhaps, thanks to it, were pushing the Church where it could not go except at the price of losing herself.

Certainly, de Corte's words did not ring out in a vacuum. There were many faithful who felt disorientated and confused. Some seminarians and parents turned to Archbishop Lefebvre, now free of his obligations as superior of the Holy Ghost Fathers from which he had resigned due to the impossibility of reconciling his positions with the progressive opinions of his confreres. Those who turned to him asked him to do something to preserve the traditional priesthood.

Archbishop Lefebvre at first scoffed at this proposal and suggested some other solutions to remedy the problem, but then realized that he would have to act personally. After the Council, he had tried not to allow the experience of the *Coetus* to be forgotten, an experience that had permitted the conservative front to organize resistance to the sweeping spread of progressive thought. Archbishop Lefebvre focused on the battle for the communications media. He sought to organize the media with a traditional orientation in order to form a united front for the battle. He understood how important priestly formation was as well.

In August 1970, the bishop of Lausanne, Switzerland, granted Archbishop Lefebvre permission to open a seminary. At first, it was the St. Pius X International School. Bishop François Charrière (1893–1976) welcomed the approach of Archbishop Lefebvre and on October 7 opened the Seminary of Ecône in Vallese Canton, a location chosen because of the growing demand. On November 1, Bishop Charrière gave canonical approval to the Society of St. Pius X, the new institute of Archbishop Lefebvre for the formation of priests according to the traditional discipline of the Church. Meanwhile, the situation was not improving for the Church; on the contrary. Emblematic of this, in 1970, is the story of the Turin community of the Vandalino. They told their own story as follows (www.ilfoglio.info):

> In July of 1969, we actively participated in an Agape camp dedicated to the base communities around Europe. Protestant churches were also harshly criticized. But the very emotive aspect that characterized our action, the exasperated desire to change everything, this human, delirious expectation of a new world ... *could not last.* Little by little, from 1969 to 1970, sympathizers stopped participating in our liturgical assemblies; even many of the old friends of the community were leaving it. The continuous rush toward all and any change, the end-of-the-world atmosphere of those times, caused in some a growing distress. This put to the test the resistance of many. Given the downsizing of our community, it no longer made sense to keep the venue in Via Vandalino. In the same neighborhood, in Via Arnaz, we found space in a little villa. We moved in the summer of 1970. Two priests had asked if they could celebrate their weddings, even though they had not been laicized. That September we carried out this

gesture as a little sign of freedom, aware that this
would lead to a complete break with the official
Church. And so it happened. Suspension *a divinis*, excommunication, condemnation for all the
members of the community. It was the last
clamorous act acknowledged by the media.
Then weariness and silence. We celebrated another wedding of a priest still a "priest," but the
media ignored the fact. Over the course of 1971
and 1972 our activities dwindled. Every now
and then we were in touch with dissident communities in Milan, Genoa, with Catholics in
Holland, France, and Spain. We also participated in the movement advocating the abolition
of the Concordat. But the decline seemed inexorable. In January of 1973, the community
ceased all of its activities.

It was certainly not a sign of a return to order; it was just one
of many symptoms of the progressive disintegration.

This naturally accompanied the ongoing estrangement
of society from Catholic teaching. In Italy, the law on divorce was introduced on December 1, a death blow to the
Christian family. The state vacillated as well: just a few days
later there was a failed coup attempt, the Golpe Borghese.

Meanwhile, on February 18, 1971, Archbishop Lefebvre
received a letter of encouragement from the American Cardinal John Joseph Wright, Prefect of the Congregation for
the Clergy. It seemed that things might go well between the
Vatican and the Society of St. Pius X, but this was not to be.

THE INDULT OF AGATHA CHRISTIE

Protest reached England as well. In a text edited by Alcuin Reid, *A Bitter Trial*, we find a letter by the writer Evelyn Waugh (1903–1966) to the *Catholic Herald* on August 7, 1964. In it he states:

> Finally, a word about the liturgy. It is natural for the Germans to make a ruckus. The torches and noisy assemblies of the Hitler Youth expressed a national passion. It is good that this is channeled into the Church. But it is essentially not English. We do not seek "Sieg Heils." We pray in silence. "Participate" in the Mass does not mean listening to our own voices. It means that God listens to our voices. He alone knows who is "participating" at Mass. I believe, to compare little things with the big, that I "participate" in a work of art when I study it and love it silently. There is no need to yell. Whoever has taken part in a show knows he can rant and rave on stage with his mind elsewhere. If the Germans want to be noisy, let them. But why should they disturb our devotions?

This entirely British way of facing the question certainly did not end with Waugh's letters. On the contrary, England was to mobilize numerous intellectuals to lead the reaction.

In an interesting book from 2013 (with an introduction by Archbishop Luigi Negri), attorney Gianfranco Amato reconstructs the entire matter. On July 6, 1971, a group of English intellectuals published in the *Times* an appeal to

Pope Paul VI for the preservation of the Tridentine Mass. Among these was the famous writer Agatha Christie (1890–1976), to which the entire affair was to be linked. Here, I will refer to an article by Alfred Marnau on the website of the Latin Mass Society (lms.org.uk), which bears witness to the events and reconstructs the whole affair.

Here is the appeal of July 6:

> One of the axioms of contemporary advertising, both religious and secular, is that modern man in general, and intellectuals in particular, have become intolerant towards all forms of tradition and are anxious to suppress them and to put anything else in their place. But as with many other statements of our advertising machine, this axiom is false. Today, as at other times, educated people are on the cutting edge in recognizing the value of tradition, and are the first to sound the alarm when tradition is threatened. If some daft decree were to order the total or partial destruction of basilicas or cathedrals, it would obviously be the educated—whatever their personal convictions—to rise up with horror to oppose such a possibility. Now, the fact is that basilicas and cathedrals were constructed to celebrate a rite which, until a few months ago, constituted a living tradition. We are referring to the Roman Catholic Mass. Yet, according to the latest information from Rome, there is a plan to cancel that Mass before the end of this year. At this moment, we are not considering the religious or spiritual experience of millions of

individuals. The rite in question, in its magnificent Latin text, has also inspired a series of inestimable conquests in the arts, not only mystical works, but works of poets, philosophers, musicians, architects, painters, and sculptors of every country and age. It belongs, therefore, to universal culture just as it does to ecclesiastics and formal Christians. In this materialistic and technocratic civilization that increasingly threatens the life of the mind and of the spirit in its original creative expression, the word, it seems particularly inhumane to deprive man of the forms/words in one of their most grandiose manifestations. The signatories of this appeal, completely ecumenical and apolitical, belong to every branch of modern culture in Europe and elsewhere. They desire to call the attention of the Holy See to the terrible responsibility that it incurs in the history of the human spirit if it were to refuse to permit the survival of the traditional Mass, even if this survival were to occur next to other liturgical forms.

Here is the list of the signatories, many of whom we recognize still today:

Harold Acton, Vladimir Ashkenazy, John Bayler, Lennox Berkeley, Maurice Bowra, Agatha Christie, Kenneth Clark, Nevill Coghill, Cyril Connolly, Colin Davis, Hugh Delargy, +Robert Exeter, Miles Fitzalan-Howard, Constantine Fitzgibbon, William Glock, Magdalen Goffin, Robert Graves, Graham Greene, Ian Greenless, Joseph Grimond,

Harman Grisewood, Colin Hardie, Rupert Hart-
Davis, Barbara Hepworth, Auberon Herbert, John
Jolliffe, David Jones, Osbert Lancaster, F. R. Lea-
vis, Cecil Day Lewis, Compton Mackenzie,
George Malcolm, Max Mallowan, Alfred Marnau,
Yehudi Menuhin, Nancy Mitford, Raymond Mor-
timer, Malcolm Muggeridge, Iris Murdoch, John
Murray, Sean O'Faolain, E. J. Oliver, Oxford and
Asquith, William Plomer, Kathleen Raine, Wil-
liam Rees-Mogg, Ralph Richardson, +John Ripon,
Charles Russell, Rivers Scott, Joan Sutherland,
Philip Toynbee, Martin Turnell, Bernard Wall,
Patrick Wall, E. I. Watkin, R. C. Zaehner.

Cardinal John Carmel Heenan (1905–1975), a figure of high
visibility in British Catholicism at that time, was received by
Paul VI on October 29 to discuss the question. It is said that
Paul VI, while running through the names of the signatories,
exclaimed, "Ah, Agatha Christie!" noticing the name of the
creator of Hercule Poirot and Miss Marple. For this reason,
the whole affair bears her name.

On November 5, the Pope conceded English Catholics
an indult which allowed, under certain conditions, for the
celebration of the traditional Mass. Ironically, the document
was signed by Annibale Bugnini, who at the time was secretary of the Congregation for Divine Worship, who then sent
it to Cardinal Heenan.

His Holiness Pope Paul VI, with the letter of October 30, 1971, conferred special permission to

the undersecretary of this Sacred Congregation to transmit to Your Eminence, as President of the Episcopal Conference of England and Wales, the following points regarding the Order of the Mass:

1. Considering the pastoral exigencies recalled by Your Eminence, it is consented to the Ordinaries of England and Wales to concede that some groups of faithful can, on particular occasions, participate in the Mass celebrated according to the Rites and texts of the previous Roman Missal. The edition of the Missal to be used on these occasions ought to be that published newly with the Decree of the Sacred Congregation of Rites (January 27, 1965), and with the modifications indicated in the altered Instruction (May 4, 1967).

2. This authority can be conceded on condition that the groups make their request for reasons of genuine devotion, and such that the permission not disturb or harm the general communion among the faithful. For this reason, permission is limited to some groups on special occasions; in all the regular parochial and community Masses the order of the Mass given in the new Roman Missal is to be used. That the Eucharist be the sacrament of unity, it is necessary that the use of the Order of the Mass given in the previous Missal does not become a sign

or cause of disunity in the Catholic community. For this reason, the agreement with the Bishops of the Episcopal Conference on the modality of exercising this faculty will be a further guarantee of unity of practice in this matter.

3. Priests who want to celebrate occasionally the Mass according to the aforementioned Roman Missal can do so with the consent of their Ordinary and according to the norms given by the same. When these priests celebrate the Mass with the people and desire to use the rites and texts of the former Missal, the conditions and limits mentioned above for the celebration on the part of some groups on special occasions must be applied.

So, permission was accorded, though Fr. Bugnini asked that this indult not be given too much publicity.

Meanwhile, the editorial world continued to print books for both sides of the ecclesiastical divide. On the progressive side, Fr. Ernesto Balducci came out with *Diary of an Exodus* and Fr. Gustavo Gutiérrez *Liberation Theology*, a fundamental text for understanding this revolutionary movement. From the extreme side of traditionalism, we have Joaquin Saenz y Arriaga's *The New Montini Church*. "Maurice Pinay" continued his battle from sedevacantist positions against the official hierarchy, which cost him excommunication by the Mexican bishops shortly thereafter. This did not impede the author from continuing his battle, publishing another book under the evocative name, *Sede Vacante*. Remember that Mexico was one of the most fervent areas of Catholic traditionalism (or traditionalisms, because as we have seen there are various types and orientations) in Latin America, together with Bazil and Argentina.

In a homily in 1972, for the feast of Sts. Peter and Paul, the Pope offered a fine synthesis of the state of uncertainty in which the Church found herself. Here is a well-known passage taken from the Vatican website:

> Referring to the situation of the Church today, the Holy Father affirms having the sensation that "the smoke of Satan has entered the Temple of God through some fissure." There is doubt, uncertainty, problems, apprehension, dissatisfaction, conflict. The Church no longer commands people's trust; one places trust in the first secular prophet who will speak in some newspaper or at some social protest and chases after him and ask him if he has the formula for true life. And we do not realize that we are already masters and teachers. Doubt has entered our consciences, and it has entered through windows which ought to have been open to the light. From science, which is made to give us truths, not alienate us from God but make us seek Him all the more and celebrate Him with greater intensity, instead we have criticism and doubt. Scientists are the ones who most pensively and painfully doubt. In the end, they teach only: "I do not know, we do not know, we cannot know.".... We believed that the

> Council would be followed by a day of sunshine
> in the history of the Church. Instead, we have
> clouds, tempest, darkness, searching and incerti-
> tude. We preach ecumenism and we are
> increasingly detached from others. We are dig-
> ging abysses instead of filling them in.

In the poetic language used by the Pontiff, one intuits the state of disorientation in which the Church was floundering, as perhaps he was too.

In an audience on November 15, he clarified his admonition:

> The chapter on the Devil and the influence he
> exercises on individuals, communities, events, or
> on society as a whole would be an important
> chapter in Catholic doctrine to study once more,
> whereas today it is studied very little. Some think
> they can find a sufficient return in psychoanalytic
> or psychiatric studies, or in spiritualist experi-
> ences, today unfortunately widespread in some
> countries. There is the feared risk of falling once
> again into Manichean theories or into frightening
> digressions, into fantasy and superstition. Today,
> people prefer to show they are strong and unscru-
> pulous, to pose as positivists, except for the faith
> they place in many magical or popular irrational
> fears, or worse, opening their souls, their baptized
> souls, visited so often by the Eucharist and inhab-
> ited by the Holy Spirit!, to licentious sensual
> experiences, deleterious experiences with drugs, as

well as ideological seductions of the errors in vogue, fissures through which the Evil One can easily penetrate and alter one's mind. Not every sin is directly caused by diabolical action (cf. Summa Th. 1, 104, 3); but it is true that one who fails to keep guard over himself with moral rigor (cf. Mt 12:45; Eph 6:11) exposes himself to the influence of the *mysterium iniquitatis*, to which St. Paul refers (2 Thes 2:3–12), which renders the possibility of our salvation problematic. Our doctrine has become uncertain, obscured as it is by the shadows which surround the Devil. But our curiosity, excited by the certainty of his manifold existence, is legitimated in two questions. Are there signs, and what are they, of the presence of diabolic action? And what are the means of defense against such as insidious danger?

The Pontiff's words are clear and they render his memory even more enigmatic.

All of this is to be read in the context of what was being said and done in the Church in those days. Consider an article from the official newspaper of the Vatican, *L'Osservatore Romano*, and Amerio's comment on it:

> The *OR* of July 23, 1972, introducing another poetic analogy, writes that the current groanings of the Church are not the groanings of agony, but rather birth pangs, heralding a new being coming into the world, namely, a new Church. But can a new Church be born? Here in the enticement of

poetic metaphors and in the mixing of concepts is hidden the idea of something impossible according to the Catholic system, the idea, that is, that the historical realization of the Church can be a foundational realization, a substantial mutation, a transfer from one thing into something entirely other. Instead, according to the Catholic system the realization of the Church consists in a vicissitude in which the accidental forms and the historical circumstances change, maintaining identical and without innovation the substance of religion. The sole innovation which orthodox ecclesiology acknowledges is eschatological innovation with a new earth and a new heaven, namely, the final and eternal reordering of the created universe, liberated from imperfection, not of limits, but of sin, through the justice of all justices in eternal life.

Amerio's clarity seems to contrast with the confusion that reigned at that time.

Another important book for Liberation Theology came out in 1972, Leonardo Boff's *Jesus Christ Liberator*. I was curious to find a copy of this online several days ago: it was on sale for two hundred euros (perhaps because of the author's signature). Leonardo Boff, still living and no longer a priest, is one of the most notable names of the theological movement that sought the encounter between Marxism and Christianity, an encounter considered by many intellectuals to be unnatural and strongly deleterious.

How does Boff explain the genesis of this book?

To mock the structures of control and military repression, I published every month during 1971 in *Sponsa Christi* (*The Spouse of Christ*), a journal for consecrated religious, an article under the title *Jesus Christ Liberator.* In March of 1972, I compiled the articles and ventured their publication in the form of a book. I had to hide myself for two weeks because the political police were looking for me. The words "liberation" and "liberator" had been banned and could not be used in public. The editor's lawyer had much to do (she had taken part in the Brazilian expedition to Italy in World War II) to convince the surveillance agents that it was a book about theology, with many notes taken from German literature, and that it did not threaten the State of National Security. (leonardoboff.org)

Clearly, a text that was born in a situation of political oppression. He continues:

What is particular about this book (now in its 21st edition)? It represented, based on a rigorous exegesis of the Gospels, an image of Jesus as liberator from various forms of human oppression. He confronted two of these directly: religious oppression under the form of the Pharisaism of strict observance of religious laws; and the other, political, the Roman occupation that demanded the recognition of the emperor as "God" and assisted in the penetration of pagan Hellenistic culture into Israel. Jesus opposed religious oppression with a greater "law," that of unconditional love toward God and toward neighbor. Neighbor for him is any person I draw near to, especially the poor and invisible ones, those who do not count in society. As for political oppression, instead of submitting to the order of the caesars, he announces the Kingdom of God, a crime of *lèse-majesté*. This reign entailed an absolute revolution in the cosmos, in society, of every person, and a redefinition of the meaning of life in the light of God, called "Abba" that is, "papa," good and merciful who makes all feel they are his sons and daughters, brothers and sisters to each other.

Although some of the intentions which guided the writing of this book might be comprehensible, its message of "absolute revolution" which guides it and the other books referring to Liberation Theology is not.

It is true that Christ came to announce a message of liberation, but what type of liberation do we mean? Above all, from the slavery of sin, announcing a kingdom which is primarily the final *goal*, not the *content* of the journey. Terrestrial messianism led many to a fascination for Marxism, with all that it offered politically as well as religiously, and not only in Liberation Theology. God does not ask of us a revolution, but a spiritual evolution, because his reign, now and always, is not of this world.

ONCE MORE, ABBÉ DE NANTES

Those who thought Abbé de Nantes would be placated were wrong in their calculations. On April 10, 1973, he went on the counterattack, publishing his first *Liber Accusationis*. On that date, he went to Rome with some of his confreres to consign his book of accusations against the Pope, to Paul VI personally. The Pope, who must not have been very happy about the accusations, had the police obstruct his access to the Vatican. The idea contained in the book was that religion had been subjugated to the worship of man and not of God. The abbot's followers thought that this book, in some way, would halt the unbridled innovations of the Vatican, but I do not think this is accurate. In *Liber Accusationis*, Abbé de Nantes says:

> The Church cannot live in this contradiction. Our accusation obliges You, Holy Father, to examine the entire matter and to make a pronouncement. The price of this is the peace of the Church and its fidelity to Jesus Christ. I would like, we all would like, to be wrong and that You would be right. But the honor of God, the common good of the Church and the salvation of souls speak more loudly than our human sentiments: You are wrong. We pray for your spiritual conversion, that the Church might be liberated from Satan who holds it subjugated and that it be surrendered to Christ to produce once more fruits of life and sanctity.

Strong words for sure, which would not have pleased Paul VI. The defamation was to be diffused in many languages.

THE "BASE COMMUNITIES"

As we have said, base communities began to grow in the heart of radical progressive Catholicism. We saw the community of Isolotto, some years before. Now this movement would take hold precisely in Rome near the Pope: the Community of San Paolo.

The protagonist of this event was the abbot of the Benedictine community at the Basilica of St. Paul Outside the Walls, Dom Giovanni Franzoni (1928–2017). He was the youngest bishop to have taken part in the Council, and that experience changed him, so much so that he came out in favor of divorce and abortion and drew near to the Italian Communist Party. In July 1973, he was invited to resign, then forced to leave the priesthood as well on August 2, 1976. He and the people who followed him began to meet in Via Ostiense 152/B, giving life to what came to be known as the Community of San Paolo. He remained very active right up to his death in promoting the cause of ultra-progressive Catholicism, which saw in him an important reference point.

These base communities did not become the vanguard of progressive Catholicism as they had hoped to do. Rather, Modernism found a more viable incarnation in ecclesial movements, although with varying nuances.

It was also in 1973 that a film came out that would mark the historical period: the film adaptation of the musical by Andrew Lloyd Webber and Tim Rice called *Jesus Christ Superstar*. From the entertainment point of view, it was an enormously successful show, with well-written and captivating music. But the image of Jesus it portrayed was that of a hippy and was contested by traditionalist Catholicism, although it seems that Paul VI saw a preview of the film and admired it. During the showing of this musical at the opera house in Rome there was a protest organized by two Catholic traditionalist intellectuals, Duillio Marchesini (1930–2020) and Giancarlo Scafidi (1941–2022), which is narrated in the book *Nati per combattere* (*Born to Fight*).

In his general audience on August 29, Paul VI discussed

> the spirit of protest that today has become fashionable, and that everyone in the ecclesiastical field presumes is modern, popular and personable, which they often claim with irresponsible nonchalance. As such, protests should identify and correct defects worthy of being reproached, and thus aim for conversion, reform, an increase of good will; and We do not exorcise a positive protest if it remains such. But woe is me! Protesting has become a form of self-harm, too often lacking wisdom and love; it has become an easy affectation which veils one's gaze from one's own defects and opens to those of others; it is accustomed to judgment, often rash, of the failures of the Church, and indulges to the point of sympathy and connivance, those of the Church's adversaries who reject the name of God, subverters of the social order; they radically espouse audacious and dangerous reforms, and then withhold their adhesion, humble and filial, to the renewing efforts which Catholicism has tried to establish in every sector of life and human activity.

In his audience on November 21, we read a hint of self-critique
in the Pope's very severe words:

> We have been too weak perhaps, and imprudent
> in this attitude to which the school of modern
> Christianity invites us: the recognition of the
> profane world and its rites and values, even the
> sympathy and the admiration which is their due.
> We have often, in practice, gone beyond the
> mark. The so-called permissive demeanor of our
> moral judgment and of our practical conduct; the
> malleability toward the experience of evil, with
> the sophisticated pretext of wanting to know it so
> as to be able to defend against it (medicine does
> not admit this criteria; why should one who
> wants to preserve his spiritual and moral health
> allow it?); secularism, wanting to mark the
> boundaries of certain specific competencies, im-
> poses as self-sufficient and moves on to the
> negation of other values and realities; the am-
> biguous and perhaps hypocritical rejection of
> exterior signs of one's religious identity; etc., have
> insinuated in many the comfortable persuasion
> that today Christians as well must assimilate to
> the mass of humanity as it is, without taking care
> to make some distinctions, and without presum-
> ing we Christians, to have something of our own
> that is original that might, compared with others,
> bring some salutary advantage. We have gone
> beyond the mark in conforming to the mentality
> and customs of the profane world. Let us listen

again to the rebuke of the Apostle Paul to the early Christians, "Do not conform yourselves to the present world, but be transformed by the renewal of your spirit" (Rom 12:2); and that of the Apostle Peter, "As obedient children, do not be conformed to the passions of your former ignorance (of the faith)" (1 Peter 1:14). A difference between Christian life and the profane or pagan life which besieges us is needed; an originality, a proper style. Let us even say: a proper liberty to live according to the exigencies of the Gospel.

CATHOLIC TRADITIONALISM ON THE BARRICADES

The year 1973 also marked the publishing of two other books that would become important for the traditionalist front: Michel de Saint Pierre's *Églises en ruine, églises en peril* and Dietrich von Hildebrand's *The Devastated Vineyard*. Dietrich von Hildebrand (1889–1977) was a German philosopher who later taught in the United States. Several years earlier, he had published *The Trojan Horse in the City of God*, in which he dealt with the crisis in the Church. In society as well, people were becoming increasingly estranged from traditional teachings of the Church. In May 1974, for example, there was a referendum to abrogate the law on divorce introduced in Italy in 1970. The majority sided against the abrogation of the law, which thus remained in force.

At the start of 1974 (January 25), Bishop Antonio Castro Mayer sent Paul VI a critical text on religious freedom. In his supplication, he stated:

> Over the years, the conviction has matured
> within me that the official pronouncements of
> Your Holiness do not have the consonance which
> I desire to see with my whole soul, with the acts
> of Pontiffs who have preceded You. This is clearly
> not the case of proclamations guaranteed by the
> charism of infallibility. Thus, my conviction does
> not shake my unreserved faith in any way in the
> definitions of the Second Vatican Council.

The document continues with a severe critique of the Church
and of the changes underway.

Meanwhile, Rome continued to observe what was taking place in Switzerland. In November 1974, Bishop
Albert Descamps and Msgr. Guillaume Onclin were sent
on a canonical visit to the seminary of the Society of St.
Pius X. It seems this visit was embellished with cutting-
edge theological discourses on the part of the visitors,
leaving the members of the Society, especially its founder,
scandalized. On November 21, this would provoke a declaration of fidelity to Catholic Rome, but in resistance to
Modernist Rome:

> We adhere with whole heart and soul to Catho-
> lic Rome, custodian of the Catholic faith and of
> the traditions necessary for maintaining the
> faith, to Rome eternal, teacher of wisdom and of
> truth. We reject, however, and we have always
> rejected to follow the Rome of neo-Modernist
> and neo-Protestant tendencies which were

clearly manifested in the Second Vatican Council and after the Council, in all the reforms it produced.

Despite attempts at drawing nearer, this declaration firmly reestablished the distance that, despite further attempts, would not be overcome. At that point, a dance of threatened ordinations began, which in some cases would be carried out.

The new bishop of Lausanne, Pierre Mamie (1920–2008), who succeeded Bishop Charriere for whom he had served as auxiliary, was not as favorable to the Society as his predecessor. On May 6, 1975, after consultations with Rome, he obtained permission to suppress it. This was a harsh trial for the followers of Archbishop Lefebvre. On June 29, Paul VI wrote a letter to Archbishop Lefebvre which began with these words:

> Dear brother, it is with grief that We write you today. With grief because we intuit the interior laceration of a man who sees the annihilation of his hopes, the ruin of his work which he believes he has undertaken for a righteous cause. With grief because We are thinking of the anguish of the youth who have followed him, full of ardor, and who now discover the impasse. But our suffering is deepest in finding that the decision of the competent authority—despite having been formulated clearly and being entirely justified, it must be said, dictated by your refusal to modify your public and persistent opposition to the

> Ecumenical Council Vatican II, to the postcon-
> ciliar reforms and to the orientations imposed by
> the same Pope—that this decision is open to
> further discussion even to the point of seeking
> any juridical possibility to invalidate it.

The Pope, then, was offering the archbishop a way out, which naturally had to include the acceptance of the Council and what it entailed, including the new Mass.

We recall as well how Paul VI, in 1974, had prepared a booklet called *Iubilate Deo* containing some pieces of Gregorian chant for use by the faithful and given to bishops around the world. But by now it was of little use.

TENSIONS WITHIN THE CHURCH INTENSIFY

But Paul VI's problems came not only from the right wing, so to speak. We have seen how an atmosphere of remonstration had enveloped ecclesial life for many years. On May 11, 1975, the right-leaning journal *Il Borghese* published an article entitled "*Confetti verdi con la benedizione*," which accused a priest, Fr. Marco Bisceglia, of having celebrated the wedding of a homosexual couple. The authors, Bartolomeo Baldi and Franco Jappelli, posed as homosexuals to draw out the priest. The unsophisticated prose of the article nicely describes the genesis of what happened:

> The two "infiltrators" brought back the tran-
> script of their conversation with the priest, who
> at a certain point said, "I think you came to me
> precisely because of that episode that I cited in

my article in the *Radical News*, about the homosexual who came to me looking for consolation. In that case as well, I tried to take the detached attitude of the confessor but understanding, trying to understand completely, trying not to face this issue on a traditional moralistic level, but on an anthropological one, so to speak. Enough with prejudices. I've realized that human beings have a right to live their lives responsibly and according to their own personal needs. On the other hand, when two homosexuals create a full human relationship that gives sense to their lives, a relationship that's positive above all because it's affective, loving, why should they not be free to do so? It's not that I've come to absolute certainty, because in this field it's all, it seems to me, in the research phase, on the scientific plane. As I see matters today, it seems to me that all traditional morality has absolutized the heterosexual relationship in terms of procreation, for [the sake of] the demographic increase of humanity. At a certain time in history there was a need to multiply. Primitive society, the patriarchal society, was founded on quantity. In the tribe, the cult of patriarchy was strong, it was able to survive, to impose itself insofar as it was numerous. Every sexual encounter that didn't lead to procreation was banned, there was ostracism. The homosexual act was condemned because there was the so-called spilling of the seed. All legislation and morality were understood to condemn acts against nature, precisely because they didn't attain their goal of procreating."

As we can see, it was a complete negation of the traditional morality of the Church, as the priest (who later defines himself a Marxist socialist) clearly states. And not only. Later the priest pushes even farther:

> Take the Gospel: the attitude of Jesus too is always one of extreme respect and there's never that moralistic attitude steeped in absolute principles. For me, the substance of the Gospel is this: whatever doesn't offend is never negative, whatever doesn't do injustice to others. For me, when would a homosexual be morally reprehensible? When, let's say, he has recourse to the subtle arts to satisfy his instincts. If there's an affective relationship that is mutual, even if one is forty years old and the other fifteen, you certainly can't say it's a crime.

The authors of the article finish with this:

> Even love, often brought up by Bisceglia, no longer has that ancient and marvelous significance that true Catholics have always attributed to it but assumes a role as "umbrella" under the protection of which, as an inalienable right of man, any filthy sexual or homosexual behavior is permitted. And even the Christ of Fr. Bisceglia not only no longer has the ancient faculty of condemning or pardoning, but does not even

resemble the film version of the superstar hippy Jesus. He has become, in fact, a sort of squalid panderer, always ready to bless, upon request, any union, even the most obscene or the most unnatural. If these are the priests of today, and especially of tomorrow, if these individuals are still allowed to live in the bosom of the Catholic Church (the provision of "removal" adopted by the bishops in his case, at this point seems ludicrous), it's up to the laity to climb onto the barricades in the defense of those spiritual and (for God's sake!) sexual values, which these "elastic" priests are trying to upend.

On December 9, 1980, Don Marco Bisceglia founded the first ArciGay association in Italy, together with a young activist, Nichi Vendola. Thus, the groundwork for the gay rights movement in Italy was set by a Roman Catholic priest.

But the fascination with Marxism and communism was widespread in Catholic circles and still is today. Consider that at the start of 1976, a convention of worker-priests was held near Modena, northern Italy. The delegate from the Italian Episcopal Conference was Bishop Cesare Pagani, who was welcomed with the singing of the *Internationale*—the communist anthem—and the raising of a closed fist, the universal salute of the radical Left.

MEASURES AGAINST ARCHBISHOP LEFEBVRE

Despite the violent forward push of the powerful and influential progressive wing in the Church, the path marked out by Vatican II continued. The liturgical reform did not retreat; on the contrary, it was promoted with great fervor by the Pontiff himself. A commission of cardinals had been considering the Lefebvre case since 1975, but attempts at reconciliation did not produce effects, particularly because the elements for an evolution of the affair in a positive direction were objectively absent. Rome represented at that moment everything the Society of St. Pius X was born to oppose and there was no margin for a reorganization of the differences, except for the renunciation of the positions of one of the sides.

In his important discourse of May 24 during the secret consistory, the Pope reprimanded the rebels on both sides and highlighted in particular the question of Archbishop Lefebvre:

> On one side there are those who, under the pretext of greater fidelity to the Church and to the Magisterium, systematically reject the teachings of the Council, its application and the reforms derived from it, its gradual application by the Apostolic See and the Episcopal Conferences, under our authority willed by Christ. They discredit the authority of the Church in the name of Tradition, which is given only material and verbal respect; they estrange the faithful from obedience to the See of Peter as to their legitimate Bishops; they refuse the authority of today, in the name of that of yesterday. And the fact is all the more serious because the opposition of which we speak is

not only encouraged by some priests but headed
by a Bishop whom We nevertheless have always
esteemed, Msgr. Marcel Lefebvre.

The Pontiff's condemnation was unyielding, and his words
revealed how much the question weighed upon him.
Then he touched the theme of the liturgy:

> This is all the more serious, in particular, when
> introducing the division precisely where *congrega-*
> *vit nos in unum Christi amor*, in the Liturgy and
> in the Eucharistic Sacrifice, refusing the defer-
> ence to the norms defined in the liturgical field.
> In the name of Tradition, We ask all our children,
> all the Catholic community, to celebrate, with
> dignity and fervor, the renewed liturgy.

At this point, the Pontiff struck the other side: those progressives who were upsetting the liturgical doctrine and practice
of the Church. But many only remember the part in which
he castigated the traditionalist wing.

In June of that year, Archbishop Lefebvre was due to
ordain his seminarians. The Holy See, through Archbishop
Giovanni Benelli (1921–1982) at that time Secretary of
State, beseeched him not to proceed with the ordinations,
but this did not convince the French prelate, who proceeded
with the ceremony. In his homily, he explained everything
that had passed between him and Rome in the preceding
days and the significance of the distance that separated him
at that moment from Rome's positions:

In the previous twelve days, we have not ceased to receive messages and envoys from Rome intimating that we abstain from carrying out these ordinations. But if we seek in all objectivity the true motive that animates those who ask us not to carry out these priestly ordinations, if we look for the hidden motive, it is because we are ordaining these priests that they might be able to say the Mass as it always has been. It is because they know that these priests will be faithful to the Mass of the Church, to the Mass of the Tradition, to the Mass as it has always been celebrated, that they exhort us not to ordain them.

As said above, the rift was already too wide to bridge with an accord; the material foundation for this was not there. Some of the names of those who were ordained are noteworthy: Richard Williamson (b. 1940), whom we shall be forced to consider later; Daniel Dolan (1951–1922); Donald Sanborn (b. 1950); and Anthony Cekada (1951–2020), who was to play an important role in Catholic traditionalism in the years to come.

The ordination carried out was judged an act of serious disobedience and led, on July 22, to the suspension *a divinis* (prohibition to celebrate Mass) of the French archbishop. On August 9, some French intellectuals (Michel de Saint Pierre, Michel Droit, Louis Salleron, Jean Dutourd, Henri Sauguet, Colonel Remy, Michel Siry, Gustave Thibon) signed a letter in support of Archbishop Lefebvre addressed to Paul VI, in which they affirmed, "Every day [the Christian faithful] bring us the echoes—increasingly determined, increasingly numerous—of their amazement and anguish. For this reason, we turn to You, for to whom would a Catholic turn if not to the Pope, the successor of Peter, Vicar of Jesus Christ? We place our petition at your feet."

But the clash was by now too intense to allow for an immediate solution. There was also the fact that the Society had begun to inspire fear because it had gone beyond the borders of France and gained ground in other countries such as the United States, with the creation of a female branch as well.

On August 29, Archbishop Lefebvre celebrated Mass in Lille before an enormous crowd of about six thousand people. In his homily, he stated that the Church had in some way espoused the ideas of revolution, having in mind the French Revolution. The distance grew, and by now the Vatican knew what the stakes were and did not retreat.

On September 1, just three days after Archbishop Lefebvre's homily, Paul VI gave a discourse in which he defied all expectations by refusing to comment on Archbishop Lefebvre. Yet this was a response in itself: the Pope would not retreat.

THE ENCOUNTER

This attitude on the part of Paul VI can be explained perhaps by the fact that a meeting between him and Archbishop Lefebvre was in the works. It was to take place on September 11 at Castel Gandolfo, the papal summer residence. The transcript of the encounter was published by Fr. Leonardo Sapienza in *La casa di Paolo* (*The House of Paul*) and then reprinted in *La Stampa* (Andrea Tornielli) and other news agencies. Here, we present the reprint by Gelsomino Del Guercio in *Aleteia*.

The encounter began at 10:30 a.m. and lasted half an hour. The Pope stated, "I hope to have before me a brother, a son, a friend. Unfortunately, the position you have taken is that of an antipope. What can I say? You have not conceded the least measure in your words, in your actions, in your behavior. You have not refused to come to me. And I would be happy to be able to resolve a case that is so distressing. I will listen to you; I will also invite you to reflect. I know I am a poor man. But here, it is not the person that is at stake: it is the Pope. And you have judged the Pope to be unfaithful to the faith of which he is the supreme guarantor. Perhaps this is the first time in history that this has occurred. You have told the entire world that the Pope does not have the faith, does not believe, that he is a Modernist, and so forth. Yes, I must be humble. But you find yourself in a terrible position. You have committed extremely grave actions, before the whole world."

Lefebvre replied, "Perhaps there was something inappropriate in my words, in my writings." He added that he was not alone, that he had "with him bishops, priests, and numerous faithful." He stated, "The situation in the Church after the Council [is] such that we no longer know what to do. With all of these changes either we risk losing the faith or we give the impression of disobeying. I would like to kneel before you and accept everything; but I cannot go against my conscience. I am not the one who created a movement, [it was the faithful] who do not accept this situation. I am not the leader of the traditionalists.... I am behaving exactly as I did before the Council. I cannot comprehend how, suddenly, I would be condemned because I form priests in the obedience of the holy tradition of the holy Church."

The discussion continues, with Paul VI being very authoritative toward Lefebvre. Then at one point, "How can you consider yourself in communion with Us when you take a stance against Us, before the world, accusing us of infidelity, of wanting the destruction of the Church?"

"I never had the intention of...," Lefebvre defends himself.

But Pope Montini interrupts, "You have said it and you have written it. That I was a Modernist Pope. Applying the Ecumenical Council, I am betraying the Church. You understand that, if that were the case, I would have to resign; and you to take my place and direct the Church."

As we can see, Paul VI's tone was very harsh, while Archbishop Lefebvre, though defending himself, tended to be more submissive, perhaps because he realized he was speaking with the Pope. After other skirmishes, Paul VI affirmed in conclusion:

You will understand that I cannot allow, even for reasons I would call "personal," that you implicate yourself in schism. Make a public declaration in which you retract your recent declarations and behaviors, which all have recognized as actions not aimed at edifying the Church, but dividing it and doing it harm. Ever since you met with the three Roman cardinals, there has been a rupture. We must recover our union in prayer and reflection.

The Pope and Archbishop Lefebvre concluded the encounter by praying together.

It was certainly a highly dramatic meeting which, seen in hindsight, did not resolve the question of Lefebvre. Quite to the contrary. Other clouds were forming above the gulf that divided Rome and Ecône.

BUGNINI A FREEMASON?

In October, an explosive report in *Le Figaro* denounced the architect of the liturgical reform, Archbishop Annibale Bugnini as a Freemason. Bugnini denied the disparaging accusation. The journal of Mino Pecorelli, *Osservatorio Politico*, also re-launched the accusations, even publishing a photo of a check that Bugnini supposedly received from high-level masons. The masonic affiliation of Bugnini was repeated more recently in the journal *30 Days* in 1992, including new evidence; and likewise in 2009 in the American magazine *Inside the Vatican*. I repeat, Bugnini always denied the accusations.

Paul VI must have had something on him, though. Why else would he send Bugnini to Iran as Apostolic Pro-Nuncio at the beginning of 1976? Bugnini was well aware that he had been slighted. In his account of Bugnini's last years, his Lazarist confrere G. F. Rossi observed:

On January 5, 1976, Msgr. Bugnini was nominated Apostolic Pro-Nuncio to the Islamic Republic of Iran, a mission for which he felt neither prepared nor called, but which he accepted in a spirit of faith and obedience. He reached Teheran as the Pope's representative in an Islamic land, as had his superior forty years earlier (in 1936), Msgr. Marina, in the service of the Church. He returned to Italy in the summer of 1982 to undergo surgery and was admitted to the Pius XI Clinic in Rome. On July 3, in a sudden and unexpected manner, just moments after having received the Eucharist, as he was about to leave the clinic and begin a period of rest before returning to his mission in Teheran, he passed from the table that nourishes us in our earthly walk to the heavenly banquet. The Lord's call came suddenly, unexpectedly; but the thought of death was familiar to Msgr. Bugnini.

Archbishop Bugnini was certainly one of the most enigmatic figures of the years we are discussing, and much will still be said about him and his influence. The shadows that still cover his work are unmistakable.

THE COUNCIL IN QUESTION

On October 11, Paul VI sent a long letter to Archbishop Lefebvre in which he recognized the merits of the ex-missionary in Africa. He was also grieved that Lefebvre's positions had not changed. The Pope continued to manifest his stern attitude toward the rebel bishop. His words transmit a certain anger toward Lefebvre's obstinacy. There were also some who sought to convince him to be more permissive toward the archbishop, like his friend Jean Guitton. After an initial moment in which it seemed the Pope would make concessions, he decided to maintain the hard line so as not to renounce the Council and its reforms. But the French bishop would not stop. On October 24, he celebrated Mass in Friedrichshafen, Germany, and on October 31, he ordained twelve deacons. During those weeks a book came out that collected the interventions pronounced during Vatican II with the unambiguous name *J'accuse le Concile!* ("I accuse the Council!").

On November 19 in Rome, during a press conference, Fr. Noël Barbara accused Paul VI of heresy and schism. Fr. Barbara was another important figure of Catholic tradition-alism, with a more impetuous character than the diplomatic Archbishop Lefebvre. Fr. Barbara was also inclined toward sedevacantism and later towards sedeprivationism, which we shall examine later.

Archbishop Lefebvre responded to Paul VI's letter on December 3. Obviously the Council was still a central question. He asked the Pope how he could have conceded a right to error and asked for an account of the Protestant influence in the setting of the liturgical reform. He pointed out how their seminary was entirely in conformity with ecclesiastical norms.

It was difficult to imagine a restructuring of the controversy when the core dispute remained unresolved and would certainly have been very difficult to resolve in the ecclesial and social context of those years. The Church could not renounce, after so few years, its shift, regardless of whether right or wrong. They were in a state of serious deadlock, from which the way out was nowhere to be seen.

Even a certain German theology professor at the University of Regensburg who had an important role as peritus at the Council in the progressive wing (and who would soon make a name for himself) had realized exactly this. His name was Joseph Ratzinger. Responding to a letter by Wolfgang Waldstein, on December 14, Ratzinger sided in favor of the preservation of the missal from before the reform (unavoce-ve.it):

> To cut to the quick: in my opinion, permission should be obtained, for all priests, to make use of the old Missal on condition they recognize the validity of the new Missal.

We see how the position of the "progressive" Ratzinger had evolved toward one of greater comprehension of the issues involved in the liturgical evolution and was not hardened in a refusal that smacked of ideology. But even his request that those who would have celebrated with the old missal should also recognize the new one did not satisfy everyone in the vast traditionalist camp.

Two books of that year are worthy of mention. One is by Michel de Saint Pierre; the title, *Les fumées de Satan* (The Smoke of Satan), speaks volumes. In it, Saint Pierre gives an account of the pastoral aberrations in the Church in France. The other book was by a young Italian journalist, a Catholic convert, who felt it was necessary to reestablish the theme of apologetics at the center of discourse and sounded the reasons for faith in Him whom we proclaim our Savior. The journalist was called Vittorio Messori. The book was *The Jesus Hypothesis*, a text that would have resounding success, selling millions of copies with translations in dozens of languages and that is now being republished also in English thanks to Sophia Institute Press. After the ideological derailments, Messori tried to place the theme of Jesus at the center of the faith, rather than the deviations which for many had come to dominate. Although he is no traditionalist, this book would present solid arguments in favor of the traditionalist world.

THE TIME FOR ACTION BEGINS

At the beginning of 1977, we do well to consider what was moving in Latin America. In Mexico, after the death of Senz y Arriaga, a priest named Moisés Carmona di Acapulco founded the Catholic Trent Union in January, a group oriented toward sedevacantism that would carry some weight, especially in Latin American traditionalism. It would later take the name Priestly Society of Trent. This group currently has various locations in Mexico and in other Latin American countries, with a presence in the United States and Europe as well, though without a significant following.

Returning to Europe, in France to be precise, a disturbing event occurred in Paris. A group of traditionalist faithful occupied the Parisian church of St. Nicholas du Chardonnet on February 27, still today run by priests of the Society of St. Pius X. Alexandre Simonnot narrates the affair:

Forty-two years ago, on Sunday, February 27, 1977, three French priests had a brilliant idea: they would occupy a Parisian church, the soon-to-become-famous St. Nicholas du Chardonnet. The idea of Fr. Louis Choache, Fr. Vincent Serralda, and Msgr. Fran Ducard-Bourget was simple: place an announcement in the newspaper *L'Aurore* for the celebration of a solemn, traditional Mass at the *Mutualité*, in the V District. What the faithful who gathered there did not know was that they would be redirected to the nearby church, St. Nicholas du Chardonnet, which stands about ten meters from the *Mutualité*. It was in this way that a miracle occurred. Not only did the faithful occupy the church, but they have been there ever since!

Thus, a time for action was beginning, and by employing an occupation, the traditionalists were using, paradoxically, the methods of the extreme Left.

Meanwhile, the meetings between Archbishop Lefebvre and Vatican representatives continued on May 10–11. The French archbishop celebrated Confirmations on May 22 in the occupied Parisian church of St. Nicholas du Chardonnet, conferring the sacrament on 150 youth. On May 30, he celebrated Confirmations in Switzerland.

On June 6, the Roman nobility met under the hospitality of Princess Elvina Pallavicini, who welcomed them in her palace near the Quirinale. The historian Roberto de Mattei, among the organizers of the event which he would then attend, recalls the episode that preceded this event. According to a report in the *Corrispondenza Romana*:

> The news of the conference, which circulated in the month of May, at first did not sound the alarm in the Vatican. Paul VI assumed it would be easy to convince the princess to desist in her idea and entrusted the matter to one of his close collaborators, "Don Sergio" Pignedoli (1910–1980), whom he had made cardinal in 1973. The cardinal telephoned the princess using an affectionate tone of voice, asking about her health. "I was pleased," observed Elvina Pallavicini ironically, "with his interest after such long silence." After about an hour of pleasantries, the cardinal arrived at his question: "I know that you intend to receive Archbishop Lefebvre. Will it be a public or private engagement?" "In my house, it can only be private," replied the princess. The cardinal then ventured, "Would it not be better to postpone the meeting? Archbishop Lefebvre has caused the Holy Father much suffering, and he is quite pained by this initiative…" Lady Elvina's response chilled Cardinal Pignedoli. "Eminence, in my house I think I can receive whomever I wish to receive."

The attempts to convince the aristocrat did not stop. At one point, she too was threatened with excommunication. But despite this, the conference took place, and Archbishop Lefebvre explained to those gathered the reasons for the opposition to him. It concluded with the singing of the Marian antiphon, *Salve Regina*.

Archbishop Lefebvre continued with his ordinations (June 26 and 29). On June 27, during a consistory for the creation of four cardinals, Paul VI pronounced in his homily words of great suffering for these ordinations that he defined "illegitimate" and implored the rebellious bishop to be reconciled to him, obviously on conditions that Lefebvre found unacceptable. But Archbishop Lefebvre continued on his path and on July 10 consecrated the Queen of Angels Chapel in the United States, where the Society was expanding.

THE CASSICIACO THESIS

In the Swiss seminary of the Society, one of the professors was not asked to return for the fall semester. In this case, his was a prestigious name which we have already encountered: Michel Louis Guérard de Lauriers, a Dominican and a distinguished theologian. He was dismissed for hinting in his lessons at a theological thesis which, in his view, explained the crisis of the Church but was a view that was unacceptable to the Society. In an interview for *Sodalitium*, Msgr. Guérard de Lauriers remembers the affair in this way:

> I had collaborated with Archbishop Lefebvre since the beginning of his work: Fribourg and Ecône, at the end of 1970. At Midnight Mass on December 25, 1970, Archbishop Lefebvre celebrated and gave the homily. To the joy of all, the integrity of the traditional rite had returned. I celebrated the Christmas Day Mass and gave the

homily of which I still conserve the outline, and I warmly thanked Archbishop Lefebvre. I remained a professor at Ecône until September of 1977, the date on which I preached the retreat for the return to the seminary. I was dismissed a short time later. I was even prohibited from visiting the Dominican Brothers whom Archbishop Lefebvre had welcomed as students at Ecône. The motive for this exclusion: I had expressed numerous times in "private circles" [intra muros] and had made a perfectly clear allusion during a public lecture to the "thesis."

According to this thesis, which would be redacted for the first time in March of 1978 and definitively published in *Quaderni di Cassiciaco* (Notebooks of Cassiciaco), there is a defect in those who have been Pope, at least after December 7, 1965 (*Dignitatis Humanae*) — that is, those who have been Popes materially in the sense of occupying the Apostolic See, but not formally, in the sense that they do not enjoy the authority connected to it. Much has been written about this real distinction between *materialier* and *formaliter*. Those who hold this thesis take the common name of sedeprivationists, to be distinguished from pure sedevacantists who claim that the postconciliar Popes are not materially or formally Popes. The name was given by a layman and is not necessarily recognized by those who take up the thesis of Cassiciaco. I would propose a name such as sedematerialists, which is perhaps more precise. The thesis requires a certain knowledge of the subtleties of theological abstraction to understand, but what is certain is that it was to be adopted by a considerable part of the Catholic world that opposed the reforms of Vatican II.

THE END OF PAUL VI'S PONTIFICATE

In Italy, the drift of Catholic values in society continued to worsen with the passage of the law permitting abortion, *Legge 194*. Social and political tensions would then culminate in the abduction and murder of one of the most visible leaders of the majority party of Christian Democracy. Aldo Moro had been a student of then-Msgr. Montini, and his murder was a terrible blow for Paul VI, already ailing. He celebrated Moro's funeral. The words he pronounced on May 13, 1978, became famous:

> And now our lips, sealed as if by an enormous obstacle, similar to the large stone rolled over the entrance of the sepulcher of Christ, desire to open and express the *De Profundis*, the cry and lament of ineffable suffering with which the current tragedy suffocates our voice. Lord, hear us! And who could hear our lament if not you, O God of life and of death? You did not hear our supplication for the safety of Aldo Moro, of this good man, meek, wise, innocent, a friend. But You, O Lord, have not abandoned his immortal spirit, marked by faith in Christ who is resurrection and life. For him, for him.

He was profoundly anguished, and perhaps this suffering would accelerate his end, which came just three months later on August 6, the feast of the Transfiguration. One of the most dramatic pontificates in history had come to an end, and its changes are still palpable today. For some it was a time of grace, for others of disgrace. The fact is that the Church today is still in a situation of crisis in terms of numbers and vocations, and the debate over Paul VI continues—on both sides.

The Parenthesis of John Paul I

On August 26, the patriarch of Venice, Albino Luciani, was elected Pope. He took the name John Paul I. But as we all know, he was to die just over a month later, on September 28. What relationship would he have had with traditionalists? The signs he gave as a cardinal did not leave much room for hope. In fact, the preceding February 20 he had prohibited the celebration of the traditional Mass in his diocese. On that February 26, the Association *Una Voce* Venice responded to his decision:

> Even greater amazement and perplexity arouses from the prohibition of the celebration of the Tridentine Mass (as we have said, *never abrogated*), by his Eminence, considering that His Eminence demonstrates great tolerance in the face of celebrations in the diocese of irregular rites (which in some cases verge on sacrilege or at least irreverence), before the continued violations of the norms of Canon Law as concerns the ecclesiastical habit of many priests of the diocese, before the lack of compliance on the part of almost all priests charged with the cure of souls, of

the second comma of article 54 of the conciliar constitution *Sacrosanctum Concilium*; irregularities and violations of which Your Eminence is definitely aware and which we shall communicate to Your Eminence, if requested, and make public if necessary. (unavoceitalia.org)

His attitude did not seem friendly, but how it would have played out we will never know. Would the grace of his office have helped him take different decisions? Many had hoped so.

Another conclave had to be summoned, and this time the newly elected would remain Pontiff "*ad multos annos.*"

CHAPTER 4

The Age of John Paul II

A SHIFT IN THE CHURCH

ON OCTOBER 16, THE archbishop of Krakow, Karol Wojtyla, was elected and took the name John Paul II. His would be a no less historical pontificate. I cannot hope to summarize here the activity of a Pontiff who influenced the life of the Church in so many ways. Memorable, after the gaunt figure of Paul VI and the thin figure of John Paul I, was the athletic build of this man from Poland, a clear signal of attention to the problems of the silent Church.

John Paul II's stamina led him to tackle various questions with strength and resolve, and obviously even those of the traditionalist world underwent important developments during his pontificate.

He had to continue to face the challenges of Liberation Theology and of the many priests fascinated by it, like Ernesto Cardenal, who in July of 1979 entered Managua, Nicaragua, with the revolutionary troops. He was to become a minister in the government of Daniel Ortega. This did not please John

Paul II. The photo of the Pope reprimanding Cardenal on his knees during the 1983 papal visit was seen around the world. Here is how Cardenal (vita.it) remembers the episode:

> After the greetings of protocol, including those to the honor guard and the flag, the Pope asked President Ortega if he could greet his ministers, too. Naturally, he was allowed; thus, the Pope came toward us. With Daniel and Cardinal Casaroli on either side, he started giving his hand to the ministers and, when he drew near to me, I did what the Nuncio had advised us to do in this case: I removed my beret and kneeled to kiss his ring. But he did not allow me to kiss it and brandishing his finger as if it were a stick, he told me in a scolding tone: "You must regularize your situation." I didn't respond, so he repeated the brusque admonition. And this happened while we were being filmed by all the telecameras in the world. I have the impression that all this was completely premeditated by the Pope. And that the television had been warned.

Returning to 1979, we recall the death of Cardinal Alfredo Ottaviani, one of the most important reference points for the traditionalist front. It was also in this year that Hans Küng's *missio canonica* was withdrawn: a sign that his teaching was judged beyond the Catholic tradition.

John Paul II was sending out signals of having understood the state of crisis of the Church. For example, in his discourse at a missionary conference on February 6, 1981, he said:

> Today, to be effective in the work of preaching, we need first to know well the spiritual and psychological reality of Christians living in modern society. We need to admit realistically and with profound and pained sensitivity that most Christians today feel lost, confused, perplexed, and even disappointed; ideas have been spread everywhere that stand in contrast to the revealed truth that has always been taught; actual heresies have been divulged in dogmatic and moral theology, creating doubt, confusion, rebellion; even the liturgy has been tampered with; immersed in intellectual and moral "relativism" and therefore in permissiveness. Christians are tempted by atheism, by agnosticism, from vaguely moralistic Enlightenment to sociological Christianity, without defined dogmas and without objective morality.

The Pope had not closed his eyes to what was happening.

Catholic Alliance

A movement called *Civiltà Cristiana* (Christian Civilization) had been active in Italy since 1967, animated by Franco Antico (1932–1981). This traditionalist movement made use of a journal called *Vigilia Romana*. Important names of the traditionalist world wrote for it, in particular several important Dominicans. The association and the journal ceased operation in 1974.

Then, in 1962, an engineer named Giovanni Volpe (1906–1984), son of the historian Gioacchino, founded a publishing house important for the Right and for Catholic traditionalism. Thanks to Volpe Editions, the texts of Louis Salleron, Jean Madiran, Marcel de Corte, Ernst Junger, José Ortega y Gasset, and others were able to be published in Italian. Between 1973 and 1984, the Volpe Foundation was at work uniting intellectuals in various conferences. The year 1975 saw the foundation of the anti-Modernist journal *Sì Sì No No*, an idea of Fr. Francesco Maria Putti (1909–1984). This journal, which we mentioned in the previous chapter, hosted anonymous contributions from well-prepared authors, protected in this way from possible repercussions. The journal remains for many today an important alternative to mainstream Italian media, both Catholic and secular.

An even more important entity is the *Alleanza Cattolica* (Catholic Alliance), which also still exists today. This association of the faithful at first represented the traditionalist front. It was founded by Giovanni Cantoni (1938–2020). It gave space for personalities like Roberto de Mattei, Mauro Ronco, Marco Tangheroni, Massimo Introvigne, Marco Invernizzi, and Agostino Sanfratello.

The importance of this association for Italian traditionalism cannot be overstated, because it catalyzed the attention of many youths, finding inspiration in the thought of intellectuals like the aforementioned Plinio Corrêa de Oliveira. Not that there was much in Italian traditionalism at that time. As Christian Civilization collapsed, Catholic Alliance would fill the void. This movement at the time was very close to the positions of Archbishop Lefebvre, and those who wished to embrace consecrated life entered mostly into the seminaries of the Society. Running through the index of authors of *Cristianità* in the 1970s, one finds names such as Luis Salleron (1905–1992), Plinio Corrêa de Oliveira, Antonio de Castro Mayer (1904–1991), and Archbishop Lefebvre. Regarding the Brazilian scholar Corrêa de Oliveira, it must be said that one of the reference texts of the association of Cantoni was his book *Revolution and Counterrevolution*, published in Portuguese in 1959 and in Italian in 1964 by the publisher Dell'Albero, for whom Cantoni directed a series of essays.

The founder, Giovanni Cantoni, took strong positions in an edition from 1974 of *Cristianità*, the association's journal, over the indissolubility of natural law:

> The physiological conformation of the human race, its sexual subdivision, the dichotomy in male and female, clearly indicates, without the least shade of doubt, the modality our race has for perpetuating itself. This modality is the coupling between individuals of different sexes, which all throughout human existence produces a new individual, a "little man."

Obviously, those were the times in which movements in favor of divorce and abortion were strong, and obviously, Catholic Alliance was on the side of what the Church had always taught in its continuous doctrine. The themes of the counterrevolution were lively and strong, and the ample space reserved for authors representing that orientation fully is a clear proof of this.

At a certain point, toward the 1980s, this association was maturing a position that was in clear contrast with some of the historians in its ranks. The occasion was the referendum on abortion in Italy in 1981, which saw some authoritative members take a different side of the debate with respect to the directives of Catholic Alliance. The problem was more extensive and concerned the impact of Vatican II on the Church. Archbishop Lefebvre began to find some answers to the doubts he had expressed on Vatican II and the new Mass. Cantoni said, "Up until 1981, Archbishop Lefebvre asked questions; ever since 1981 he has started to find answers to them on his own."

It was a moment of great impact on the association. The sociologist Massimo Introvigne, at that time its young director, recalled to the author in a private communication:

> In 1981, the long reflection by Catholic Alliance had also come to maturity regarding the documents of the Second Vatican Council, which the association took as an integral part of the Magisterium of the Church, distinguishing between the texts of the Council and a presumed "spirit of the Council" and interpreted them according to what Benedict XVI would later call the "hermeneutic of continuity." At that time, I was twenty-six years old but had already become director of the Catholic Alliance, participating in all the meetings where these decisions were taken. I consider much more important the break with those in the association who were intending to reject the Council documents and continue their collaboration with Archbishop

Lefebvre, than the break with those who had doubts
on the question of the referendum on abortion. I
remember, in fact, that considering the effectively
problematic nature of the referendum, the National
Chapter declared that "conscientious objection" was
licit, not participating in the referendum campaign
and not even going to vote as an individual, so as
not to criticize publicly the different positions of the
Italian bishops and of the Catholic Alliance. Personally, having lived the entire matter with notable
affliction (considering that at that time Roberto de
Mattei was my best friend), I consider that as such
the question of the referendum on abortion was the
occasion for a separation that had its center in the
question of Vatican II.

Among these dissidents were Agostino Sanfratello and the
historian Roberto de Mattei, who would be expelled and then
form a new entity, which we shall consider now.

First, however, I would like to mention the encounters of
Civitella del Tronto, promoted by Pucci Cipriani, who from
the beginning of the 1970s until today has assembled important names of the Italian traditionalist world. These encounters
had a notable importance in maintaining united a world that,
as we have seen, tended to disintegrate. The acts of these meetings have been collected in published works.

Lepanto Cultural Center/Lepanto Foundation

The experience of Catholic Alliance led Roberto de Mattei to
create another entity which would perpetuate its original

objectives. Its foundation dates to April 16, 1982, in Rome, and its founding members, besides president de Mattei, were the attorneys Stefano Nitoglia and Claudio Vitelli, the scholar Guido Vignelli, and Dr. Claudio Bernabei. Later, Fabio Bernabei and Pier Luigi Bianchi Cagliesi would join the initial group.

Among its first battles was their opposition to the visit in 1983 of the secretary of the Italian Communist Party, Enrico Berlinguer, to the Basilica of St. Francis in Assisi. At that time, their battles were carried out in the newspapers, writing articles or publishing communications to spread their point of view to the general public. The battles of the Lepanto Cultural Center were directed in particular to political themes, like that against the new concordat between the Church and the Italian state (1984–1985), or the snares of the leftward shift of the Europe of Maastricht (1992), or cultural artifacts like films that were considered to be blasphemous. All of this was done with the message of Fatima in the background and attention to the traditional deposit of faith.

One theme often occupying the Center's attention was that of Islam and the danger of a multiracial society. Between 1993 and 1995, public protests were organized against the project of constructing a mosque in Rome. The protest took the form of the recitation of the Rosary in the Church of St. Louis Gonzaga at the construction site of the mosque, with the participation of a renowned Italian political personality, Irene Pivetti, the president of the lower House of Parliament, at the time quite close to traditionalist Catholic circles.

The thought of Plinio Corrêa de Oliveira was to be a source of inspiration to the Center. Professor de Mattei met him on numerous occasions and in 1996 published his biography, which would be translated into numerous languages. In 2006, Professor de Mattei left the Center due to internal divisions and continued his activity with the Lepanto Foundation, founded a few years earlier in Washington. The Cultural Center continued under the direction of Claudio and Fabio Bernabei, although since their premature deaths one after the other in 2016, the Center is much less active. A person who acted as an important connection between the Center and the Foundation was the Marquis Luigi Coda Nunziante (cited earlier), president of the association *Famiglia Domani* (Family Tomorrow) and founder of *Noblesse et Tradition*, which sponsored a number of conventions. The daughter of the Marquis, Virginia Coda Nunziante, was president of the Italian March for Life from 2011 to 2021.

The same foundation carried out intense activity from 2006 to 2021 in Italy and abroad, organizing conferences at their offices in Piazza Santa Balbina in Rome, six summer universities in Subiaco, and several international demonstrations under the name *Acies Ordinata*, carried out in Rome (February 19 and September 29, 2019) and in Munich (January 18, 2021).

Professor Roberto de Mattei was vice president of the National Research Council from 2003 to 2011. He has written thirty books that have been translated into various languages, among them *The Second Vatican Council: The Unwritten History*, winner of the 2011 Acqui Storia Prize.

The Lepanto Foundation promotes Catholic information through the online magazine *Corrispondenza Romana* and the journal *Radici Cristiane* (Christian Roots). Professor de Mattei was also one of the promoters of the "Filial Correction" addressed to Pope Francis in 2017, although he defended the Congregation for the Doctrine of the Faith's position on vaccines and the consecration of Russia and Ukraine by Pope Francis on March 25, 2022. The Lepanto Bulletin, a service used first by the Center and then by the Foundation, celebrated its fortieth birthday in 2022. Professor de Mattei stated, in a private correspondence with the author, "In these forty years we have sought to serve with consistency the Church and Christian civilization, against attacks from the outside as well as from within, trusting always in the triumph of the Immaculate Heart promised by Our Lady at Fatima. This is still our great ideal today after so many trials."

CONTACTS WITH ROME AND DIVISIONS WITHIN THE SOCIETY OF ST. PIUS X

Contacts between the Society of St. Pius X and Rome continued at a fast pace. Back under Paul VI there had been the letter of Cardinal Franjo Seper (September 28), then Prefect of the Congregation for the Doctrine of the Faith (until 1981 when Cardinal Ratzinger would succeed him). The Congregation, at Paul VI's orders, contested Archbishop Lefebvre's positions regarding religious freedom, the new Mass, the Rite of Confirmation, the papacy, and of course the Council. The letter was sent through the apostolic nuncio in Switzerland.

Archbishop Lefebvre responded on the following February 26, stating: "It is out of my attachment to the infallible doctrine of the Church and to the Successor of Peter that we find ourselves forced to express, in our words and in our actions, reservations regarding the new and singular direction taken by the Holy See on the occasion of the Second Vatican Council and after the Council." He then responded at length to all the objections raised by the Congregation, delivering his response to them personally.

Cardinal Seper responded again on March 16, thanking the French bishop but asking him for further clarifications in his answers. On April 13, Archbishop Lefebvre's response arrived, stating in the accompanying letter that "the underlying problem with our perseverance in the Tradition despite the orders imparted by Rome to abandon it, is that of the serious and profound change in the relationship of the Church with the world."

Cardinal Seper responded on June 16, assuring that the documents would be studied, hinting at a possible meeting with the bishop, and trying to avert the ordinations that had been announced. On August 8, just days after the death of Paul VI, Archbishop Lefebvre responded, looking to the future conclave. In fact, the following October 6, after the brief parenthesis of John Paul I, he wrote to forty cardinals (among whom was the future John Paul II) to steer their decisions in the direction of tradition in the conclave.

Cardinal Seper responded to Archbishop Lefebvre on November 30, inviting him to a private interview in Rome. Archbishop Lefebvre proposed the coming January 11 and 12, and asked if he could come accompanied. The cardinal denied this request. Meanwhile, in November of that year, John Paul II received Archbishop Lefebvre in a private audience, and the French bishop was able to express directly to the Pope his motivations. We have confirmation of this encounter thanks to a letter which Archbishop Lefebvre sent to the Pontiff on December 24, in which he began:

> Most Holy Father, for the honor of Jesus Christ, for the good of the Church, for the salvation of souls, we implore you to say just one word, just one word to the bishops of the entire world, as the Successor of Peter, as Pastor of the Universal Church: Let them do so; we authorize the free exercise of that which the centuries-old Tradition has used for the sanctification of souls.

This was certainly not an innocuous request, whatever Archbishop Lefebvre wished people to believe, because at bottom, he was asking the bishops to renounce the ideological vision of the Council which had insinuated itself widely throughout the Church.

As concerned his audience at the Holy Office, Lefebvre published the questionnaire with the questions and answers to which he had been subjected, and the themes always focused on questions that rose like unbreachable walls between the two positions: religious freedom, the new Mass, ecumenism, the Council on one side and obedience to ecclesial authority on the other. The themes of the Council and the Mass were important in future developments as well. Archbishop Lefebvre said that the new Mass could foster heresy, although not going so far as to say openly that it was heretical. Concerning the Council, Lefebvre said he was willing to sign his acceptance of it, on condition that it be read in the light of tradition. After this meeting, there was an exchange of letters between Archbishop Lefebvre and the Prefect, because the French bishop had learned from a bulletin of the Press Office that the questionnaire with the questions and answers would not be submitted directly to the Pope but to a commission of cardinals composed of those who had previously condemned him. This commission would then present to the Pope their judgment. Obviously, this was not advantageous for Archbishop Lefebvre, who then appealed to Seper and finally to John Paul II against this decision. In the end, he decided to sign his declaration and send it directly to the Pope and not to the Congregation for the Doctrine of the Faith.

SCHISM IN THE SOCIETY OF ST. PIUS X

On March 25, 1983, nine American priests communicated their perplexity regarding several positions of the Society by means of a letter to Archbishop Lefebvre and to the General Chapter. Concerning the liturgy, for example, they stated:

> The First General Chapter of the Company, held in Ecône in 1976, adopted the principle that the Districts and the formation Houses must follow the Missal, Breviary, Calendar, and the Rubrics that were usual at that time. This decision has never been revoked and was not even discussed in the Second General Chapter held last year, at which your successor was chosen. In the case of the United States, we have always followed the Missal, the Breviary, the Calendar, and the Rubrics

of our holy patron, Pope St. Pius X, a practice sanctioned by the First General Chapter. Lately, however, there has been an attempt to force all priests and seminarians in the United States to accept the liturgical reforms of Pope John XXIII for the sake of uniformity and loyalty in the Company, implying in this way that adhesion to the unreformed traditional Rites of St. Pius X constitute disloyalty. Can it be that the Society has reached the point at which it considers loyalty to the tradition as disloyalty to the Society?

A month later, those nine priests—Fathers Clarence Kelly, Donald J. Sanborn, Daniel L. Dolan, Anthony Cekada, William W. Jenkins, Eugene Berry, Martin P. Skierka, Joseph Collins, and Thomas P. Zapp—were expelled. Anthony Cekada (1951-2020) and Clarence Kelly would later establish the Society of St. Pius V. In 2019, Fr. Cekada also wrote an important book criticizing the Mass of Paul VI on theological grounds.

THE ORDINATIONS OF ARCHBISHOP THUC

At this point we must examine a subject that would become controversial in the traditionalist world, namely the episcopal ordinations conferred by the Vietnamese Archbishop Pierre Martin Ngô Dinh Thuc, an important chapter in the complex history of traditionalism.

Archbishop Thuc, born in 1897, had held important ecclesiastical positions in Vietnam, thanks also to important family ties. His brother was Ngô Dinh Diem, who became president of South Vietnam and was then assassinated with their other brothers. Thuc was not in Vietnam at the time, and so escaped death. He participated in Vatican II and at a certain point decided that, due to a state of emergency within the Church, new bishops should be provided to preserve Catholic identity. He began consecrating new bishops without a mandate from the Holy See, including those who would later give rise to the so-called "Palmarian Church," which today receives visitors to its website in this way:

> We want to welcome everyone who desires to learn about the Apparitions of the Most Holy Virgin Mary and the heavenly manifestations in the Sacred Place of the Lentisco of El Palmar de Troya, which began in the year 1968.
>
> Likewise, it is our desire to make clear that the true Church of Christ ceased to be in Rome on August 6, 1978, and from there was transferred to El Palmar de Troya, with the election of Pope Saint Gregory XVII as Vicar of Christ directly by Our Lord Jesus Christ.

It is said that Archbishop Thuc repented of these ordinations, but nevertheless continued to ordain many other candidates, among them Fr. Guérard de Lauriers on May 7, 1981. There has been widescale debate in the traditionalist world over the validity of these ordinations, over the true motives of Archbishop Thuc, and so forth. The Vietnamese bishop's intentions are difficult to discern.

The Congregation for the Doctrine of the Faith, under the direction of its new Prefect Cardinal Joseph Ratzinger, issued a Notification of Condemnation on March 12, 1983, which followed a previous condemnation:

His Excellency Mons. Pierre Martin Ngô-dinh-Thuc, titular Archbishop of Bulla Regia, in the month of January 1976 ordained several priests and bishops in the village of Palmar de Troya in Spain, in a way which was completely illicit. Consequently, the Sacred Congregation for the Doctrine of the Faith, on 17 September of the same year, issued a decree (cf. *AAS* LXVIII, 1976, p. 623), mentioning the canonical penalties incurred both by himself and by the others who were thus illicitly ordained by him.

Later the same Prelate requested and obtained absolution from the excommunication most specially reserved to the Holy See which he had incurred.

It has now come to the knowledge of this Sacred Congregation that His Excellency Mons. Ngô-dinh-Thuc, since the year 1981, has again ordained other priests contrary to the terms of canon 955. Moreover, what is still more serious, in the same year, disregarding canon 953, without pontifical mandate and canonical provision, he conferred episcopal ordination on the religious priest, M.-L. Guérard des Lauriers, O.P., of France, and on the priests Moises Carmona and Adolfo Zamora, of Mexican origin. Subsequently Moises Carmona in his turn conferred episcopal ordination on the Mexican priests Benigno Bravo and Roberto Martínez, and also on the American priest George Musey.

As we have said, the issue of the "Thuc-line bishops" is very complex and has divided the traditionalist world between the sedevacantist and the sedematerialist sides. It is often said that the ordinations could be valid but not licit, but the debate is still ongoing concerning Thuc and the reasons behind his ordinations and whether he was entirely in his right mind in carrying them out. It is said that before dying he reconciled with the Holy See, but some say he was compelled to make this act.

THE SECOND *LIBER ACCUSATIONIS*

The following May 13, Abbé de Nantes presented his second *Liber Accusationis*, which begins thus:

> To our Holy Father Pope John Paul II, by the grace of God and the law of Church sovereign judge of all Christ's faithful, we present a complaint against our brother in the faith, Karol Wojtyla, for heresy, schism and scandal.

It was a bit strange insofar as he was asking the Pope to judge himself. We see how the approach is quite aggressive, and this was eventually to marginalize fatally Abbé de Nantes and those who followed him. It must be said that Archbishop Lefebvre, though admitting his intransigence, knew how to use diplomatic means and sought in every way possible to reconstruct relations with Rome, without of course placing in doubt the principles on which his battle was founded. A fundamental difference in the approaches of the two churchmen also led to different results in the scope of their battles.

THE INDULT OF 1984

The Holy See had to maneuver amid pressures from the left as well; for example, the turmoil caused by Liberation Theology. On August 6, 1984, the Sacred Congregation for the Doctrine of the Faith promulgated an *Instruction on Some Aspects of Liberation Theology*. An interesting document, it shed light on the positive aspects of the motivations behind the struggle of those who made use of Liberation Theology, but raised caution about its even greater dangers.

The Holy See had carried out a survey in 1980, hoping to determine to what extent the liturgical reforms had been implemented around the world. It seems the results were encouraging, even though only a small part of the faithful continued to be attached to the traditional form. On October 3 of the same year, the Congregation for Divine Worship promulgated a circular letter *Quattuor Abhinc Annos*, which affirmed:

> Four years ago, by the will of the Holy Father, the bishops of the entire Church were invited to present a report:
>
> > — regarding the way in which priests and the faithful of their dioceses have received the missal promulgated in 1970 by Pope Paul VI in compliance with the decisions of the Second Vatican Council;

— regarding the difficulties that have arisen in the fulfillment of the liturgical reform;

— regarding the eventual resistance that might have occurred.

The result of the consultation was sent to all the bishops. Based on their answers it seems the problem of the priests and faithful still tied to the "Tridentine Rite" has been almost entirely resolved.

Should the problem perdure, the Holy Father, desiring to find common ground with said groups, offers the diocesan bishops the possibility of making use of an indult, whereby those priests and faithful indicated in the letter of request to be presented to their bishop, may celebrate the Holy Mass using the Roman Missal according to the 1962 edition and respecting the following indications:

1. With all clarity it must be shown publicly that these priests and faithful in no way share the positions of those who place in doubt the legitimacy and the doctrinal precision of the Roman Missal promulgated by Pope Paul VI in 1970.

2. These celebrations are only for the usefulness of the groups requesting them, in the churches and oratories indicated by the bishop (not, however, in parish churches,

unless the bishop has conceded this as an extraordinary case); and on days and under the conditions established by the bishop, whether habitually or in individual cases.

3. These celebrations must be carried out according to the 1962 Missal and in Latin.

4. Any comingling of texts and rites of the two missals must be avoided.

5. Each bishop shall inform this Congregation of the concessions he has given and, in a year's time from the concession of the indult, shall report the results of its application.

This concession, indicative of the solicitude that the common Father has for all his children, must be used in a way that will not create prejudice toward the faithful observance of the liturgical reform in the life of the respective ecclesial communities.

And so, an opening was made by Rome. It was an important gesture, which sought to recover those who were fascinated by Archbishop Lefebvre and his Society. It was certainly not an easy move for Rome, because it could not hide the fact that many bishops, to whom the application of the norms of the letter was entrusted, were less than enthusiastic to concede approval to have traditional Masses in their dioceses.

INSTITUTE MATER BONI CONSILII

In 1985, the Society of St. Pius X would suffer other losses, and this time from the Italian district, when four priests broke with Lefebvre. Their names are Fr. Francesco Ricossa, Fr. Franco Munari, Fr. Giuseppe Murro, and Fr. Curzio Nitoglia. They were angered by the letter *Quator Abhinc Annos*, which as we have seen, permitted the celebration of the traditional Mass on condition of acceptance of the Council and all that this implied as well as the new Mass. But this was not the only problem. The question had already come up some years earlier and had to do with whether participation in the new Mass was licit or not.

It must be said that at this point the superior general was no longer Archbishop Lefebvre, who was now quite elderly, but Fr. Franz Schmidberger (superior from 1982 to 1994). There was division on how to face the question of the renewed liturgy. It seems that Archbishop Lefebvre and Fr. Schmidberger also did not share the same line on this issue. This pushed the four Italian priests, not sharing Fr. Schmidberger's position, to leave the Society and to create a new entity in December 1985 with the foundation of the Institute Mater Boni Consilii, still in existence today. This institute adhered to the theological position expressed by the Theses of Cassiciaco (which some called sedeprivationist and which I call sedematerialist). The four priests decided to consider the possible theological options and were convinced by those of Guérard de Lauriers, whom they visited in France and who (as we explained) had been ordained bishop by Archbishop Thuc. During their visit, Guérard de Lauriers explained his complex theological position, which in written form comprises six volumes in French, and is yet to be translated into Italian or English.

The Institute is currently one of the most representative of that particular fringe of Catholic traditionalism and is led still today by one of its founders, Fr. Francesco Ricossa. Fr. Giuseppe Murro is still part of the Institute, while Fr. Curzio Nitoglia abandoned it in 2007, finding its theological positions (i.e., the famous Theses) no longer convincing. Today, he is chaplain of the Disciples of the Cenacle, who publish the anti-Modernist journal *Sì Sì No No,* which we have already mentioned. For Fr. Franco Munari, the story is even more complicated: after having been ordained bishop in 1987 by Guérard de Lauriers, he abandoned in 1990 not only the Institute but also the priesthood.

The Institute propagates its positions through various means, including the journal *Sodalitium,* which originally belonged to the Society but, having been registered under the name of one of the priests who left the Society, departed with him. In this journal one finds historical studies of great interest to those of the integral Catholic perspective, inspired by the figure of Msgr. Umberto Benigni (1862–1934), founder of the *Sodalitium Pianum,* which served as inspiration for Fr. Ricossa's institute. There is also a publishing house that prints texts on history, spirituality, apologetics, and so forth. The Institute also promotes its activities through social media, especially on YouTube, where one can find videos on many talks, conferences and homilies, especially by Fr. Ricossa. It is a numerically limited movement, but one which has acquired a distinct following among those who accept the theological positions of the Institute in the world of traditional Catholicism.

Two Important Books

In 1985, two very important books were published that merit our attention. In 1985, Vittorio Messori published a book based on an interview with the Prefect of the Congregation for the Doctrine of the Faith, Cardinal Joseph Ratzinger. The book was called *The Ratzinger Report* in English and enjoyed enormous success. Above all, it sounded the alarm for the situation in which the Church found herself and for the reckless interpretations being made of the Council. It was an encouragement for certain sectors of the traditionalist world as well, who found some of their complaints being made by the Pope's closest collaborator.

Another book, of which we have already said much, was written by a Swiss professor, naturalized in Italy, Romano Amerio. The book is *Iota Unum*, a very important text for its analysis of the variations in the postconciliar Church. Archbishop Luigi Negri said of Amerio,

> His level of culture is extraordinary: if John Paul II used for Hans Urs von Balthasar the expression "the most cultured Christian of our time," I believe I offend no one by considering Amerio one of the most cultured Italians of the twentieth century. His culture is limitless, embracing theology, Church history, history of philosophy, cultural anthropology, and ethics, synthesized in classical literature; his was the discovery of the

ancient world in profound, synergistic dialogue with the Christian world, almost parallel to what Romano Guardini was doing contemporaneously. Every one of Amerio's lines is imbued with citations, which only those with a broad grasp of the history of philosophy or literature or theology can draw out, beyond the nearly limitless multiplicity of the notes that document his writings and in particular *Iota Unum*.

The mystic Divo Barsotti described him thus:

> In essence, Amerio says that the gravest evils present in Western thought today, including Catholic thought, are due mainly to a general mental disorder which places *caritas* before *veritas*, without realizing that this disorder overturns the proper conception that we ought to have of the Most Holy Trinity. Christianity, before it took to heart and affirmed the thought of Descartes, had always proceeded in the holy fashion of making *veritas* precede *caritas*, such as we have from the divine mouth of Christ who breathes out the Holy Spirit and not vice versa.

Amerio spoke of the crisis of the Church in this way:

> The crisis in the Church, as confessed and as we have indicated in the initial paragraphs of this book, is a crisis of faith, but the existing bond between the natural constitution of man and the

supernatural life, which is not juxtaposed but rather connatural, demands that the Catholic scholar research the etiology of the crisis on a more profound level than the philosophical. On the basis of the current confusion there lies an attack on the cognitive power of man, and this attack sends us back ultimately to the metaphysical constitution of being and most ultimately to the metaphysical constitution of the Prime Being, namely to the divine Monotriad.

The book is a must-read for understanding the reasons for the particular evolution of the Church and the consequences that derive from it.

THE MEETING AT ASSISI

Meanwhile, it was announced that the Pope would go to Assisi to encounter all the other religious leaders for a great ecumenical gathering. The meeting at Assisi was one of the moments of greatest tension between the Holy See and the traditional Catholic world. Archbishop Lefebvre was shocked by this news and thought it heralded the end of the Church's missionary activity. On August 27, he sent a letter to a group of cardinals in which he said,

> In light of the current events in the Church and of which John Paul II is the author, in view of the activities proposed in Taizé and in Assisi this October, I cannot refrain from addressing you with my supplications, in the name of the many

priests and faithful, to save the honor of the
Church, humiliated as it has never been before in
the course of its history. The discourses and the
actions of John Paul II in Togo, in Morocco, in
India, in the Synagogue of Rome, raise a holy
indignation in our hearts. What shall the Saints
of the Old and New Testaments think of this?
What would the Holy Inquisition do if it existed
still today?

The cardinals to whom the letter was sent were Siri, Zoun-
grana, Oddi, González Martín, Thiandoum, Stickler, and
Gagnon. Archbishop Lefebvre referred to other events in his
letter, such as the meeting the Pope would hold with the ecumenical Community of Taizé in October of that year, the
discourses the Pope made during his apostolic journeys and
during the historic visit on April 13 to the Synagogue of
Rome, at which he famously expressed hope that "the Church
of Christ rediscover its 'bond' with Judaism, 'scrutinizing its
own mystery.' The Jewish Religion is not 'extraneous' to us,
but in a certain way is 'intrinsic' to our religion. We have
toward it a relationship which we have with no other religion.
You are our dearly beloved brothers, and, in a certain way,
one could say our elder brothers."

For the followers of Archbishop Lefebvre, and for himself, these affirmations were the straw that broke the camel's
back. The meeting of Assisi, with its syncretic flavor, with
the idea that Catholicism was on the same plane as all the
other religions, was truly too much. Could error have the
same rights as the truth?

On the occasion of the repetition of this event twenty-five years later, an attempt was made to read the event in a way that would save the idea and the doctrine of the Church. In a collection of essays edited by Luisealla Scrosati, the theologian Fr. Mauro Gagliardi says, "The 'spirit of Assisi' is above all a spirit of constant request to God of the gift of peace on the part of all men of good will, among whom are counted religious men, despite the errors and lacunae in their worship." In the same text, the philosopher Corrado Gnerre comments on the motto for the twenty-fifth anniversary commemoration of Assisi thus:

> We return to the theme chosen by the Holy Father for the day of reflection in Assisi: "Pilgrims of truth, pilgrims of peace." This presents us with a clear logical succession, which in this case is also ontological. It is not "Pilgrims of peace, pilgrims of truth," but "Pilgrims of truth, pilgrims of peace." The recognition of the Truth precedes all else. After all, this is also in the nature of the Monotriad. One says: Father, Son, and Holy Spirit and not otherwise. It is always the truth that judges everything. And when this is not the case, aberration results. In fact, all can be justified in the name of a love that judges itself.

On November 11 of that same year, Abbé de Nantes wrote his old seminary companion who had become the archbishop of Paris, Cardinal Jean-Marie Lustiger, in his usual inflammatory style:

I imagine that no one in your entourage, neither you yourself, would dare pray for 365 days that the Heavens would take my life that the edifice from which my entire faith draws inspiration be demolished. To give it a more exact name, this edifice is the Faith of Pius X. Shall you ask in your pious prayers: "O Christ, O Lord and King of my heart as you are of the Church of Heaven and of earth, destroy St Pius X?" No, certainly not! Thus, I formulate the desire that, urged by this threat of God's judgment, you would see within yourself, Eminence, that you abjure your errors and your hatred before this year the hour would arrive of the just Truth and of the true Justice. The consequences of said abjuration would be considerable and you would be then much better off than I was in these twenty years of tribulations and diabolical disorientation, the better defender of the Catholic Faith. Eminence, I kiss your pastoral ring, with the most profound and firm hope that you might enter willingly into this judgment of God that is our last resource, our sacred resource, that which cannot be refused. You shall be heard.

The Abbot had proposed for Lustiger a sort of challenge that year, to pray that whichever of them was in error would be seized by death, while the other saved. I imagine Cardinal Lustiger was not well pleased with this proposal.

Nor were the traditionalists pleased with what John Paul II said in his Advent discourse to the Roman Curia on

December 22. "Men will often fail to grasp the radical unity of their origin, destination and place in the same divine plan," he declared; "and when they profess different and incompatible religions, they might feel that their divisions are insurmountable. But despite this, they are encompassed within the great and unique design of God, in Jesus Christ, who 'united himself, in a certain way, to every man' (*Gaudium et Spes*, 22), even if they are not aware of this."

A very daring theological statement, certainly. There were those who noted that in this way he seemed to want to include all religions in the saving design of God, as if salvation could be attained in all of them.

THE POINT OF NO RETURN?

In those years, two of the protagonists of these decades of great tension between Rome and Catholic traditionalism passed away. On June 18, 1987, the writer Michel de Saint Pierre died, who with his novels described the crisis in the Church and in French society in those postconciliar years. Then, on February 27, 1988, Guérard de Lauriers died. By means of his Theses, he offered a middle way to Catholic traditionalism between those who wanted to remain under pontifical authority although with resistance (called "recognize and resist" by Americans), and sedevacantism.

During the last months of 1987, Cardinal Eduard Gagnon carried out a canonical visit to the Society and his impressions seemed positive, judging from his declarations. On April 8, 1988, John Paul II sent a letter to Cardinal

Ratzinger concerning the Society of Pius X. In it, the Pope declared the benefits of the Council and how this event had a central role in the life of the Church. Then he confronted the problem with the Society:

> Among the topics which the Congregation for the Doctrine of the Faith had to consider in recent times appear the problems connected to the "Society of Pius X," founded and guided by Archbishop M. Lefebvre. Your Eminence knows very well how much effort the Holy See has given from the beginning of the existence of the "Society," to ensure ecclesial unity in relation to its activity. The most recent of these efforts was the canonical visit carried out by Cardinal E. Gagnon. You, Lord Cardinal, have followed this case in a particular way, as did your predecessor of venerable memory, Cardinal F. Seper. All that the Apostolic See does, which is in continual contact with the bishops and the interested episcopal conferences, aims at the same objective: that the words of the Lord in the priestly prayer for the unity of all his disciples and followers be fulfilled in this case as well.

This letter was important because it marked the willingness to reach an agreement with the Society on the part of the Holy See. Why was the Holy See so concerned? The motives for concern were essentially two, as I see it. The first was to recognize that the Society was growing and expanding throughout the world and thus was catalyzing the attention of those who were dissatisfied with the way the Church was facing the postconciliar period. The second was the fear that Archbishop Lefebvre might carry out his threat to ordain a bishop, fearing for the future of his Society once he too was dead. From the Pope's point of view, these were doubtless legitimate concerns. The ordination of a bishop would be one of the elements that led to the degeneration of the situation.

The meetings between Rome and the Society continued and seemed fruitful even to the point of leading to a protocol of agreement which Archbishop Lefebvre signed on May 5. Its first words were,

> I, Marcel Lefebvre, Archbishop-Bishop emeritus of Tulle, and the members of the Priestly Society of St. Pius X founded by me:
>
> 1. promise to be always faithful to the Catholic Church and to the Roman Pontiff, the Supreme Pastor, Vicar of Christ, Successor of Blessed Peter in the primacy and Head of the Body of Bishops.
>
> 2. declare to accept the doctrine contained in n. 25 of the Dogmatic Constitution *Lumen Gentium* of the Second Vatican Council on the ecclesiastical Magisterium and adhesion due it.
>
> 3. As concerns some points taught by the Second Vatican Council or concerning the successive reforms of the liturgy and canon law, which seem difficult to reconcile with Tradition, we

shall commit ourselves to a positive attitude of study and communication with the Apostolic See, avoiding any controversy.

4. Furthermore, we declare to recognize the validity of the Sacrifice of the Mass and Sacraments celebrated with the intention of doing what the Church does and according to the rites indicated in the typical editions of the Roman Missal and of the Rituals of the Sacraments promulgated by the Popes Paul VI and John Paul II.

5. Finally, we promise to respect the common discipline of the Church and the ecclesiastical laws; in particular, those contained in the Code of Canon Law promulgated by Pope John Paul II, except for the special discipline conceded to the Society by particular law.

It seemed a turning point had been reached, but something was not right for Archbishop Lefebvre. He was troubled by the vagueness of the promise from the Pope about the permission of ordaining bishops. The night was tormented, and the day after he entrusted a letter to an interlocutor, by which he communicated to the Holy See his desire to retract his signature. He had decided to proceed with episcopal ordination.

At this point, a back-and-forth struggle with the Holy See began concerning the ordination of a bishop for the Society. On May 24, Lefebvre encountered Cardinal Ratzinger in Rome. On this occasion, Ratzinger communicated to the

French bishop that the Pope would have consented to the nomination of a bishop within the Society for August 15, but Archbishop Lefebvre asked for three bishops and wanted them to be ordained at the end of June. Clearly, Rome and the Society were at loggerheads.

On May 30, Cardinal Ratzinger wrote Archbishop Lefebvre and concluded thus:

> Excellency, in conclusion, I cannot but repeat, as was said last Tuesday, and—if possible—with even greater seriousness: considering the positive evaluation of the content of the agreement to which the benevolence of Pope John Paul II has allowed to come to pass, there is no proportion between the latest difficulties you have expressed and the damage that a failure would now constitute, a rupture on your part with the Apostolic See and only for these reasons. You need to trust the Holy See; its goodness and comprehension recently manifested toward you and toward the Society constitute the best guarantee for the future. Finally, you must—and we all must—have faith in the Lord, who has permitted the path of reconciliation to be opened as it is today, and that the goal appears now so close.

But on June 2, Lefebvre responded directly to the Pope. Though cordial in tone, it was not so in substance:

> Radically opposed [as we are] to this destruction of our faith and resolved to remain in the doctrine

and the traditional discipline of the Church, especially in what concerns priestly formation and religious life, we feel the absolute necessity of having ecclesiastical authority that espouses our concerns and helps equip us against the spirit of Vatican II and the spirit of Assisi. Thus, we ask for a number of bishops, chosen in the Tradition, and the majority of members of the Roman Commission, with the aim of protecting us from every moral compromise. Given the refusal to consider our request, and given that it is evident that the aim of this reconciliation is not the same for the Holy See as it is for us, we believe it would be preferable to await a more propitious time for Rome's return to the Tradition. For this reason, we ourselves shall ensure the means for continuing the work which Providence has entrusted to us, reassured by the letter of His Eminence Cardinal Ratzinger, dated May 30, that the episcopal ordination is not contrary to the will of the Holy See, given that it has been agreed to for August 15.

This was practically the announcement of a rupture, and there was little room left to maneuver. Archbishop Lefebvre's lack of trust toward the Holy See was evident. They had decided to go ahead with the episcopal ordinations so as to guarantee a future for his Society.

Obviously, the Holy See showed concern about the intentions of the French bishop and on June 9, John Paul II sent an ardent letter to Lefebvre:

> With paternal heart, but with the full gravity of
> the present circumstances, I exhort you, Venera-
> ble brother, to renounce your project which, if
> carried out, can only be seen as a schismatic act,
> whose inevitable theological and canonical conse-
> quences are known to you.... Dear Brother, do
> not allow that this year dedicated in a particular
> way to the Mother of God yield another wound
> to her motherly heart!

Archbishop Lefebvre did not stop, however. Just several days
later he announced the names of the four priests to be ordained
bishop: the Swiss Bernard Fellay, the Frenchman Bernard
Tissier de Mallerais, the Spaniard Alfonso de Galarreta, and
the Englishman Richard Williamson. Not one bishop was
ordained, or even three, but rather four! On June 17, the
Vatican gave him a formal warning, asking him not to proceed
with the episcopal ordinations, but by now Archbishop Lefebvre had made his choice.

On June 30, the ceremony took place in Ecône, with the
ordination of the four priests before the eyes of the international press. Bishop Antonio de Castro Mayer participated
with Lefebvre at the ordinations. During the homily, the
French bishop said:

> It is necessary that you understand that we do not
> wish in any way that this ceremony become a
> schism. We are not schismatics. If excommunica-
> tion has been meted to the Chinese bishops who
> separated from Rome and who submitted to the

Chinese government, one can understand why the Pope excommunicated them. But for us it is not in the least a question of separating from Rome and of submitting to some power extraneous to Rome, and to constitute a type of parallel Church as the bishops of Palmar de Troya have done, for example, by nominating a pope and constituting a college of cardinals. Our case has nothing to do with such things. Far be it from us to think such miserable thoughts of distancing ourselves from Rome. To the contrary: it is to manifest our attachment to Rome that we are celebrating this rite.

The die had been cast. Rome was silent.

In effect, after an action such as this it was obvious that the supreme condemnation had to come, and it came the following day from the Congregation for Bishops, signed by the Cardinal Prefect Bernardin Gantin: Archbishop Lefebvre and the newly ordained bishops were excommunicated. The condemnation of Rome was clear, but how could they still allow those who refused to renounce the traditional Mass to find their place in the Catholic Church?

ECCLESIA DEI

The Vatican had been farsighted and evidently knew well that Archbishop Lefebvre intended to go forward with his battle. In fact, the day after the excommunication, July 2, the apostolic letter in the form of a motu proprio, *Ecclesia Dei*, was promulgated. It offered to those who would leave the Society of St. Pius X the possibility of living traditional Catholicism within the Church—albeit with the risk of facing a hierarchy that was entirely unfavorable to that choice. This would see the creation of several traditional institutes in full communion with the Holy See. That same July 18, in the Monastery of Hauterive in Switzerland, the Priestly Fraternity of St. Peter was founded by Fr. Josef Bisig and others who had left the Society of St. Pius X. In 1990 in Gabon, the Institute of Christ the King Sovereign Priest was founded by Msgr. Gilles Wach (former assistant to Cardinal Siri) and Fr. Philippe Mora. On September 8, 2006, the Institute of the Good Shepherd was founded by Philippe Laguérie, who had been an important figure within the Society of St. Pius X. But there were other realities that would take shape under the umbrella of the Ecclesia Dei Commission created by John Paul II.

Returning to 1988, however, one must say that John Paul II's document caused debate on both sides of the dispute. On July 13, Cardinal Ratzinger, speaking to the Chilean bishops, stated:

> The liturgy is not a party; it is not a meeting with the aim of enjoying time together. It does not matter in the least that the parish priest pulls his hair out to come up with who knows what ideas or imaginative novelties. The liturgy is what makes possible the presence of the Thrice Holy God among us; it is the burning bush; it is the covenant between God and man in Jesus Christ, who died and came back to life. The greatness of the liturgy is not to be found in interesting entertainment,

but in rendering tangible the Totally Other, whom we (on our own) are not capable of evoking. He comes because he wills it. In other words, the essential in the liturgy is the mystery, which is realized in the common rituality of the Church; all the rest diminishes it. Some seek to experience it in a vivacious manner, and they are left deceived: when the mystery is transformed into distraction, when the main actor in the liturgy is not the living God but the priest or the liturgical animator.

Although he criticized the rebellious bishop, he also criticized the liturgical excesses and abuses.

On October 18, meanwhile, the Pope gave new faculties to the president of the Ecclesia Dei Commission. It seemed the traditionalist "problem" was moving toward normalization. At that point, there would be one traditionalism within the visible confines of the Church and another outside it. But was Archbishop Lefebvre's act to have a schismatic nature? Recently, on the website of the Society (May 4, 2022, unavox.it), Fr. Jean-Michel Gleize, leading theologian of the Society, contested the schismatic nature of Lefebvre's actions and considered various points, among which is the concept of "living tradition":

One thing is the transmission, and another is the perception of that which is transmitted. This perception is always improving; effectively, it progresses above all, thanks to the preaching of the Pope and the bishops. But the transmission does not progress under the assumption that the

Church does not already possess in a definitive manner the fullness of the truth. With this evolutionistic conception of the living Tradition, the Council opened the door to the "hermeneutic of reform," theorized by Benedict XVI in his discourse on December 22, 2005.

The discussion remained open.

On April 28, 2005, Eric Vermehren died. He was also known as Eric de Saventhem (1919–2005) and, along with his wife, Elisabeth, had been a major figure in the world of Catholic traditionalism, and was one of the founders of the International Federation *Una Voce,* of which he was the president. In 1992, Michael Davies (1936–2004) succeeded him, author of many works investigating the reasons for the liturgical and theological decline of the Church (cf. Porfiri 2020).

ARCHBISHOP LEFEBVRE IN THE TWILIGHT

The passing of the years was making itself felt for Archbishop Lefebvre, as is only natural. But on November 14, 1989, during a press conference at the Hotel Crillon in Paris, he did not refrain from warning against some of the dangers that he judged incumbent upon Christianity. One of these dangers was the Islamic invasion, and for this he was denounced for religious defamation and sentenced on July 12, 1990, to pay a fine of five thousand francs.

It was to be the last bitter pill the archbishop would have to swallow. He died on March 25, 1991, at the age of 85. On his tomb, as he wanted, was written *tradidi quod et accepi*: "I transmit to you what I have received."

How can one judge such a complex life? It is not easy. One must acknowledge that he reacted to a period of enormous change in the life of the Church and the criticism of this change led him to the actions we have described. Now he stands before the only judge who matters: God Almighty.

MISSAL NEVER ABROGATED

Glenn Tattersall, president of the Ecclesia Dei Society in Australia, wrote to Cardinal Augustin Mayer, head of the Vatican Commission Ecclesia Dei, asking for clarifications. A rich exchange of letters took place between April and May of 1990.

The cardinal assured Tattersall of the benevolence of the Holy Father toward those faithful to the Tridentine Mass and then made this affirmation:

> Perhaps it is questionable to hold that "the intention of the Holy Father is not to perpetuate the Tridentine Mass as an alternative liturgy, but to favor the people who truly merit to be favored." One can also hold that the intention of the Holy Father is certainly not to abrogate the use of the former missal. This Pontifical Commission knows from experience that those who desire the use of the former missal is a relatively small portion of the faithful, but where the possibility of using it is given to those who wish to, they find therein an efficacious means for helping them enter into the Eucharistic sacrifice.

This statement about the abrogation of the former missal was to have an importance that we shall see later.

TRADITIONALISM IN MOVEMENT

On May 13, 1993, Abbé de Nantes came into the light again with the publication of his third *Liber Accusationis*. This time he took aim at the *Catechism of the Catholic Church*, condemning it harshly for wanting to set man in the place due to God. In 1996, he published a book against Vatican II and in 1997 was suspended and placed under interdict by his bishop. The path of Abbé de Nantes became increasing polemical toward the shifts in the Church, moving toward a point of no return in his opinion.

It must be said that Abbé de Nantes, though he preceded Archbishop Lefebvre in his battle against the "postconciliar Church," was not able to recruit such a large following.

Meanwhile, in the United States, two bishops were ordained illicitly (i.e., without pontifical mandate) by Archbishop Thuc: Clarence Kelly and Daniel Dolan, who would become important exponents of sedevacantism.

RATZINGER SPEAKS

Cardinal Joseph Ratzinger took important stances in this period. On October 24, 1998, he spoke at a conference at the Hotel Ergife in Rome, on the ten years of *Ecclesia Dei*:

> It was not the Council that reformed the liturgical books; it only ordered their revision and, to this end, established some fundamental principles. In the first place, the Council gave a definition of what the liturgy is, and this definition furnishes a standard for judgment for every liturgical celebration. If these essential rules are ignored and the "*normae generales*" formulated in

numbers 34–36 of the Constitution *De Sacra Liturgia* are set aside, then the Council is truly being disobeyed!

As we can see, the cardinal was quickly transforming into the spokesman for a new kind of conservative Catholic: one that defended the Council but deeply understood the merits of the traditionalist camp and shared many of their concerns. Today, followers of this tendency are sometimes known as the "Reform of the Reform" camp. The cardinal would also be at the heart of much controversy when he promulgated the Declaration *Dominus Iesus* on August 6, 2000. In it, he sought to resist ecumenism that saw in all religions a way of salvation. At a certain point, the document affirms,

> Not infrequently it is proposed that theology should avoid the use of terms like "unicity," "universality," and "absoluteness," which give the impression of excessive emphasis on the significance and value of the salvific event of Jesus Christ in relation to other religions. In reality, however, such language is simply being faithful to revelation, since it represents a development of the sources of the faith themselves.

Ferment in the opposite direction to this affirmation was abundant. One thinks of the Jesuit Fr. Jacques Dupuis and his book *Towards a Theology of Religious Pluralism.* On January 24, 2001, the Congregation for the Doctrine of the Faith issued a warning against the erroneous theses contained in this text, reiterating that Jesus Christ is the sole mediator in light of the salvation of all men. Ratzinger's resistance to Modernism—which was largely supported by John Paul II—was powerful. One book of 1999, for example, by the philosopher Pietro Prini, emphasized the distance between the Church and its teachings and that which is to be found in the consciences of the faithful. *The Submerged Schism*, as the text called it, was discussed widely. But protests arose from all sides and were confronted with the bonds of mutual loyalty and trust that yoked Ratzinger and John Paul II together, especially as the Pope entered his twilight years.

At the start of this new millennium there were texts which shed light on the dramatic situation the world found itself in, such as that of the German Martin Mosebach, published in 2002 under the title *Heresies of Formlessness: The Roman Liturgy and Her Enemy*. The work clearly denounces the uglification of the liturgy's aesthetic aspect and precisely for this reason enjoyed great success. The American attorney Kenneth C. Jones published at the start of 2003 an *Index of Leading Catholic Indicators: The Church since Vatican II*, in which the dramatic decline of the American Church is made visible in all its parameters.

The reigning Pontiff was by now gravely ill, and this personal decline was made manifest in the images of the Via Crucis of March 25, 2005, in which he was shown from behind clutching the cross while following on TV the Way of the Cross meditations at the Colosseum, listening to the meditations of his trusted Ratzinger. At the ninth station, Ratzinger gave a dramatic cry:

What can this third fall of Jesus under the weight of the cross tell us? Perhaps it draws our thoughts to the fall of man in general, the distancing of many from Christ, the deviation toward a secularism without God. But should we not also think about how much Christ must suffer in His own Church? How often is the holy sacrament of His presence abused, in what empty hearts filled with evil does He so often enter! How often do we celebrate just among ourselves without recognizing His presence! How often is His Word distorted and abused! How little faith there is in so many theories, how many empty words! What filth there is in the Church, precisely among those who, in the priesthood, ought to belong completely to Him! How much arrogance, how much self-sufficiency! How little we respect the Sacrament of Reconciliation, in which He awaits us to lift us up from our falls!

John Paul II would die a week later, on April 2. His funeral was attended by millions of people. That event bore witness to how, if faith in Catholic doctrine was decreasing dramatically, the personality of the Polish Pontiff compensated for this seemingly inexorable decline. As John Paul II would have said, people followed the minstrel and not the song.

CHAPTER 5

The Age of Benedict XVI

AN ELECTION IN CONTINUITY

AMONG THOSE INDICATED AS *papabile*, or probable candidates for election at the conclave, there was certainly Joseph Ratzinger, who enjoyed enormous prestige: in addition to his position as Prefect of the Congregation for the Doctrine of the Faith (essentially the Catholic Church's chief theologian), he was also the Dean of the College of Cardinals. He was indeed elected on April 19 and would choose the name Benedict XVI. Obviously, in the Catholic traditional world this election was looked upon with favor. Here was a Pope who seemed very attentive to their needs. Yet they saw in him also a degree of continuity with his predecessor, and this fact was interpreted in various ways.

In 1994, Bishop Bernard Fellay became the new superior of the Society of St. Pius X. Commenting on the June 13, 2005, election of Benedict XVI during a press conference in Brussels, he said that certainly Cardinal Ratzinger was the one who best knew the Society's concerns, and that he had sought reconciliation between them and Rome; on the other hand, it had been his idea to undercut the Society by forming the Priestly Fraternity of St. Peter. Thus, diffidence continued on the part of the Society.

Nevertheless, an important gesture was made on the following August 29, when Benedict XVI received Bishop Fellay. The Vatican Press Office published this communication:

> The Holy Father Benedict XVI has received this morning at the Apostolic Palace in Castel Gandolfo the Superior General of the Society of St. Pius X, Msgr. Bernard Fellay, who had requested the audience. The Pope was accompanied by His Eminence Cardinal Dario Castrillon Hoyos, President of the Pontifical Commission "Ecclesia Dei." The meeting was carried out in a climate of love for the Church and the desire to reach perfect communion. Although aware of the difficulties, the will to proceed by degree and at a reasonable pace was manifest.

Bishop Fellay issued a communication as well:

> The meeting lasted about thirty-five minutes, in a serene atmosphere. The audience was an occasion for the Society to show that it has always been and always will be attached to the Holy See, Eternal Rome. We recalled the serious difficulties already known to us in a spirit of great love for the Church. We found consensus in proceeding by stages in the attempt to resolve the problems.

There was prudence in moving forward, but at any rate the desire to move forward was manifested.

We cannot forget that at the end of this same year there was the famous discourse of Benedict XVI on the hermeneutic of continuity and of rupture, a discourse to go down in history. The discourse, still important today, was given to the Roman Curia on December 22, during the usual Christmas greetings.

NEW IMPULSE TO THE TRADITIONALIST MOVEMENT: *SUMMORUM PONTIFICUM*

The advent of the papacy of Joseph Ratzinger served as an encouragement to the entire traditionalist world. New groups were born, like the *Foederatio Internationalis Iuventutem* in May 2006. Important traditionalist authors such as Romano Amerio now found a place in the Vatican journal *Civiltà Cattolica,* and mainstream Catholic editors began publishing works oriented to a traditionalist public.

Then, on July 7, 2007, Benedict XVI promulgated his motu proprio *Summorum Pontificum*, which granted greater leeway for the use of the missal prior to the liturgical reform. In article 1, it says:

> The Roman Missal promulgated by Pope Paul VI is the ordinary expression of the *lex orandi* (rule of prayer) of the Catholic Church of the Latin rite. The Roman Missal promulgated by Saint Pius V and revised by Blessed John XXIII is nonetheless to be considered an extraordinary expression of the same *lex orandi* of the Church and duly honoured for its venerable and ancient

usage. These two expressions of the Church's *lex orandi* will in no way lead to a division in the Church's *lex credendi* (rule of faith); for they are two usages of the one Roman rite.

It is therefore permitted to celebrate the Sacrifice of the Mass following the typical edition of the Roman Missal, which was promulgated by Blessed John XXIII in 1962 and never abrogated, as an extraordinary form of the Church's Liturgy.

Many concessions were made to the traditional Catholic world, and this alarmed the progressives. In the letter that accompanied the motu proprio sent to the bishops, the Pope sought to preempt the criticism:

> It is not appropriate to speak of these two versions of the Roman Missal as if they were "two Rites." Rather, it is a matter of a twofold use of one and the same rite.
>
> As for the use of the 1962 Missal as a *Forma extraordinaria* of the liturgy of the Mass, I would like to draw attention to the fact that this Missal was never juridically abrogated and, consequently, in principle, was always permitted.

This was a balanced, objective analysis of the situation, though it failed in calming the waters. Certainly, this motu proprio gave an important impulse and encouragement even among priests to rediscover the treasures of the ancient Mass, despite the opposition (at times quite violent), even within the hierarchy of the Church. Some liturgists distinguished themselves in their opposition to Benedict XVI's document and to the wider application of the Mass in the old rite. Among the most visible of these liturgists is Andrea Grillo, professor of sacramental theology and philosophy of religion at St. Anselm in Rome, and of liturgy at the Institute for Pastoral Liturgy at Santa Giustina in Padua. Grillo is not the only one to express his opposition to this document. An entire generation of liturgists formed in the atmosphere of Vatican II closed ranks in their efforts to reject this "danger" of the Mass of St. Pius V.

TURBULENT 2009

Bishop Fellay, in a letter to Cardinal Darío Castrillón Hoyos, at the time head of the Commission Ecclesia Dei, on December 15, 2008, asked that his canonical situation and that of the other bishops excommunicated at the time of their consecration in 1988 be reconsidered. By a decree of the Congregation of Bishops, on January 21, 2009, signed by Cardinal Giovan Battista Re, the excommunication was lifted by Benedict XVI.

One would have expected a time of peace to ensue. One would be wrong.

Bishop Fellay responded with a communication on January 21:

> We express our filial gratitude to the Holy Father for this act which, reaching beyond the Priestly Society of St. Pius X, benefits the entire Church. Our Society desires always to assist the Pope in bringing remedy to the unprecedented crisis that currently engulfs the Catholic world and that Pope John Paul II defined as a situation of "silent apostasy."

But then a media bomb exploded. Bishop Richard Williamson, one of the four reconciled bishops, was accused of spreading denialist ideas concerning the Holocaust, provoking a media storm. How could the Pope remit the excommunication of a Holocaust-denying bishop? Bishop Fellay did damage control with a communication on January 27:

> It is evident that a Catholic bishop can speak with ecclesiastical authority only on questions regarding faith and morals. Our Society does not claim any authority on other issues. Its mission is the spreading and restoration of authentic Catholic doctrine, expounded in the dogmas of the faith. For this reason, we are well known, accepted, and esteemed around the world. It is with great regret that we see how the transgression of this mandate can cause harm to our mission. The statements of Msgr. Williamson reflect in no way the position of our society. For this reason, I have prohibited him, until further notice, to make any public statement on matters political or historical.

The next day, January 28, Benedict XVI returned to the issue during a general audience, trying to explain his gesture toward the Society and to block criticism for the declarations of Bishop Williamson:

> In these days when we remember the Shoah, images come to mind from my repeated visits to Auschwitz, one of the concentration camps in

which the heinous slaughter of millions of Jews occurred, innocent victims of a blind racial and religious hatred. As I affectionately renew the expression of my full and unquestionable solidarity with our fellow receivers of the First Covenant, I hope that the memory of the Shoah will lead humanity to reflect upon the unfathomable power of evil when it conquers the heart of man.

May the Shoah be a warning for all against forgetfulness, denial or reductionism, because violence committed against one single human being is violence against all. No man is an island, as a famous poet wrote. May the Shoah teach both old and new generations that only the arduous path of listening and dialogue, of love and forgiveness leads peoples, cultures and religions of the world to the desired goal of fraternity and peace in truth. May violence no longer degrade the dignity of man!

On January 29, the four bishops addressed a letter of thanksgiving to Benedict XVI:

With an act of thanksgiving, we wish to express to Your Holiness our profound gratitude for the act of Your paternal goodness and apostolic courage with which You have rendered null the measure which struck us twenty years ago following our episcopal consecration. Your decree of January 21, 2009, rehabilitates in some way the venerable founder of our Priestly Society, His Excellency Msgr. Marcel Lefebvre.

> It seems this gesture procures much good for
> the Church as well, rendering justice to priests
> and to the faithful of the whole world who, at-
> tached to the Tradition of the Church, would no
> longer be unjustly stigmatized for having main-
> tained the faith of their fathers.

On January 31, Bishop Fellay was interviewed by *Monde &
Vie* and could not hide his satisfaction for the developments
in Rome. But given the degeneration of the Williamson case,
Rome was forced to clarify further. In a Note on February 4,
the Secretary of State affirmed:

> The nullification of the excommunication has
> liberated the four bishops from a grave canonical
> punishment but has not changed the juridical situ-
> ation of the Society of St. Pius X, which, at this
> current moment, enjoys no canonical recognition
> in the Catholic Church. Also, the four bishops,
> while unbound of the excommunication, do not
> have a canonical function within the Church and
> do not exercise a legitimate ministry in it.

And then it confronted the sensitive issue:

> The positions of Msgr. Williamson on the Shoah
> are absolutely unacceptable and firmly rejected
> by the Holy Father, as he himself remarked this
> past January 28 when, referring to that heinous
> genocide, repeated His full and indisputable soli-
> darity with our brother beneficiaries of the First

Covenant, and affirmed that the memory of that terrible genocide must induce "humanity to reflect on the unforeseeable power of evil when it conquers the human heart," adding that the Shoah remains "for everyone a warning against hatred, against negation or reductionism, because violence committed against just one human being is violence against all." Bishop Williamson, given his admission to the episcopal function in the Church, must distance himself in an absolutely unequivocal and public manner from his positions regarding the Shoah, of which the Holy Father was not aware at the moment he remitted the excommunication.

On February 11, Bishop Tissier de Mallerais would give an interview to *Catholic Family News* in which he affirmed:

> Most especially when she fights heresies does the Church shed full light on her principles. Today as well, the Church must condemn false principles, in order to shed light on her principles, revealed principles. It is a necessity. The Church cannot teach the truth without fighting errors. This is the providential path established by the Good God for the Magisterium of the Church.

On March 5 came a communication from the German episcopate, substantially critical of the revocation of the excommunication. Then as now, Germany was a hub of progressive Catholicism. Having a Pope who was friendly to traditionalists was irksome to the Germans. The fact that this Pope was one of their own countrymen was more than they could tolerate.

On March 10, responding to the media storm and other matters, Benedict XVI addressed a letter to the bishops in which he said:

> It has been a tribulation for me, the fact that the Williamson case has coincided with the remission of the excommunication. The discrete gesture of mercy toward four bishops validly ordained though not legitimately, appeared suddenly as something totally different: as a denial of the reconciliation between Christians and Jews, and therefore as the revocation of what in this matter the Council had clarified for the path of the Church.... Another error, which I sincerely regret, is the fact that the scope and limits of the provision of January 21, 2009, was not illustrated in a sufficiently clear manner at the moment of its publication. The excommunication was inflicted on people, not institutions. An episcopal ordination without a pontifical mandate signifies the danger of schism because it places in doubt the unity of the college of bishops with the Pope. Thus, the Church must react with the harshest of punishments, excommunication, so as to recall the person punished in this way to repentance and to a return to unity. Twenty years after the ordinations, this objective unfortunately has not yet been obtained.

Unfortunately, the Pontiff's words would not be able to calm the waters. Bishop Fellay displayed his willingness, however, and issued a communication on March 12 affirming:

> The Priestly Society of St. Pius X reassures Benedict XVI of its desire to engage in doctrinal discussions recognized as "necessary" by the Decree of January 12, with the desire to serve the revealed Truth, which is the first charity to be shown to all men, Christian and otherwise. It assures Him of its prayers that His faith would not fail and that He might confirm all of his brothers (cf. Lk 22:32).

The talks went forward. Bishop Fellay was very active also in making known to the press his position, giving interviews to newspapers, for example.

At one point, Cardinal Angelo Bagnasco, president of the Italian Bishops Conference, had to defend the Pope against attacks which continued due to the remission of the excommunication. In his keynote speech of March 23 to the Permanent Council of the Conference, he said:

> An oppressive activity of criticism, beyond all good sense, has certainly been protracted, in Italy and abroad, against our most beloved Pope, first regarding the remission of the excommunication of the four bishops consecrated by Archbishop Lefebvre in 1988, and then regarding the Williamson case which inexplicably coincided. Regarding these two matters, what was important to say we have said in

a timely fashion during the previous speech. No one, however, could have expected that the controversy would have continued and in such a presumptuous manner, becoming a downright burden, to which the Pontiff himself has sought to put a stop with his admirable Letter of March 10, 2009, addressed to the bishops of the Catholic Church.

Neither would this placate the critics. On March 24, Bishop Fellay stated he was "disgusted" with the attitude of the German episcopate. On June 17, the Holy See issued a communication declaring the Society's ordinations to be illicit:

> In response to the frequent questions we have received in these days concerning the priestly ordinations of the Society of St. Pius X programmed for the end of June, we must refer to what the Holy Father stated in His Letter to the Bishops of the Catholic Church last March 10:
>
> As long as the Society of St. Pius X does not have canonical status in the Church, its ministers do not exercise legitimate ministries in the Church … as long as questions concerning doctrine have not been clarified, the Society has no canonical status in the Church, and its ministers … may not exercise any ministry in the Church. The ordinations are therefore still to be considered illegitimate.

On July 2, the motu proprio *Ecclesiae Unitatem* came out, in which the Prefect for the Doctrine of the Faith was put in charge of the Commission *Ecclesia Dei*:

In the same spirit and with the same commitment to encouraging the resolution of all fractures and divisions in the Church and to healing a wound in the ecclesial fabric that was more and more painfully felt, I wished to remit the excommunication of the four Bishops illicitly ordained by Archbishop Lefebvre. With this decision I intended to remove an impediment that might have jeopardized the opening of a door to dialogue and thereby to invite the Bishops and the "Society of St Pius X" to rediscover the path to full communion with the Church. As I explained in my Letter to the Catholic Bishops of last 10 March, the remission of the excommunication was a measure taken in the context of ecclesiastical discipline to free the individuals from the burden of conscience constituted by the most serious of ecclesiastical penalties. However, the doctrinal questions obviously remain and until they are clarified the Society has no canonical status in the Church and its ministers cannot legitimately exercise any ministry.

It was precisely to resolve the doctrinal questions that the Pope had decided to make that change.

On October 15, the Vatican spokesman announced the beginning of negotiations:

This coming Monday morning, October 26, the first of the scheduled meetings with the Society of St. Pius X will take place. Participating, on the part of the Commission *Ecclesia Dei*, will be the Secretary of the Commission, Msgr. Guido Pozzo, the Secretary of the Congregation for the Doctrine of the Faith, His Excellency Msgr. Luis F. Ladaria Ferrer, S.J., and the experts already nominated: Rev. Fr. Charles Morerod, O.P., Secretary of the International Theological Commission, Consultant of the Congregation for the Doctrine of the Faith, Rev. Msgr. Fernando Ocariz, Vicar General of Opus Dei, Consultant of the Congregation of the Doctrine of the Faith, Rev. Fr. Karl Josef Becker, S.J.

The meeting will take place in the Palazzo of the Holy Office. The content of the conversations concerning open doctrinal questions, shall remain strictly confidential.

The meetings could now begin. Despite being confidential, we have some information from a homily of Bishop Alfonso de Galarreta during ordinations in Argentina:

Last October 26, the first meeting with the Roman Commission took place, and although I cannot report certain details, certain circumstances, or certain things that were said, I can however tell you in general what happened and what we did. This first meeting went relatively well. I say "relatively" because we need to consider some of the circumstances in which we find ourselves and the expectations we can realistically foster. Considering these circumstances and what we can expect, the meeting went well.... We agreed to carry out a doctrinal discussion on all these topics. And what is most important, and which was established in a very clear way, is that the only common, possible criterion, the only criterion we accept, and which constitutes the *conditio sine qua non* for this discussion is the Magisterium before the Second Vatican Council, the Magisterium of always, the Tradition.

It seemed to have gotten off to a good start. Fr. Franz Schmidberger referred as well to the first meeting in an interview with *Kathnews* from February 2010:

According to the information available, which is quite scarce, the discussions on theological clarifications are off to a good start. For the first time we are able to expound serenely to the competent authorities our concerns about the declarations of the Second Vatican Council and regarding the developments since the Council. These discussions will go forward certainly for a long time, perhaps for years. But it is possible that our interlocutors quickly recognize that it is impossible to deny that the Society of St. Pius X is Catholic, even though there are areas of disagreement. It is an enormous step forward. The highly discrete form of the discussions is absolutely necessary for their success. The good makes no commotion and a commotion generates no good.

THE LONG DEMISE OF A PONTIFICATE

Pope Benedict XVI found himself forced to manage several fronts, and traditionalism was but one of these. The major problems which agitated the Church were to explode in 2012 with the scandals that took the name "Vatileaks." It was a moment of enormous tension for the Church, a scandal of global proportions that would weigh heavily on the Pontiff.

However, on October 27, 2011, the Pope had to face a crossroads: the twenty-fifth anniversary of the Meeting of Assisi, of which the former Cardinal Ratzinger was not a great fan. Now the Pope could not absent himself from the event, risking a disaster in ecumenical relations, but he obviously had to avoid every accusation of syncretism. Remember that the Meeting of Assisi represented a moment of serious difficulty in relations with traditionalists. Benedict XVI sought to make it clear that his approach would avoid accusations of syncretism, but suspicions accompanied him.

On April 15, Bishop Fellay sent a doctrinal declaration to Cardinal Levada, Prefect of the Congregation for the Doctrine of the Faith, in which he stated:

> We declare to accept the doctrine on the Roman Pontiff and on the College of bishops, with its head, the Pope, taught by the Dogmatic Constitution *Pastor Aeternus* of the First Vatican Council and of the Dogmatic Constitution *Lumen Gentium* of the Second Vatican Council, chapter three (*De constitutione hierarchica Ecclesiæ et in specie de episcopatu*), explained and interpreted by the *Nota explicative praevia* to

this same chapter. We recognize the authority of the Magisterium, the only one entrusted with the task of authentically interpreting the Word of God written and transmitted in fidelity to the Tradition, remembering that "the Holy Spirit was not promised to the successors of Peter that they might make known, through his revelation, a new doctrine, but that, with his assistance, they preserve in holiness and express faithfully the revelation transmitted by the Apostles, namely the deposit of faith." The Tradition is the living transmission of Revelation "*usque ad nos*," and the Church, in her doctrine, in her life, and in her worship, perpetuates and transmits to all generations that which she is and all that she believes.

That a different climate had taken shape is evident, also in September of that year, when a documentary on Archbishop Lefebvre, *A Bishop in the Tempest*, was presented, which discussed his life and his struggle.

RENUNCIATION!

The climate was not favorable to the Pope, as we have seen, attacked on all sides and put in the corner by various scandals and powerful opposition inside the Church. This did not help his already fragile health, especially the insomnia from which he suffered, and which would worsen due to the heavy stress he was under daily. At a certain point, the idea matured within him of stepping down. And so he did.

On February 11, 2013, he announced the renunciation of his papacy, effective February 28. This renunciation, and the way in which it came about, was to open another front in the traditionalist world, which we shall turn to shortly. Nevertheless, it was shocking news for most: a Pope had not abdicated for centuries. Still today there is various speculation as to the motivations behind his renunciation, speculation that remains unanswered. The images of the Pope abandoning the Apostolic Palace circled the globe.

He chose to be called "Pope Emeritus" and to continue to wear white. Then he retired to a monastery inside the Vatican. This, quite honestly, would cause great confusion for many people, giving rise to various theories, which we shall consider in a moment. If the judgment on Ratzinger the man, by those who met him even briefly—and I am among these—is largely positive, that on the work of Ratzinger as theologian, cardinal, and Pope is not easy to decipher, and is marked by contrasting opinions. But that time has not yet come.

A new Pope must now be elected.

CHAPTER 6

The Age of Francis

BUONASERA!

ON MARCH 13, THE papal conclave made a stunning decision,
electing Cardinal Jorge Mario Bergoglio. Bergoglio, the media
reported, would take the name Francis. The choice of the
name, his informal style, the choice to live in Casa Santa
Marta rather than in the papal apartments fascinated many,
but problems soon arose. An Argentinian Pope presented a
host of cultural differences with the Popes who had preceded
him. Discord was not long in coming, and the Pope himself
would make his contribution.

During his return from Brazil on July 28, as he was responding to journalists' questions, at a certain point he
seemed to criticize surreptitiously the loss of a sense of ado-
ration in the new liturgy:

> In the Orthodox Churches they preserve that
> pristine liturgy, so beautiful. We have lost a bit
> the sense of adoration. They preserve it, they

praise God, they adore God, singing, time stops. The center is God, and this is a wealth that I would like to say on this occasion that you ask me this question. Once, speaking about the western Church, of western Europe, above all the grown-up Church, they told me this phrase: *"Lux ex oriente, ex occidente luxus."* Consumerism, well-being, have done much harm. Instead, you preserve this beauty of God at the center, the point of reference. When reading Dostoyevsky, I believe that for all of us he must be an author to read and reread, because he has a wisdom, one perceives the Russian soul, the oriental soul. It is something that will do us all good. We need this renewal, this fresh air from the East, this light from the Orient.... But many, too often, the *luxus* of the West causes us to lose the horizon. I don't know, this is what I'm moved to say.

Then they asked him about Msgr. Ricca, one of his preferred prelates accused of homosexual behavior:

About Msgr. Ricca: I did what Canon Law requires, which is the *investigatio previa*. And from this *investigatio* there's nothing of what they're accusing him of, we didn't find anything. This is the answer. But I'd like to add something else to this: I see that so often in the Church, beyond this case, one goes looking for "the sins of youth," for example, and then publishes this. Not the crimes, eh? The crimes are another thing: the abuse of minors is a crime. No, the sins. But if a person, lay or priest or nun, committed a sin and then converted, the Lord forgives, and when the Lord forgives, the Lord forgets, and this is important for our lives. When we go to confession and we really say, "I sinned in this," the Lord forgets and we do not have the right to forget, because we run the risk that the Lord might not forget our [sins]. This is a danger, this is important: a theology of sin. Often, I think of St. Peter: he committed one of the worst sins, renouncing Christ, and with this sin they made him Pope. We have to reflect. But returning to your question, more concrete: in this case, I did the *investigatio previa* and we didn't find anything. This is the first question. Then, you spoke of the Gay Lobby. Bah! They write a lot about the gay lobby. I still haven't found anyone who could give me his ID card in the Vatican that says "gay" on it. They say there are some. I believe that when you find yourself with that kind of person, you have to distinguish the fact of being a gay person from the fact of making a lobby, because lobbies, not all of them are good. That is bad. If a person is gay and seeks the Lord and has good will, who am I to judge him? The *Catechism of the Catholic Church* explains this in such a beautiful way, it says, wait a minute, how does it say... it says, "these people must not be marginalized for this, they must be integrated into society." The problem is not having this tendency, no, we have to be brothers, because this is one, but if there is

another, another. The problem of making a lobby
out of this tendency: lobby of the greedy, lobby of
the politicians, lobby of the Freemasons, so many
lobbies. This is the more serious problem for me.
And I thank you so much for having asked this
question. Thank you very much.

I apologize for the long citation, but this response gave rise
to much controversy, which some considered to have opened
wide a door. Perhaps it did not, but the style of this Pope
would lead to many misunderstandings like this one, where
the exact interpretation of many of his statements is not simple.
Still today there is controversy over these words spoken years
ago, whose sense, judged by many as progressive, would be
confirmed by the encouragement given to the American Jesuit
James Martin, actively working for a greater involvement of
people with a homosexual tendency in the Church.

On November 24, Pope Francis promulgated the Apostolic Exhortation *Evangelii Gaudium*, in which, speaking of
spiritual worldliness, he stated:

> This worldliness can be fuelled in two deeply inter-
> related ways. One is the attraction of gnosticism, a
> purely subjective faith whose only interest is a cer-
> tain experience or a set of ideas and bits of
> information which are meant to console and en-
> lighten, but which ultimately keep one imprisoned
> in his or her own thoughts and feelings. The other
> is the self-absorbed promethean neopelagianism of
> those who ultimately trust only in their own

powers and feel superior to others because they observe certain rules or remain intransigently faithful to a particular Catholic style from the past....

In some people we see an ostentatious preoccupation for the liturgy, for doctrine and for the Church's prestige, but without any concern that the Gospel have a real impact on God's faithful people and the concrete needs of the present time. In this way, the life of the Church turns into a museum piece or something which is the property of a select few.

For whom was the ax being whetted? The targets are not hard to identify. Slowly, throughout his pontificate, he will make clear his thought on the traditionalist world, with actions and gestures that leave little room to the imagination. The word *indietrismo* (backwardism) has become part of the Pontiff's vocabulary and is synonymous with traditionalism but not in a positive sense. He has often allowed himself to use contemptuous judgments which, though without naming the traditionalist world directly, make it clear what his opinion of it is.

Amoris Laetitia

On March 19, 2016, the Apostolic Exhortation *Amoris Laetitia* was promulgated, in which an opening toward the divorced and remarried is evident. Roberto de Mattei (*Corrispondenza Romana*) reflected in 2021 on the impact of this document, saying:

In fact, even more than *Amoris Laetitia*, the innumerable criticisms that have been made of this document have made history, in books, articles, interviews. Among these critiques, two stand out in particular. The first is represented in the *Dubia* submitted to the Pope and the Congregation for the Doctrine of the Faith on September 19, 2016, by Cardinals Walter Brandmüller, Raymond Burke, Carlo Caffarra, and Joachim Meisner; the second is the *Correctio filialis de haeresibus propagates*, addressed to Pope Francis by more than sixty Catholic scholars and pastors of the Church on August 11, 2017. A month after its publication, the number had grown to 216 theologians, professors, and scholars of all nationalities.

Here we see two important initiatives that spring from the Pope's document: the *Dubia* proposed by the four cardinals, which sought to resolve their doubts over the interpretation of *Amoris Laetitia*; and the *Correctio Filialis*, signed by representatives of the traditionalist world, including Roberto de Mattei, Fr. Claude Barthe, Bishop Bernard Fellay, Christopher Ferrara, Antonio Livi, Martin Mosebach, Ettore Gotti Tedeschi and others. The *Correctio* was disseminated on July 16, 2017:

> Scandal has been given to the Church and to the world, in matters of faith and morals, through the publication of *Amoris Laetitia* and through other acts by which Your Holiness has rendered sufficiently clear the scope and the aim of this document. Consequently, heresies have been spread as well as other errors in the Church; while some bishops and cardinals have continued to defend the truths

divinely revealed regarding marriage, the moral law, and the reception of the sacraments, others have denied these truths and from Your Holiness have received not a reprimand but a favor.

Through this document, an attempt was made to show the Pope how much concern there was for his positions, words, and actions. But these efforts did not seem to bring about the desired change.

THE ACTIONS OF POPE FRANCIS

Returning to 2016, the Pope participated in a meeting with Lutherans on October 13. The media appreciated the image of Martin Luther, a statue, placed directly behind the Pope. A little later, with *Misericordia et Misera*, the Pope granted priests of the Society of St. Pius X the faculty to hear Confessions licitly. Then, on June 20, 2017, he visited Bozzolo to render homage to Fr. Primo Mazzolari, and then Barbiana to honor Don Lorenzo Milani, two bulwarks of progressive Catholicism.

On November 20, the Pontifical Council for Culture, presided over by Cardinal Gianfranco Ravasi, asked for the removal of the *Monito* that had been imposed on the work and ideas of the Jesuit Teilhard de Chardin, a major (if idiosyncratic) figure of Catholic Modernism. This is indicative of the type of thought that has informed the Church in recent decades and how dialogue with the contemporary world is one of the reefs on which the barque of Peter continues to dash itself.

Meanwhile Pope Francis continued with his style that at times derides those who try to maintain decorum, both interior and exterior. Consider his August 18 remarks about religious dress (seeming to imply that wearing religious dress was not relevant) or his refusal to allow his ring to be kissed.

Even more importantly, the Declaration at Abu Dhabi of February 4, 2019, raised concern. It was signed together with the Grand Imam of Al-Azhar, Ahmad Al-Tayyeb. Among the various things stated by the Declaration were:

> Freedom is a right of every person: each individual enjoys the freedom of belief, thought, expression and action. The pluralism and the diversity of religions, colour, sex, race and language are willed by God in His wisdom, through which He created human beings. This divine wisdom is the source from which the right to freedom of belief and the freedom to be different derives. Therefore, the fact that people are forced to adhere to a certain religion or culture must be rejected, as too the imposition of a cultural way of life that others do not accept.

Thus, there would no longer be a true religion but a plurality of religions, all desired and created by God. For the traditionalist world this was outright blasphemy. It is certainly very complex to harmonize this with Catholic doctrine in general.

It was also that year that that fire severely damaged the Basilica of Notre Dame in Paris, one of the symbols of Christian civilization. The tragedy seemed to have deep symbolic value.

In 2020, other documents came out which raised eyebrows, such as *Querida Amazonia* and *Fratelli Tutti*. The Pope, as always, leaves no doubt as to what his opinion might be concerning those belonging to the traditionalist world, which he describes as "rigid" at best. This deep division had not been seen under previous Pontiffs. In the audience of February 2, 2022, the Pope offered a singular interpretation of what the communion of saints might be:

> In Christ no one can ever truly separate us from those we love because the bond is an existential bond, a strong bond that is in our very nature; only the manner of being together with each of them changes, but nothing and no one can break this bond. "Father, let us think about those who have denied the faith, who are apostates, who are the persecutors of the Church, who have denied their baptism: Are these also at home?" Yes, these too, even the blasphemers, everyone. We are brothers. This is the communion of saints. The communion of saints holds together the community of believers on earth and in heaven.

These words generated a lot of discussion, and not only among traditionalists. The clash has become increasingly evident.

The Viganò Case

We need to take a step back to August 2018, to give an account of important news that would have an impact on the traditionalist world. The former nuncio to the United States,

Archbishop Carlo Maria Viganò, revealed a dossier to various news agencies which accused Pope Francis of having protected then-Cardinal Theodore McCarrick, well-known for his sexual abuse of young seminarians and adolescents. Archbishop Viganò accused the Pontiff of having done nothing about it, protecting the cardinal known for his progressive positions and for his ability as a fundraiser. One of the protagonists (among others, we also recall the Vaticanist Aldo Maria Valli), the journalist Marco Tosatti remembers the way the Viganò case broke. He says:

> The history of the Viganò dossier, and of all that came of it, began one morning at the end of July. A friend called me, asking if I had read an article on a website tied to the Vatican Secretary of State, on the McCarrick affair, the cardinal accused by the authorities of abuse of minors many years ago; he was subsequently punished by the Vatican, which removed him from the college of cardinals and sent him to a secluded life of prayer and penitence, after years of having traveled here and there, being a sort of unofficial ambassador. I hadn't read it; my friend gave me the scoop: "Msgr. Viganò will call you, he is indignant about the allusions being made to the two Nuncios who preceded him, and who have since died, and can no longer defend themselves; and about accusations toward Benedict XVI, who had punished McCarrick." I had met Carlo Maria Viganò a few times at social events; an acquaintance, nothing more. My friend told me that he followed *Stilum Curiae*, and it

seemed he might be the right person, given the freedom with which he handled matters of the Church, to give an interview. "Why not?" I answered. And effectively a few days later the former nuncio to the US called me. We agreed to see each other at my house in Rome. He arrived one morning, and I told him I was ready, showing him my [voice] recorder. "No, not yet. First, I want to tell you a story," he responded. We sat down and he told me everything that you later read in the first testimony. In the end, I asked, "So, should we do the interview?" "Not yet," he answered, "First I have to arrange some personal matters." We got in touch again a few days later. Some time passed, and when the Report of the Grand Jury of Pennsylvania came out, which spoke extensively of Cardinal Wuerl, one of the factotums of the reigning Pontiff in the US, I took the initiative to telephone him. "Did you see that the Grand Jury Report came out? If you still want to do that interview, this might be the right moment." He responded: "Let's meet next week." It took place again at my house; and he immediately said, "I thought I might write something, instead of the interview. Would you like to read it?" We read the text a couple of times together, editing just the bare minimum to clarify the terms and concepts for nonspecialists, and to eliminate what was superfluous. Then we had to choose an Italian newspaper to launch it in; I thought of *La Verità*, I had high esteem for Maurizio Belpietro, and I thought it might be one of the few newspapers that would not raise alarm in the Vatican, in a precautionary way. He agreed. I called Belpietro, whom I didn't know, I explained the situation, and he said he would be happy to publish the testimony. The archbishop wanted it to come out in both English and Spanish. He knew Edward Pentin and spoke with him; for the Spanish I got in touch with Gabriel Ariza of *Infovaticana*. Some days were needed for the translation (there were more than ten pages of text). We met on August 22 and decided it would come out four days later, at seven o'clock on Sunday morning. We said goodbye. I asked where he would go. He answered he was going to disappear and didn't tell me where, so I wouldn't be forced to lie if they were to ask me. That afternoon I wasn't at peace until I had sent the text to those who had to receive it. It was a heavy burden. The embargo should have kicked in at seven on Sunday, but I hadn't calculated one fact. At midnight on Saturday, the Rai (Italian State Television) displays the front pages of the following day's newspapers. Naturally *La Verità* ran the entire front page with the Pope and Mc-Carrick … someone mentioned it to their American colleagues who then ran their articles anticipating the embargo by a few hours.

Some time later, the Pope denied the accusations raised by the former nuncio. In the meantime, Archbishop Viganò acquired an increasingly important role in the traditionalist world, at times uniting factions, at other times creating new ones. An intense media activity led him to make pronouncements on many hot topics, such as the New World Order, Covid, vaccines, the Russia-Ukraine conflict, and so forth. His theological positions are completely aligned with those of some in the traditionalist world (which, as I said in the introduction, is much less homogeneous than one thinks), and his clash with the Pontiff has become increasingly intense.

Recently (2024), Archbishop Viganò believed it was necessary to found a priestly college in Viterbo, near Rome, where he could welcome priests and seminarians with a traditionalist orientation. This initiative is supported by the Exsurge Domine foundation, created by the archbishop himself. Furthermore, according to some press reports, Archbishop Viganò would be reconsecrated bishop by Bishop Williamson, becoming part of that sector of fringe traditionalism called the "resistance." Archbishop Viganò continues his battles which, beginning in the religious sphere, often also touch on social and geopolitical issues.

FRANCISCANS OF THE IMMACULATE

Another problem that has erupted under Francis is that of the Franciscans of the Immaculate, a congregation founded by Fr. Stefano Maria Manelli in the 1970s, flourishing with vocations and pastoral, cultural, editorial, and liturgical activities. In 2013, it was placed under external administration by the Congregation for Religious and later underwent distressing judiciary investigations for presumed abuses that were later revealed to be unfounded.

The founder, Fr. Manelli, was encouraged after the promulgation of *Summorum Pontificum* to use the Missal of 1962. This did not please certain parties within and outside the Congregation for Religious. Journalists Alessandro Gnocchi and Mario Palmaro commented on the matter in 2013 for *Corrispondenza Romana*:

> According to Fr. Volpi, the terrible vice of the ancient rite might lead to the crime of *"lesa ecclesialità"*: a concept that means everything and nothing. Perhaps, to comprehend what this term contains, one needs to look back at what happened in Rio de Janeiro during the World Youth Day there, precisely while the Franciscans of the Immaculate were relegated to external administration. It suffices to consider just one example of what the media baptized as "the Woodstock of the Church," the grotesque exhibition of the bishops dancing in the flash mob led by an amateur Belushi type, a spectacle that not even Las Vegas at its best could put on stage. If this is *"ecclesialità,"* (the way of being Church) it's understandable how the Franciscans of the Immaculate violate it constantly: they wear their habit, they fast and do penance, pray, celebrate Mass, practice and teach rigorous morality, go on mission to take Christ and not just aspirin to the needy, they don't fight AIDS with condoms, they have a Marian doctrine that the separated brethren of every type cannot endure. And then, they're poor and humble in deeds and not in words. Given all this, the

disciplinary resoluteness toward this institute leaves one speechless, but only to a certain point. Of course, such rigidity in the context of the contemporary Church is just amazing.

The painful affair continues even today, and many of the members who were prominent before the external administration began have continued their religious life in different orders. Fr. Manelli bears this bitter trial in solitude.

Recently, the Franciscans of the Immaculate elected new leadership for the order (April 2022). The newly elected leaders support the new policies of the Congregation for Bishops. This is how their official website gave the news:

> On the Feast of Our Lady of Fatima, with confirmation on the part of the Holy See of the religious indicated for the General Chapter inaugurated on April 18, 2022, the period of external administration has come to an end. The Institute is grateful to the Church for its maternal concern which witnessed the indefatigable efforts of the appointed fathers Fidenzio Volpi, OFM Cap, and Sabino Ardito, SDB, with the arrival of Fr. Gianfranco Ghirlanda, SJ, who was assisted by Fr. Carlo Calloni, OFM Cap, who were able with competence and generosity to project the Institute toward new horizons. We express our best wishes to Fr. Immacolato M. Acquali as new Minister General and to Fr. Massimiliano M. Zangheratti (Vicar General), Fr. Alfonso M. A. Bruno and Fr. Gianfrancesco M. Lim (Councilors General).

Many see this as the conclusion of the process of normalization by the Vatican.

"BENEVACANTISM"

There is also the story of the Sicilian priest Fr. Alessandro Minutella, who was excommunicated by the bishop of Palermo in 2018 and who was recently reduced to the lay state. Minutella represents a particular position in the traditional world. According to him, Benedict XVI remained Pope after his renunciation and Francis was therefore an antipope. This position is called by some "Benevacantism." It must be said that Don Minutella has a not-so-small following and that he richly benefits from the possibilities offered by social media (as in the case of other figures we have discussed) such as Facebook and YouTube. Through a platform called *Radio Domina Nostra* he spreads his message to his fans around the world.

A reference point for those who defend this position is the journalist Andrea Cionci, a "Benevacantist" who has been studying this issue for some time. He has written abundantly, especially for the newspaper *Libero Quotidiano*, his most important book being *Codice Ratzinger* (The Ratzinger Code), published in Italian, English, and Spanish, and enjoying wide success. He claimed that Benedict was in a state of *sede impedita* (obstructed see) and therefore renounced the papacy in an imperfect, invalid manner when he resigned. Various priests and scholars take this thesis seriously, which surely channels some of the increasing discontent over Pope Francis into its fold.

Although some refuse to give credence to this question, nevertheless, one must acknowledge that these ideas have been gaining increasing visibility. This merits serious reflection, both in the traditionalist world as well as in the official Church.

THE DEATH OF BENEDICT XVI

On the last day of the year 2022, Benedict XVI passed away. This event not only gave renewed energy to the Benevacantists, who now consider the see vacant, but also to a certain discontent in the traditionalist world. What does the death of Joseph Ratzinger mean? He was a Pope who had been benevolent toward the traditionalist world. As if this had not sufficed, ten days later the Australian Cardinal Pell passed away unexpectedly. With a few other high-level prelates, he had been considered a point of reference for the traditional Catholic world, a victim of disgraceful accusations of which he had been absolved, and author of denunciations of the confused situation in which today's Church finds herself.

But let us return for a moment to the days following the death of Benedict XVI, the first week of 2023.

AN END THAT NEVER ENDS

We spoke of *Traditionis Custodes* at the beginning of this study. This document introduced new tensions between the official hierarchy and the traditionalist world. Further actions have done nothing but reinforce this division, although the Pope did receive representatives of the Society of St. Pius X and the Priestly Fraternity of St. Peter. We are referring to the Congregation for Divine Worship's *Responsa ad Dubia on Certain Provisions of the Apostolic Letter Traditionis Custodes* of December 18, 2021, in which the restrictive measures regarding the traditional Missal were reinforced. We are witnessing in many dioceses an attempt to dismantle traditionalist groups, an attempt that will not be successful. On February 21, 2023, Pope Francis issued a directive demanding that bishops more tightly enforce *Traditionis*.

The question of Catholic traditionalism remains an open one, a thorn in the side of the postconciliar Church, and we do not know what future developments might bring. This will depend on an eventual new Pope, and no one knows when this will be. At any rate, the divisions are profound, and difficult to overcome. In the Catholic setting, traditionalists have a few reference points like Cardinals Burke, Sarah, and Zen, and Bishops Schneider and Strickland, but they and a few others are naturally a minority in the worldwide episcopal body, which in human terms is not encouraging. There also exists a magmatic world that draws inspiration from traditionalism, some even going beyond the boundaries of obedience to the visible Church. How can dialogue with them be reestablished? We are all — I really mean *all* — in the hands of God.

Bibliography

AA.VV. *Mons. Lefebvre e il Sant'Uffizio (Archbishop Lefebvre and the Holy Office)*. Rome: Giovanni Volpe Editor, 1980.

Agasso Jr., Domenico. Il Concilio, l'11 ottobre 1962 dall'alba al tramonto. (The Council: October 11th from Dawn to Dusk). *La Stampa*, published October 11th, 2012, and consulted February 5th, 2022 at https://www.lastampa.it/vatican-insider/it/2012/10/11/news/il-concilio-l-11-ottobre-1962-dall-alba-al-tramonto-1.36368357.

Amato, Gianfranco. *L'indulto di Agatha Christie (The Indult of Agatha Christie)*. Verona: Fede & Cultura, 2013.

Amerio, Romano. *Iota unum*. Verona: Fede & Cultura, 2012.

Andreucci, Silvio. Note to the work "Contestazioni contestabili" ("Contestable Contestations") by Jean Danielou: amid light and shadows. *Radio Spada*, published on December 2nd, 2020, and consulted on February 14th, 2022 at https://www.radiospada.

org/2020/12/da-leggere-note-all-opera-contestazioni-contestabili-di-jean-danielou-tra-luci-e-ombre/.

Andreucci, Silvio. The Criticism of Fr. Cornelio Fabro Regarding the Anthropological Shift of Karl Rahner. *Radio Spada*, published May 24th, 2020, and consulted on February 12th, 2022 at https://www.radiospada.org/2020/05/da-leggere-la-denuncia-di-padre-cornelio-fabro-della-svolta-antropologica-di-karl-rahner/

Andreotti, Giulio. *I quattro del Gesù. (The Four from the Il Gesù Church)*. Milano: RCS libri, 1999.

Anonimo. *Il programma dei Modernisti (The Program of the Modernists)*. Torino: Fratelli Bocca editori, 1911.

Balducci, Ernesto. *Io e don Milani (Don Milani and I)*. Cinisello Balsamo: edizioni san Paolo, 2007.

Barra, Gianpaolo; Iannaccone, Mario A.; Respinti, Marco. *Dizionario elementare del pensiero pericoloso (Elementary Dictionary of Dangerous Thought)*. Milan: Istituto di Apologetica, 2016.

Béguerie, Philippe. *Vers Écône (Towards Écône)*. Paris: Desclée de Brower, 2010.

Belli, Carlo. *Altare deserto (Deserted Altar)*. Rome: Giovanni Volpe, 1983.

Byrne, Carol. *Born of a Revolution*. Holyrood Press, 2020.

Bonanata, Eugenio. January 25th, 1959 Mons. Capovilla: i sentimenti di Giovanni XXXIII (Msgr. Capovilla: The Sentiments of John XXIII). *VaticanNews*, published

January 25th, 2019 and consulted on February 5th, 2022 at https://www.vaticannews.va/it/vaticano/news/2019-01/papa-giovanni-xxiii-sentimenti-conciliointervista-capovilla.html.

Bouyer, Louis. *Il rito e l'uomo (The Rite and Man)*. Brescia: Morcelliana, 1964.

Brienza, Giuseppe. Il movimento Civiltà Cristiana e la rivista cattolica Vigilia Romana (The Christian Civilization Movement and the Catholic Journal Vigilia Romana) (1969-1974) in *Fides Catholica*, year V, n. 2, 2010.

Bugnini, Annibale. *La riforma liturgica (The Liturgical Reform)*. Rome: CLV, 1997.

Buonaiuti, Ernesto. *La Chiesa e il comunismo (The Church and Communism)*. Tiemme digital edition, 2018.

Capanna, Mario. *Formidabili quegli anni (Those Tremendous Years)*. Milan: Garzanti, 2007.

Cavalcoli, Giovanni. *Schillebeeckx: un domenicano accusa (Schillebeeckx: A Dominican Accuses)*. Hong Kong: Chorabooks, 2016.

Cavalcoli, Giovanni. *Rahner e Küng. Il trabocchetto* di Hegel *(Rahner and Küng: Hegel's Trick)*. Hong Kong: Chorabooks, 2021.

Cekada, Anthony. *Frutto del lavoro dell'uomo (Fruit of Man's Labor)*. Verruà Savoia: Sodalitium, 2019.

Chiron, Yves. *L'Église dans le tourmente de 1968 (The Church in the Turmoil of 1968)*. Paris: Ártege, 2018.

Chiron, Yves. *Annibale Bugnini: Réformateur de la liturgie (Annibale Bugini: Reformer of the Liturgy)*. Desclee de Brower, 2016.

Chiron, Yves. *Histoire des traditionalists (History of Traditionalsits)*. Parigi: Tallandier, 2022.

Davies, Michael. *Liturgical Time Bombs in Vatican II*. Charlotte (NC): Tan Books, 2003.

De Mattei, Roberto. *Il crociato del secolo XX: Plinio Corrêa de Oliveira (The Twentieth Century Crusade: Plinio Corrêa de Oliveira)*. Casale Monferrato: Piemme, 1996.

De Mattei, Roberto. *Il Concilio Vaticano II: una storia mai scritta (The Second Vatican Council: The Never Written History)*. Turin: Lindau, 2010.

De Mattei, Roberto. *Apologia della Tradizione (Apology for Tradition)*. Turin: Lindau, 2011.

De Mattei, Roberto. *Plinio Corrêa de Oliveira, Apostolo di Fatima, Profeta del Regno di Maria (Plinio Corrêa de Oliveira, Apostolo of Fatima, Prophet of the Reign of Mary)*. Rome: Edizioni Fiducia, 2017.

De Proença Sigaud, Geraldo. *Catecismo Anticomunista*. Campinas, Brazil: Caritatem, 2022.

De Simone Leo. *Liturgia medievale per la chiesa postmoderna? (Medieval Liturgy for the Post-Modern Church?)*, Panzano in Chianti: Edizioni Feeria, 2013.

Domergue, Raymond. FOI ET RÉVOLUTION: l'itinéraire de "Frères du monde" (*Faith and Revolution:*

The *"Brothers of the World" Itinerary)*. *Esprit* (1940-), 21 (9), 70–87. http://www.jstor.org/stable/24265546, 1978.

Fesquet, Henri. *Diario del Concilio (Diary of the Council)*. Milan: Mursia, 1967.

Fogazzaro, Antonio. *Il Santo (The Saint)*. Milan: Baldini, Castoldi & Co, 1906.

Gennari, Gianni. Quel Modernista amico di papa Giovanni (That Modernist Friend of Pope John). *La Stampa*, published October 4th, 2013 and consulted February 7th, 2013 at https://www.lastampa.it/vatican-insider/it/2013/10/04/news/quel-Modernista-amico-di-papa-giovanni-1.36067351.

Gnerre, Corrado. *La rivoluzione nell'uomo (The Revolution in Man)*. Verona: Fede & Cultura, 2008.

Gugelot, Frédéric. *La messe est dite: Le prêtre et la littérature d'inspiration catholique en France au xxe siècle (The Mass is Said: The Priest and Catholic Literature in 20th Century France)*. Rennes: Presses universitaires de Rennes, 2015.

Horn, Gerd Rainer. *The Spirit of Vatican II*. Oxford: Oxford University Press, 2015.

Inaudi, Silvia; Margotti, Marta ed. *La rivoluzione del Concilio (The Revolution of the Council)*. Rome: Edizioni Studium, 2017.

Ingrao, Ignazio. *Il Concilio segreto (The Secret Council)*. Segrate: Piemme, 2013.

Innocenti, Ennio. *Influssi gnostici nella Chiesa d'oggi (Gnostic Influences in the Church Today)*. Rome: Sacra Fraternitas Aurigarum in Urbis, 2000.

Invernizzi, Marco. *Alleanza cattolica dal sessantotto alla nuova evangelizzazione (Catholic Alliance from 1968 to the New Eveangelization)*. Casale Monferrato: Piemme, 2004.

Jugie, Louis-Michel. Ecône: *Le Séminaire de l'espoir (*Ecône: *The Seminary of Hope)*. FeniXX, 1986

Küng, Hans. *Di fronte al Papa (Before the Pope)*. Milan: Rizzoli, 2016.

Lamendola, Francesco. Anche de Lubac, alfiere dei progressisti, mise in guardia contro le derive post-conciliari (De Lubac, Standard Bearer of Progressives, Also on the Defensive Against Post-Conciliar Deviations). *Accademia Nuova Italia*, republished February 1st, 2018 and consulted February 11th, 2022 at http://www.accademianuovaitalia.it/index.php/cultura-e-filosofia/teologia-per-un-nuovo-umanesimo/4442-de-lubac-e-derive-post-conciliari.

Lefevbre, Marcel. *Un Vescovo parla (A Bishop Speaks)*. Rusconi, 1975.

Madiran, Jean. *L'accordo di Metz (The Agreement of Metz)*. Rome: Pagine, 2011.

Madrid, Patrick; Vere, Pete. *More Catholic than the Pope*. Huntington (IN): Our Sunday Visitor, 2004.

Mancinella, Andrea. *1962: rivoluzione nella Chiesa (1962: Revolution in the Church)*. Brescia: Edizioni Civiltà, 2010.

Manetti, Carlo, ed., *Un caso che fa discutere (A Controversial Case)*. Verona: Fede & Cultura, 2013.

Marchesini, Duillio; Scafidi, Giancarlo. *Nati per combattere (Born to Fight)*. Chieti: Solfanelli, 2020.

Martínez Villegas, Austreberto. Fragmentación católica sedevacantista en Guadalajara (Fragmentation of Catholic Sedevacantists in Guadalajara). *Estudios Jaliscienses* 99, 2015.

Messori, Vittorio, ed. Porfiri, Aurelio. *La luce e le tenebre (Light and Shadows)*. Milan: Sugarco, 2021.

Monfeli, Tommaso. *Cattolici senza compromessi (Catholics without Compromise)*. Rome: Edizioni Fiducia, 2019.

Mores, Francesco. Ernesto Buonaiuti e Angelo Roncalli, tracce di un'amicizia (Ernesto Buonaiuti and Angelo Roncalli, Signs of a Friendship). *Modernism*, Year II, Brescia: Morcelliana, 2016.

Nocilli, Giuseppe Antonio; Nocilli, Pio Benedetto (sd). *Quale musica liturgica e chi la deve interpretare? (Which Liturgical Music and Who Shall Interpret It?)* Edizioni Carroccio.

Nitoglia, Curzio. Il vero volto di von Balthasar (The True Face of von Balthasar). *Sì Sì No no*, published January

12th, 2021 and consulted February 12th, 2022 at doncurzionitoglia.wordpress.com.

Omlor, Patrick Henry. *Questioning the Validity of the Masses using the New, All-English Canon*. Menlo Park (CA): Aladextra Press Editions, 1968.

Petrolino, Enzo. *Sacrosanctum Concilium*. Padova: Edizioni Messaggero, 2005.

Pinay, Maurice. *Complotto contro la Chiesa (Plot Against the Church)*. Viterbo: Edizioni Effedieffe, 2015.

Porfiri, Aurelio. *Il canto dei secoli (The Song of the Centuries)*. Venice: Marcianum Press, 2013.

Porfiri, Aurelio. *Pulpitazioni (Pulpitations)*. Venice: Marcianum Press, 2014.

Porfiri, Aurelio. *Ci chiedevano parole di canto (They Asked Us for Songs)*. Hong Kong: Chorabooks, 2017.

Porfiri, Aurelio. *Delle cinque piaghe del canto liturgico (On the Five Wounds of Liturgical Song)*. Hong Kong: Chorabooks, 2018.

Porfiri, Aurelio; Valli, Aldo Maria. *Sradicati (Uprooted)*. Hong Kong: Chorabooks, 2018.

Porfiri, Aurelio. *Uscire nel mondo (Going Out into the World)*. Hong Kong: Chorabooks, 2019a.

Porfiri, Aurelio. *Messa a punto (Mass Clarity)*. Hong Kong: Chorabooks, 2019b.

Porfiri, Aurelio. *Cantate inni con arte e con suono melodioso (Sing Songs with Skill and Melodious Sound)*. Hong Kong: Chorabooks, 2020a.

Porfiri, Aurelio. *A Future in Tradition*. Hong Kong: Chorabooks, 2020b.

Porfiri, Aurelio; Valli Aldo Maria. *Decadenza (Decadence)*. Hong Kong: Chorabooks, 2020.

Porfiri, Aurelio. *Un canto nuovo (A New Song)*. Hong Kong: Chorabooks, 2021.

Porfiri, Aurelio. *Il paradiso degli inadeguati (The Paradise of the Inadequate)*. Hong Kong: Chorabooks, 2022a.

Porfiri, Aurelio. *Benedetto XVI, l'inizio della fine (Benedict XVI: The Beginning of the End)*. Hong Kong: Chorabooks, 2022b.

Porfiri, Aurelio. *Non nova sed noviter (Not New Things, But in a New Way)*. Hong Kong: Chorabooks, 2022c.

Reid, Alcuin, ed., *A Bitter Trial*. San Francisco (CA): Ignatius Press, 1996.

Rizzi, Filippo. Gumpel: Pio XII voleva un Concilio (Pius XII Wanted a Council). *Avvenire*, published November 15th, 2013 and consulted February 6th, 2022 at https://www.avvenire.it/agora/pagine/pio-xii-voleva-un-concilio-gumpel-#google_vignette.

Saint-Pierre, Michel de. *Ces prêtres qui souffrent (Priests Who Suffer)*, Paris, La Table ronde, 1996.

Schneider, Athanasius, with Porfiri, Aurelio. *The Catholic Mass*. USA: Sophia Institute Press, 2022.

Scrosati, Luisella, ed., *Le religioni ad Assisi (Religions at Assisi)*. Verona: Fede & Cultura, 2011.

Sorrel, Christian (dir.). *Renouveau conciliaire et crise doctrinale. Rome et les Églises nationales (1966-1968) [Conciliar renewal and doctrinal crisis. Rome and the national churches (1966-1968)]*. Nuova edizione [online]. LARHRA (Created on April 1st, 2022). Available on the Internet: <http://books.openedition.org/larhra/4945>. ISBN: 9791036543081. DOI: https://doi.org/10.4000/books.larhra.4945, 2017.

Tillloy, Pierre. *L' "Ordo Missae," l'unità nell'eresia (The "Ordo Missae:" United in Heresy)*. Rome: Giovanni Volpe, 1969.

Tissier de Mallerais, Bernard. *Mons. Marcel Lefebvre. Una vita (Archbishop Lefebvre: A Life)*. Chieti: ed. Tabula Fati, 2005.

Turoldo, David Maria. *O sensi miei… (Oh My Senses…)*. Milan: Rizzoli, 1990.

Turoldo, David Maria. *Il mio amico don Milani (My Friend Don Milani)*. Gorle: Servitium, 2003.

Viganò, Carlo Maria. *Il nuovo ordine mondiale (The New World Order)*. Hong Kong: Chorabooks, 2022.

Villa, Luigi. *Yves Congar*. Brescia: Edizioni Civiltà, 2007.

White, David. *The Voice of the Trumpet*. Saint Louis (MO): BRN Associates, 2018.

Zoccatelli, PierLuigi; Cantoni, Ignazio ed., *A maggior gloria di Dio, anche sociale (To the Greater Glory of God, Social Too)*. Siena: Cantagalli, 2008.

Zoccatelli, Pier Luigi; Sanguinetti, Oscar. *"Costruiremo ancora Cattedrali" ("We Shall Build Cathedrals Once More")*. Crotone: D'Ettoris Editori, 2022.

JOURNALS CONSULTED

Adista
Bulletin of Una Voce
Chiesa viva
Corrispondenza Romana
Échanges
Frères du monde
La Civiltà Cattolica
Le Chardonnet
L'Homme Nouveau
Osservatore Romano
Sì Sì No No
Sodalitium
Testimonianze
The Remnant
The Wanderer

REFERENCE WEBSITES

Agerecontra
Circolopliniocorreadeoliveira.blogspot.com
Duc in altum
Il Sismografo

Inter multiplices una vox
La nuova bussola quotidiana
Le Salon Beige
Messa in Latino
New Liturgical Movement
One Peter Five
Rorate Coeli
Stilum Curiae
Vatican News
Preti Operai

About the Author

AURELIO PORFIRI IS AN Italian composer, conductor, educator, and writer. He is a renowned expert in sacred music and a scholar on China and Catholic traditionalism. He is the co-author, with Bishop Athanasius Schneider, of the bestselling *The Catholic Mass*, already translated in multiple languages. He is a contributor to major Catholic and conservative blogs in Italy, France, and the United States. The popular American magazine *Inside the Vatican* included him in the top-ten most influential people in 2021.

Sophia Institute

SOPHIA INSTITUTE IS A nonprofit institution that seeks to nurture the spiritual, moral, and cultural life of souls and to spread the gospel of Christ in conformity with the authentic teachings of the Roman Catholic Church.

Sophia Institute Press fulfills this mission by offering translations, reprints, and new publications that afford readers a rich source of the enduring wisdom of mankind.

Sophia Institute also operates the popular online resource CatholicExchange.com. *Catholic Exchange* provides world news from a Catholic perspective as well as daily devotionals and articles that will help readers to grow in holiness and live a life consistent with the teachings of the Church.

In 2013, Sophia Institute launched Sophia Institute for Teachers to renew and rebuild Catholic culture through service to Catholic education. With the goal of nurturing the spiritual, moral, and cultural life of souls, and an abiding respect for the role and work of teachers, we strive to provide materials and programs that are at once enlightening to the mind and ennobling to the heart; faithful and complete, as well as useful and practical.

Sophia Institute gratefully recognizes the Solidarity Association for preserving and encouraging the growth of our apostolate over the course of many years. Without their generous and timely support, this book would not be in your hands.

www.SophiaInstitute.com
www.CatholicExchange.com
www.SophiaInstituteforTeachers.org

Sophia Institute Press is a registered trademark of Sophia Institute.
Sophia Institute is a tax-exempt institution as defined by the
Internal Revenue Code, Section 501(c)(3). Tax ID 22-2548708.